WOMEN AT WESTMINSTER

WOMEN AT WESTMINSTER

An Account of Women in the
British Parliament
1918-1966

PAMELA BROOKES

With a foreword by

MARY STOCKS

'. . . There's no such thing as a woman M.P.
We're all individuals.'

Miss Alice Bacon M.P.
reported by *The Sunday Times*
1 November 1964

PETER DAVIES : LONDON

Printed in Great Britain by
Clarke, Doble & Brendon Ltd.
Cattedown, Plymouth

*For my Mother
and, with respect,
for the women in Parliament*

CONTENTS

ILLUSTRATIONS

FOREWORD
by Mary Stocks

MRS BROOKES' *Women at Westminster* is a study of integration.
At first sight the reader may be tempted to suggest that reissues at
short intervals will be necessary to keep it up to date with the advent
of new women. On second thoughts, it becomes clear that the author
has reached the end of a definite phase. Women have *arrived*—in
both Houses, on front benches and back benches. They are no longer
news. If they still have to run faster than men to get to the same
place, and are still conscious of sex-conditioned male attitudes, this
is not peculiar to Westminster. Here, then, is the story of their arrival,
excellently documented and with penetrating character sketches of
the women concerned, to make it enthralling reading.

But history has been kind to Mrs Brookes in providing her opening chapter with a drama more unexpected, more colourful and
more piquant than any event in the long austere history of women's
emancipation: the appearance of Nancy Astor as first woman to
take her seat in the British Parliament. Mrs Brookes deals faithfully
with this event. But only feminists who lived through the early
twenties will be able fully to recapture the successive sensations of
horror, stunned surprise, and dawning adulation, provoked by the
advent of the first woman at Westminster. Here, as heir to long years
of feminist endeavour, was a wealthy American society hostess, with
no academic education, no record of feminist or even social service
activity, and no claim to a vacant seat beyond the fact that it had
been vacated by her husband. She was personally unknown to all
the leading feminists, with the exception of Mrs H. A. L. Fisher
who said: don't worry, you will be surprised. We were.

It soon became clear that Nancy Astor was the fiercest feminist
of the lot of us, that she cared for all the things we hoped a woman
M.P. would care for, and that she was prepared to fight for them
like a tiger, but in her way, not in ours. She was recklessly impulsive
and mingled irreverence with puritanism in a way never previously
encountered by men inside the House or women outside it. In a
matter of months organized women were at her feet—and she
deserved their support because for these first years, as a woman

alone at Westminster, she lived under an unblinking arc-light of publicity which involved intense nerve strain. Perhaps because she was married to a saint and addicted to the works of Mary Baker Eddy she was able to endure it.

It is fortunate that she was never offered ministerial office; equally fortunate that the women who, in due course, were, carried their burdens with the wisdom and ability that all good feminists expected of them. Mrs Brookes has indeed been able to record the achievements of a magnificent regiment of women, advancing into untrodden territory, led by a very gallant standard bearer riding two years ahead.

MARY STOCKS

INTRODUCTION

THIS BOOK is about a small group in Parliament. It is a minority that, contrary to initial predictions, hopes, and fears, has remained small, growing slowly from one in 1919 to a figure fluctuating between twenty-five and twenty-nine in recent years with a further twenty or so in the House of Lords. It is a group which has always attracted a good deal of attention and controversy and is unlike any other minority in the Houses of Parliament in that its members are bound together by no common party, policy, or regional interest and do not, in fact, voluntarily belong to it at all; they are members simply because they are women.

The members of this group have constantly engaged the attention of newsmen and political commentators but no very clear verdict has emerged about them, although much of the comment has tended to be critical: on the one hand they have been accused of being ineffectual; on the other of being 'bossy janes'; they have been said to include too many spinsters or alternatively too many married women who have inherited their seats from their husbands; they have been accused of being too feminist and not feminist enough; of having spent too much time on domestic affairs and of having meddled in matters 'outside their sphere'.

The aim of this book is to try to discover, by tracing their history over the last forty-seven years, what sort of women have sat in Parliament, what their contribution has been and whether it has differed from that of men, and why after nearly half a century there are still comparatively few of them. I must anticipate and say at once that I have not been able to do more than indicate in bare outline the interests and work of women members of both Houses of Parliament, particularly in more recent years, and in this I may have done them less than justice; but this book was never intended to be a *catalogue raisonné* of each member's activities. I trust however that I have drawn the outline accurately enough for the contribution of women in Parliament as a whole to be correctly assessed.

I would like to express my gratitude to those members past and present of both Houses of Parliament from whom I have had invaluable help in writing this book. I would also like to thank my old friend, Charles Gordon, Fourth Clerk at the Table of the House of Commons, and Mr R. W. Perceval, Clerk Assistant to the House of Lords, for their advice on points of detail. I owe a great debt of gratitude to the staff of the Fawcett Library, particularly to the Librarian, Miss Vera Douie O.B.E., who helped me in many ways, not least by reading through a great part of the book. I would also like to thank the Clerk to the Trustees of the Library, Mrs H. V. Horton.

I must record my indebtedness to Mrs Ida Barker for information about her sister, Mrs Wintringham, and to the late Viscount Astor who was kind enough to read through part of the book and help me with points of detail before his untimely death. I also wish to thank for their assistance Mr H. R. Underhill, the Assistant National Agent of the Labour Party and Miss Jean Denham of the Labour Party Press and Publicity Department; the Rt Hon. Edward du Cann M.P., Chairman, and Mr Geoffrey Johnson Smith M.P., Vice Chairman, of the Conservative and Unionist Party, and Miss Elisabeth Sturges-Jones, the Conservative Press Officer; Mr P. C. Chitnis, General Secretary of the Liberal Party; Mr Edward Macalester, Director of the Hansard Society; Mr Henry Durant of the Gallup Poll and Mr M. J. G. Cox of the National Opinion Polls Ltd.

I am indebted to the following for permission to use material from their published works: Faber & Faber Ltd and Dutton & Co. Inc. (*Nancy Astor* by Maurice Collis); the Baroness Stocks (*Eleanor Rathbone: A Biography*); William Heinemann Ltd (*As It Happened* by Earl Attlee); Mrs Braddock M.P. and Macdonald & Co. Ltd (*The Braddocks*); Arthur Barker Ltd (*Working Partnership* by Katherine, Duchess of Atholl); the Hutchinson Publishing Group Ltd (*A Life's Work* by Margaret Bondfield); Frederick Muller Ltd (*Life is Good* by Edith Picton-Turbervill, *Call Back Yesterday, The Fateful Years* and *High Tide and After* by Hugh Dalton, *British Hustings 1924–1950* by Arthur H. Booth); Odhams Books Ltd (*Woman in Parliament* by Jean Mann); Curtis Brown Ltd (*Lord Morrison of Lambeth: An Autobiography*); Oxford University Press (*A Diary with Letters 1931–1950* by Thomas Jones).

I am grateful to *The Times* for allowing me to reproduce material from my articles on women parliamentary candidates of 21 September 1964 and 14 March 1966 which first suggested the idea for this book to me and for allowing me to quote from other issues of the newspaper. I am also grateful to *The Daily Telegraph, Evening*

Standard, Daily Mirror, Guardian, The Observer, Punch, The Spectator and *The Sunday Times* for allowing me to quote from their columns.

Finally I have to thank J.G.J. whose help and encouragement throughout the writing of this book were indispensable.

January 1967

PAMELA BROOKES

PART ONE
1918-1929

Heirs and Warming Pans

1918 The First Candidates

ON WEDNESDAY, 23 October 1918 the members of the House of Commons met at 2.45 p.m. in the certain knowledge that the end of the First World War and the dissolution of the Parliament that had been sitting since 1911 could not be long delayed. The newspaper headlines spoke of 'Good Day for the British on the Scheldt', 'Big British Advance—in the Suburbs of Valenciennes', and the members gathering in the Chamber already felt relief and exhilaration at the prospect of an armistice to be followed by a general election. When Questions and Orders of the Day had been disposed of the Right Honourable Herbert Samuel, Liberal member for Cleveland, rose to move the motion 'that, in the opinion of this House, it is desirable that a bill be passed forthwith making women eligible as Members of Parliament.'

There was a stir in the Press and Strangers' Galleries. This was the high point in what was otherwise a dull day's business. There was conjecture, particularly in the Ladies' Gallery where some potentially interested parties like Mrs Edith How Martyn were sitting, as to whether the honourable members who had fought stubbornly against the provisions of the Representation of the People Act, passed in February, giving women the vote at the age of thirty, would stage another full-scale battle; several of them could be discerned in the Chamber. The anti-suffrage lobby had in the past often used as a powerful plank in its campaigns the argument that giving votes to women would make possible 'that menace to sanity in legislation, the woman M.P.' An anti-suffrage pamphlet of 1909 entitled *The Woman M.P.—A Peril to Women and the Country*[1] held that: 'To give votes to women with . . . its corollary, the woman M.P., would lower the quality of our legislation, would increase the number of capricious, emotional and meddlesome laws and would therefore in many cases bring the law into contempt and render it a dead letter. . . .' Even those who fought for women's suffrage did not believe that the vote would be quickly followed by the right to stand for Parliament, and often attempted to calm public fears by forecasting an interval of as long as ten years after the franchise was granted. During the Speaker's Conference, which reported in 1917, nothing specific had been said about the issue, but women's contribution to the war effort had done much to soften the opposition with the result that the second reading of the Representation of the People Bill had been passed by 385 votes to 55.[2] Now, with an election drawing near, the Coalition Government had decided to put the question of admitting women to the House to a free vote of the Commons. It was, in fact, one pressing for settlement, for the law as it stood was ambiguous.

In May Miss Nina Boyle, a member of the Women's Freedom League, had put the matter to the test by presenting herself as a candidate in a by-election at Keighley, but the returning officer had declared her nomination papers out of order. This, he said, had nothing to do with her sex. If her papers had been in order he would have accepted them, 'the question of her qualification as a candidate being determined elsewhere'. In the same month the Independent Labour Party announced that they were adding the names of Miss Margaret Bondfield and Mrs Philip Snowden to their list of parliamentary candidates, and in August the first prospective woman candidate, Miss Mary Macarthur, had been adopted by the Labour Party at Stourbridge. But would she or any other women be able to stand?[3] Nobody knew.

Now in a closely reasoned speech Mr Samuel pointed out that this motion was the logical outcome of the enfranchisement of some six million women voters. He maintained that the views of women would be badly needed in the House in the post-war period and added prophetically : 'It is rather more probable that too few will be elected rather than too many.' He believed that the age limit of thirty should not apply to women candidates. After all, he reminded the House, this limit had been temporarily imposed on women voters so that they should not outnumber men in the post-war period. No age barrier should be put in the way of any woman whom the electorate might wish to choose. 'I myself,' he added frankly, 'was a candidate for Parliament some years before I was a voter.'[4]

But, as *The Times* reported the following day, Mr Samuel had not been speaking long before it became clear that he was preaching to the converted and the rest of the discussion proved that the anti-women's suffrage lobby had accepted defeat on this whole issue with fairly good grace.

Mr Arnold Ward, Unionist member for Watford and the son of

Mrs Humphry Ward, who had led the campaign against giving women the vote, signalled its complete collapse by saying his associates would offer no opposition to the bill, and Mr Asquith, another convert, in a rather unfortunate turn of phrase advised the House, 'You have the camel; you ought not to strain at the gnat.' It was left to Admiral of the Fleet Sir Hedworth Meux, the Conservative member for Portsmouth South, to fight a rearguard action on behalf of those who had opposed the Representation of the People Act, and this he did with all flags flying in a speech that still leaps from the page of Hansard, full of wit and vigour. He did not oppose this motion, he said, because he did not love women—'he adored them' —but because he did not think that 'this House is a fit and proper place for any respectable woman to sit in. . . .' What, he asked, about all night sittings, 'sitting up till two or three in the morning?' ' "Who goes home?" ' he snorted. 'It will be a case of "Who will take me home?" . . .' However, Lord Robert Cecil, the Assistant Secretary of State for Foreign Affairs and a well-known advocate of women's suffrage, summed up the feeling of the House by saying that it had broken with the 'point of view that rests on distrust of women, and now I think we should treat them as human beings with absolutely equal rights with men. . . .' The discussion petered out and was wound up by the Irish Nationalist member for Galway, Mr Hazleton, who said it had really been unnecessary to have a debate at all and called for the closure.[5]

When the question was put at 6.30 p.m. after just over two hours' discussion 274 members went into the Ayes lobby (among them the Prime Minister, Mr Lloyd George, and the Chancellor of the Exchequer, Mr Bonar Law, as well as several members of the Government), and 25 into the Noes. The only sound that was heard in the Chamber when the figures were announced was an involuntary burst of laughter from the Ladies' Gallery.[6]

Once the views of the House were known the Government acted quickly. On 31 October Lord Robert Cecil, supported by the Solicitor General and the Minister of Blockade, presented the Parliament (Qualification of Women) Bill 'to amend the law with respect to the capacity of women to sit in Parliament' and it was given its first reading. On 4 November it was read the second time and the debate was brief.[7] In committee, amendments to raise the age limit to thirty for women parliamentary candidates and to disqualify peeresses in their own right from sitting in the Commons were unsuccessful. A further amendment to extend the provisions of the bill to enable women to sit in the House of Lords was exposed by Lord Robert Cecil as a last-ditch attempt to block the bill's passage in another place. In a speech that carried weight with those members who would have liked the amendment to go through for its own sake Lord Robert pointed out that the Lords would inevitably throw out the whole bill if it were to impose on them too the acceptance of women members.[8] The bill was reported without amendment, read the third time, and passed.

In the Lords there was an attempt to delay the bill by three months, and later, in committee, Lord Haldane supported by Lord Selborne, made another determined effort to allow peeresses in their own right to sit in the Upper House; this Lord Islington, the Under-Secretary of State for India, opposed, pleading serious constitutional difficulties which the bill as it stood was not empowered to remove.[9] On 21 November, the day Parliament was prorogued, the Speaker was able to inform the Commons that the Parliament (Qualification of Women) Bill had received the Royal Assent.

And so in three weeks the bill was rushed through and the matter settled. Women could stand for Parliament. It was not a moment too soon, for the general election was announced for 14 December. There was a tremendous scramble for seats in which a record number of candidates fighting under many different banners took part. The Government created a confusing and unsatisfactory situation by issuing certificates or 'coupons' to those Coalition candidates whom they favoured. These were not the easiest of circumstances in which the new women candidates could find seats. As the political correspondent of *The Times* pointed out : 'The experience of other countries shows that it is one thing to give women votes and quite another to induce them to plump for a woman candidate.'[10]

Nevertheless there were women ready to stand and in the following weeks seventeen were adopted to fight the election; they accounted for little more than one per cent of the 1,623 candidates contesting 707 seats. Their party affiliations were as follows :

CONSERVATIVE[11] (UNIONIST)	LABOUR	LIBERAL	OTHERS	TOTAL
1	4	4	8	17

Since these were the first women to stand for Parliament in these islands it is worth taking a closer look at them.

The Labour and the Liberal parties each put up four women. The Labour Party had always supported women's suffrage and it is perhaps surprising that, the battle won, it did not put forward more women in 1918. Mary Macarthur's early adoption for Stourbridge in August had been regarded as the first outcome of the affiliation of the women's trade union organizations with the Labour Party. This remarkable woman, coming from a middle-class background, had found a vocation in organizing women workers; she was honorary secretary of the National Federation of Women Workers and secretary of the Women's Trade Union League. Earlier she had achieved a great success in representing the women chain-makers of Cradley Heath during a strike. So great was her popularity in the Black Country that she was given her choice of seven constituencies and her nomination was supported by all the men's unions. In private life she was the wife of Will Anderson, a former chairman of the Labour Party and member for the Attercliffe division of Sheffield. The Andersons thus became the first of a small select band of married couples who over the years have contested parliamentary elections.

Another well-known woman, Mrs Emmeline Pethick Lawrence, was Labour candidate for the Rusholme division of Manchester. She was the only woman in this election to contest a Lancashire constituency. She and her husband (who has been aptly called 'the prince consort of militancy') had been actively engaged in the suffrage movement, first as leaders with Mrs Pankhurst of the Women's Social and Political Union until they broke with her in 1912; together they had edited the paper *Votes for Women* until the outbreak of war.

The Labour candidate for Battersea North, Mrs Charlotte Despard, was another famous suffragette. She came of an Irish family and was the sister (to his occasional embarrassment) of Field-Marshal Sir John French. In 1907, an erect impressive figure with snow-white hair, she had led the march of women on the House of Commons, where she was arrested. Later she too differed from Mrs Pankhurst and set up the Women's Freedom League of which she became president. At the time of the 1918 election Mrs Despard was seventy-four (she lived to be nearly ninety-five) and a firm supporter of the Labour Party because she believed it had been the most sympathetic to the women's movement. She had done a great deal of social work in south London and was very popular there.

The fourth Labour candidate was Mrs H. M. Mackenzie who was contesting the Welsh Universities seat, the only woman candidate in the principality. She had for many years been Professor of Educa-

tion at the University College of South Wales and Monmouth-
shire.

For the Liberals Mrs Corbett Ashby, an able woman who had
taken the classical tripos at Cambridge, was adopted to contest the
Ladywood constituency of Birmingham against a Coalition 'coupon'
candidate called Neville Chamberlain who was also fighting his first
parliamentary election. At Portsmouth South (Sir Hedworth Meux
for his peace of mind was not offering himself for re-election) Miss
Alison Garland, a dynamic lady known as 'the Lloyd George in
petticoats', was the Liberal candidate and was said to have a pro-
nounced following among women voters. Mrs J. McEwan, the wife
of a City businessman, was the Liberal candidate for Enfield where
she had a long record of public work. In her election address she
said she wanted to do something about the housing problem in
Enfield (a proposal that has a timeless ring) and to remove the restrictions on women, particularly in the legal profession. The fourth
Liberal candidate was Miss Violet Markham (Mrs Carruthers). She
had already proved her ability in various forms of social work and
is exceptional in this campaign because she had been an active supporter of the anti-women's suffrage movement. During the war she
was converted to the suffrage cause and with high hopes put up
as an Independent Liberal for Mansfield, a seat which her brother
had held for many years until his death during the war. She seems
to have taken rather a high hand with everybody, announcing at the
outset that she was standing as as Independent Liberal because
'there is something in the Markham temperament that does not
take kindly to the crack of the whip. My brother never allowed outside interference between his constituents and himself, and neither
will I.'[12] Furthermore she suspended her campaign for a few days
while her husband, Colonel Carruthers, was on leave for, as *The
Times* reported: 'It is part of Miss Markham's doctrine that if
political life clashed irrevocably with her own life, the latter must not
suffer.'[13]

Half of the women whose nominations were received by 4 December were standing as Independents. This was hardly surprising since
most of them had been suffrage fighters to whom party affiliations
were of secondary importance. The best known of this group was
Mrs Pankhurst's daughter, Christabel, who felt that 'if a woman were
elected to Parliament the opinion of women who had served in war-
time might be better heard at the Peace Conference.'[14] She was herself an outstanding personality and a brilliant speaker who in 1908

at Bow Street, during her trial for militant activities, had ably cross-
examined in the witness box both the Chancellor of the Exchequer,
Mr Lloyd George, and the Home Secretary, Mr Herbert Gladstone.
Eventually she had fled to Paris to escape imprisonment but she continued to help her mother conduct the suffrage campaign from there
until the war began. Now representing the Women's Party she was
the only woman candidate to get the 'coupon': at the eleventh
hour Mr S. N. Thompson, the Coalition candidate for Smethwick,
was induced to stand down in her favour. 'This chivalrous action',
reported *The Times*,[15] 'has been in deference to a request from Mr
Lloyd George and Mr Bonar Law. If it should ensure Miss Pankhurst's election, a new Parliamentary era will open at the assembly
of the next House of Commons.'

The Women's Party which Miss Pankhurst was representing was
the direct successor of the Women's Social and Political Union, the
suffrage society founded by her mother. It is unique in that it seems
to have been the only attempt to create a party exclusively for
women—a contingency that opponents of women's suffrage had
often predicted and feared. A pamphlet published by this party after
the passing of the Representation of the People Act in 1918 maintained that 'Victory, National Security and Social Reform are the
watchwords of the Women's Party,' and went on to say, 'while the
Women's Party is in no way based on sex antagonism it is felt that
women can best serve the nation by keeping clear of men's party
political machines and traditions, which, by universal consent, leave
so much to be desired. . . .'

The formation of the Women's Party had met with a mixed
reception from women. At a meeting of the National Council of
Women at Caxton Hall in October various speakers, including the
future Labour M.P.s, Miss Susan Lawrence and Dr Marion Phillips,
criticized it in downright terms, and Christabel's left-wing sister,
Sylvia Pankhurst, said of it, 'Here is obviously a Tariff Reform,
Tory, Imperial jingo organization and we who are Socialist and inter-
nationalist have other ideas.'[16] However, under its banner and with
the accolade of the all-important 'coupon', Christabel was fighting a
straight fight against the Labour candidate, directing her campaign
mainly against the 'Bolshevist' threat.

Two other lively participants in the suffrage campaigns had been
Mrs Dacre Fox who was now contesting Richmond and Mrs Edith
How Martyn, now contesting Hendon. Mrs Dacre Fox had always
been in the thick of militant activities; she was imprisoned three

times and once planted herself on Lord Lansdowne's doorstep saying that she was seeking refuge with his lordship since he had managed to incite violent resistance to Home Rule for Ireland without incurring arrest and imprisonment. Mrs How Martyn was well known in Hendon for her work in the Hampstead Garden Suburb. She declared herself in favour of setting up a League of Nations and pledged herself to do all in her power to promote an equally high moral standard for men and women, to open all professions and occupations to women, and to remove all women's artificial disabilities. In Scotland Mrs Eunice Murray, a leading member of the Women's Freedom League, shared a three-cornered contest for the Glasgow constituency of Bridgeton with James Maxton, the Independent Labour candidate.

In Chelsea a redoubtable feminist was opposing Sir Samuel Hoare, the Coalition Conservative candidate. She was Miss Emily Phipps, a former headmistress who was President of the National Federation of Women Teachers. She had the active backing of the Federation, which had raised £330 towards her expenses and whose members were canvassing tirelessly for her. Her campaign was under all-female direction : her election agent and her campaign manager were both women. Miss Phipps demanded the opening of all trades and professions to women and the appointment of women judges and magistrates. She called for social improvements well ahead of her time, such as the endowment of motherhood and pensions so that deserted and widowed mothers would be in a position to support their families. In this she anticipated Eleanor Rathbone's campaign for family allowances.

Meanwhile in Brentford and Chiswick a mass meeting of electors, disgruntled at the way the 'coupon' Unionist candidate, Lieut.-Colonel Grant Morden, had been adopted, decided to set up an all-party Coalitionist committee to choose another candidate to represent them. After seeing several applicants they chose as Independent Coalition candidate Mrs Ray Strachey, wife of an officer in the Intelligence Department. Their choice is not surprising since she was by any standards a woman of distinction. She published a novel at the age of eighteen, went up to Newnham College, Cambridge, became involved in the suffrage campaign as Mrs Henry Fawcett's[17] right-hand woman in the National Union of Women's Suffrage Societies, and during the war had given excellent service organizing women workers. Apart from her qualifications she was a woman of charm and magnetism. In her election address she made a broad appeal in refreshing contrast to the narrow feminism of some of her colleagues :

'. . . I believe with profound conviction that men and women should work together for the progress and good government of the nation, as they must for that of their homes. I hold that the interests of men and women are so closely bound together that they cannot be divided and that what is for the good of the one sex must certainly be for the good of the other. . . .'[18]

Finally there were two women Sinn Fein candidates for Irish seats: Miss Winifred Carney contesting the Victoria division of Belfast, and the Countess Constance Markievicz, the St Patrick's division of Dublin. Both had been leaders of the Easter Rising in 1916 and both had been imprisoned at Aylesbury for this. To both of them the question of women's rights and place in the British Parliament was of minor consequence; they stood in 1918, like others of their party, as part of their campaign for Home Rule. If elected they did not mean to take their seats. One of them, Countess Markievicz —or 'Madame' as she was known by her supporters in Dublin— was a figure of some importance. She had the wildness of the true Irish rebel combined with indomitable courage and strength of character. She was born Constance Gore-Booth of an Anglo-Irish family with a seat at Lissadell, County Sligo. She and her sister Eva were both strikingly good-looking. Eva, who wrote poetry, broke away from her family to work for pacifist and social causes in Manchester, while Constance, having been presented at Court, created consternation by going to Paris to study painting. There she met and married Casimir Markievicz, a Polish count. They settled in Dublin where Constance soon got embroiled in Irish politics. She made one dramatic incursion into suffrage campaigns by driving a four-in-hand through the streets of Manchester in support of the right of barmaids to serve behind bars (surely one of the strangest issues at any election) at a by-election in 1908 in which the Liberal candidate, Mr Winston Churchill, lost his seat. During the war her husband returned to Poland to join the Russian Army and Constance joined the Republican Army wearing a dark-green uniform and hat with waving plumes of her own design. For her part in the Easter Rising she was condemned to death, but because of her sex her sentence was commuted to penal servitude for life. She was freed under an amnesty in 1917 but reimprisoned in May 1918 in a round-up of Irish rebels suspected of conspiring with Germany (though there is no evidence that she did so). It was from Holloway that she contested the 1918 election with her usual insouciant bravado. 'By the way, shall you "stand" for Parliament?' she had written to her sister. 'I wouldn't mind doing it as a "Shinner", as an election sport, and one does not have to go to Parliament if one wins, but oh! to have to sit there and listen to all that blither!'[19] Later when she was adopted for St Patrick's she was allowed a big sheet of prison paper on which to write her election address and did it in such a hurry that she feared that it did not make sense.

By the time nominations closed on 4 December only sixteen women had been adopted, but later one more was added to their number. The Unionist candidate for Kennington, Lambeth, Colonel Lucas, died suddenly during the campaign and in the new election polling on 24 December, his widow was adopted to fight in his place, thus giving the Conservative party their first woman candidate.

Reading the Press comment of the time it is clear that women as voters and as parliamentary candidates for the first time were bringing some interest to an election that was rushed, confused and not very edifying with its cries of 'Hang the Kaiser' and 'Make the Germans pay.' In many constituencies women voters held meetings to hear and question the candidates, which they did so thoroughly in Dundee that Mr Winston Churchill under fire from women hecklers was constrained to protest that he was only a man and not an encyclopaedia. In divisions where women were candidates the interest was intensified. 'When a woman enters the lists the novelty of the situation and the freshness of her point of view contrive to banish indifference and apathy',[20] ran a typical Press comment. There was a body of opinion that believed that women would automatically attract the votes of their sex, though *Punch* had a drawing of a female candidate soliciting the support of a country yokel who retorts, 'You want my vote, Missy? W'y wot might you know about beer and baccy?'[21] Everywhere the reception of women candidates was said to be courteous and sympathetic. Emmeline Pethick Lawrence was reported well received in Rusholme where she was arousing considerable attention; Mary Macarthur, although suffering from a certain amount of mud-slinging on account of the Labour Party's supposedly pacifist policy, felt confident enough of her chances to go to speak for the Labour candidate at Smethwick against Christabel Pankhurst, the Women's Party candidate. But Christabel felt her victory was a foregone conclusion. 'Give the woman a chance' she reported to be the attitude of the electorate, and help was coming in from all quarters.

In Hendon Edith How Martyn was making a wonderful impression and her supporters were very hopeful of success. Her committee room was in a perambulator shop which *The Times* correspondent felt could not possibly be an accident. Emily Phipps was putting up a stout fight in Chelsea, although Sir Samuel Hoare had taken some of the wind out of her sails by declaring himself in favour of equal pay. Her workers were even parading the streets at night with election posters illuminated by hand lamps. Violet Markham in Mansfield was being helped by Eleanor Rathbone, the secretary of the Liverpool Women's Suffrage Society and herself a future Member of Parliament, while in Chiswick Ray Strachey received a great deal of sympathy as a result of the Coalition candidate's unmannerly taunt that she would be better employed at home looking after her children, to which she replied that she could do this better in Parliament where it was high time they had someone who knew one end of a baby from another. By all accounts she was making a very good impression, asking the electors to support her not because she was a woman but because she was a candidate who would represent them well. A special correspondent of *The Times* waxed quite lyrical about her under the headlines 'Eggs at Brentford—Mrs Oliver Strachey's Popularity'. The eggs, he reported, were not being flung, but presented as gifts by well-wishers, which in a time of scarcity was a mark of high esteem.[22]

In Holloway Gaol Constance Markievicz was writing to her sister, wishing that Eva could impersonate her in Dublin and commenting scornfully : 'The English Election is like *Alice in Wonderland* or a Gilbert and Sullivan opera. . . .'[23]

As polling day drew near the Press tipped Miss Pankhurst, Miss Macarthur, Miss Markham, and Countess Markievicz for success and said that Mrs Strachey and Mrs McEwan had good outside chances. 'None of the results of the polling will be awaited with more eagerness than those in which this constitutional experiment is being made', declared *The Times*.[24]

The results, delayed because of the service votes, were announced on 28 December. The Coalition had a sweeping victory, winning 484 seats; but the high hopes of all but one of the women pioneers came crashing to the ground. At Smethwick (already the scene of surprising results) Christabel Pankhurst lost by 775 votes, although she polled over 8,000, the highest vote achieved by any of the women candidates in this election in which the total number of votes cast was low. At Stourbridge Mary Macarthur trailed the Liberal victor by

1,333 votes having polled 7,587. She felt her chances had been jeopardized by the returning officer's insistence that she should appear on the ballot paper in her little-known married name which perplexed many supporters to whom she was, anyway, simply 'our Mary'. (To add to her bitterness her husband had also been unexpectedly defeated at Attercliffe.) Violet Markham, who had been allowed by her returning officer to fight in her maiden name, received what she called 'a clout on the head' by coming third of four candidates at Mansfield, with 4,000 votes. Mrs McEwan at Enfield just saved her deposit with 1,987 votes, but Ray Strachey lost hers with only 1,263 at Brentford and Chiswick. Edith How Martyn lost her deposit at Hendon, as did Eunice Murray (Glasgow, Bridgeton) and Winifred Carney (Belfast, Victoria).

Mrs Despard (Battersea North), Mrs Dacre Fox (Richmond), and Miss Garland (Portsmouth South) all did well, Mrs Despard polling over 5,000 votes. In addition to these three women there was Mrs Lucas, the widowed Conservative (Unionist) candidate, who in a three-cornered fight in Kennington gave the Liberal a mere 832 majority; probably she was the first woman to discover that there is nothing like bereavement, injury or childbirth to commend a candidate to the British electorate.

By a typically ironic twist of political fortune the only one of the seventeen women to be elected was the one who had taken no part in the campaign at all and did not want to take her seat anyway. Countess Constance Markievicz, detained in Holloway Gaol, swept her Nationalist opponent, a gentleman in the meat trade, from the Dublin seat that he had held since 1892, by polling 7,835 votes to his 3,752. Her only recorded comment is in a letter to her sister, 'My election was a foregone conclusion. I must know a lot of those who voted for me. . . .'[25] Subsequently she received a letter signed by Lloyd George, which is now preserved in the National Museum of Dublin, summoning her to take her seat at the opening of Parliament. It was forwarded to Holloway Gaol. Although Constance Markievicz was released in March she never took her seat and the only sign of her in the House of Commons was her name inscribed below a coatpeg. She is said to have gone there once incognito to look at it.

So the first attempt of women to enter the House of Commons ended in anticlimax. *The Times*, pleased to have had its doubts justified, drew the conclusion that, far from helping woman candidates, the votes of their own sex had been cast against them.[26] In the light of later election statistics this was too sweeping a generalization, since party affiliation more than anything else has been shown to be the determining factor. In this muddled, hasty election held in the aftermath of a world war, with new constituency boundaries and an inaccurate register, it was difficult to predict any candidate's chances. It is difficult too to draw many worth-while conclusions about the showing of these pioneers, least of all to prove that they lost votes because they were women. It is truer to say that only a very few of them such as Christabel Pankhurst and Mary Macarthur had real prospects of success. Of the defeated candidates half were standing as Independents, and independence, as Violet Markham for one found to her cost, does not often pay electorally. There are however two interesting facts about this group of women candidates which indicated trends for the future. First, as far as can be ascertained from those who gave their date of birth, none was under thirty years of age. The youngest may well have been Mrs Corbett Ashby who was thirty-one and the average age for the rest seems to have been just over forty. Secondly, all of them contested urban seats. In 1918, as in later elections, townsfolk were more willing to adopt women candidates than were electors in the rural seats.

In quality the candidates compared favourably with any subsequent group: no fewer than five of the seventeen had had the benefit—rare in those days—of a university education. Yet none of them ever reached the House of Commons and only three of them tried again: Mrs Corbett Ashby, Miss Garland, and Mrs Strachey. (Mrs Dacre Fox, as Mrs Norah Elam, was to become one of Sir Oswald Mosley's Fascist candidates in the 1930s but never fought an election.[27]) Mary Macarthur was dead, at a tragically early age, by the time of the next election; Emmeline Pethick Lawrence preferred to help her husband into Parliament; Edith How Martyn became the first woman to sit on the Middlesex County Council; Violet Markham had a distinguished career but decided Parliament was not for her. Many of the other suffrage campaigners probably felt that they had made their point by standing for this election and left it to others to carry the advance further. The Irish Treaty transferred Countess Markievicz's activities to the Irish Free State where she was elected to the Dail but she was in and out of prison for her political activities until her death in 1927. Nevertheless these pioneers had shown that women could contest an election and do so creditably.

But, if Parliament, Press and public drew the conclusion that women's entry into the House of Commons was a long way off, they were in for a shock. Within twelve months the first woman had taken her seat there—a woman moreover with the wit and fire of a Christabel Pankhurst, the charm of a Rachel Strachey, and the devil-may-care courage of a Constance Markievicz.

1919 'A Lady in the House'

IN THE summer of 1919 the death of an eccentric American-born millionaire, the first Viscount Astor, indirectly caused a by-election in the Sutton division of Plymouth which was represented by his heir, Waldorf. The fact that he had to go to the Lords was a heavy blow to this Conservative M.P. who had embarked on a successful parliamentary career, becoming Parliamentary Private Secretary to Lloyd George, the Prime Minister, in 1918. He and his American wife, Nancy, were popular in Plymouth where they had done a great deal of social work and where they had a house on the Hoe. Both the Astors and the Plymouth Conservatives were loth to break their connection and when Lord Astor proposed that his wife should stand in his place his suggestion was readily accepted. On 4 November Viscountess Astor was formally adopted as the Conservative candidate to fight the by-election.

Nancy Astor was then aged forty-one, small and delicate in appearance but endowed with great vitality. Her first marriage in the United States to an alcoholic had ended in divorce, leaving her with a son and a hatred of drink. Since her second marriage she had been busy bringing up a family that had grown to six children and entertaining at Cliveden, a grand mid-Victorian house near Taplow where the Astors founded a hospital for the Canadian Army during the First World War. She had never taken a direct part in the suffrage campaigns.

Almost at once she made a remarkable impression on the electorate and the public at large. Not only the novelty of her candidature but also her vivacity, charm and wit attracted the Press irresistibly. She flung herself into the election campaign with great energy, finding as many other women were to find out after her what tremendous fun it could be. In her adoption speech she told her party not to expect her to be 'a sex candidate' or simply 'a warming pan' to keep the seat aired for someone else. She meant to represent everyone in the constituency though she saw herself as having a special responsibility towards women and children.[1]

Her husband became her campaign manager and helped with all her speeches, but she spoke best extempore and, once launched into a speech, forgot about her notes. Although she supported the policies of the Coalition Government her independence soon became manifest and she did not hide her views on temperance (although denying that she was a 'pussyfoot' or prohibitionist), or her dislike of war profiteers, brewers, and certain other categories of the human race. Her meetings were always crowded. She spoke well in a good clear voice and the audience loved her gift of repartee. Her opponents were Mr Isaac Foot, the Liberal candidate (father of Sir Dingle and Mr Michael Foot, the M.P.s, and Lord Caradon) and Mr W. T. Gay, a Labour man who was said to have pacifist tendencies. 'Mr Gay represents the shirking classes, I represent the working classes,' she told an audience.[2]

'The House of Commons will be a vastly more interesting place if she enters it', declared the *Ladies' Field* with some insight, while the *Evening Standard* reported, 'Lady Astor is laughing her way into Parliament.'[3] But *The Times* disagreed: 'Lady Astor can be very serious and is by no means the frivolous creature some of the reports suggest.'[4]

She was said to be expecting a 14,000 majority and the Prime Minister, Lloyd George, sent her a cautious message of encouragement saying, 'I think it important that there should be a certain number of women in Parliament in order to represent the women's point of view.'[5] His wife came to speak in her support at a women's meeting on the eve of poll. When asked why she was not supporting Mr Foot, the Liberal candidate, Mrs Lloyd George replied that this was a time for unity under a Coalition Government and not for party strife. (The fact that Mr Foot was a supporter of Mr Asquith may also have had something to do with it.) She added that she 'always thought women would be greater politicians than men if they had the chance'.[6] The eve-of-poll meeting at the Guildhall was enthusiastic and crowded to the doors.

Polling took place on 15 November and the results announced on 28 November were as follows:

Viscountess Astor (C.)	14,495
Mr Gay (Lab.)	9,292
Mr Foot (Lib.)	4,139

If Lady Astor did not get the majority she had forecast, her comparatively large one of 5,203 surprised a great many people. After it was announced sailors and workmen dragged her carriage to the Conservative Club where she declared, 'I cannot say the best man has won, but I can say the best policy has won.' She was presented with a silver cup on behalf of the women and children of the division 'in honour of the return of the first lady M.P.'[7]

A great historic event had occurred : a woman was about to take her seat in the House of Commons for the first time. The papers were prepared to make the most of it. *The Times* under the headline 'A Lady in the House' thundered that no such event had taken place since abbesses had sat in the Saxon Witenagemot.[8] It then went on to consider certain delicate matters. Where, for instance, was the lady to sit? It seemed inconceivable to 'the Correspondent' that a lady of any party could be expected to sit huggermugger on the benches with male M.P.s. Of course, he said (with more truth than he can have realized), the place for her would have been on the crossbenches—if there had been any in the Commons. The alternative, he thought, was a corner gangway seat to be reserved for her. He then brought up the question of hats for the first time in connection with women politicians : Should she wear one or not? 'The Correspondent' thought that she would wear a hat in the House as she would in church; but should she remove it when she rose to speak as men do? (In the event the Speaker sensibly decided that women could wear hats or remain uncovered as they pleased.) Yet another matter of moment was whether she should be referred to as 'the noble lady' or 'the honourable member for the Sutton division of Plymouth'. (The first address was generally used although the two used together was in order.) Unanswered questions came thick and fast.

In all the excitement the irony of a situation in which an American-born woman was to be the first to sit in the British Parliament and moreover a woman who had never campaigned for women's political rights, was generally overlooked. There was but one poignant reminder of past struggles when the train bearing the newly elected member drew in to Paddington Station. There, among the crowd on the platform to greet her was a small band of veteran suffragettes, some of whom had known imprisonment and forcible feeding. Lady Astor, small, elegant, light-hearted and rich must have been quite unlike the woman they had envisaged as their first M.P. Yet one came forward to present her with a badge saying : 'It is the beginning of a new era. I am glad to have suffered for this.' Lady Astor was deeply moved. The tension was relieved by an ugly-looking chap in the crowd bawling, '*I* never voted for you.' 'Thank heaven for that', she retorted.[9]

1 December was fixed as the date for Lady Astor to take her seat and that morning readers of *The Times* learned that 'she was sure of a cordial reception. However, it cannot be denied that her coming is causing a grave shaking of heads among the more conservative elements of all parties.' Perhaps it was not so much the thought of a woman sharing their counsels that was disturbing members, as the invasion of the privacy of what has often been described as 'one of the best clubs in London'. Until August 1917 lady visitors had to listen to debates seated behind a grille in the Ladies' Gallery like nuns in an enclosed convent. On 15 August 1917 a resolution was passed recommending the removal of the grille and authorizing the expenditure of a sum 'not exceeding £5 for that purpose'.[10] Thereafter ladies sat in full view of honourable members. In October 1918 a motion was passed, on the same day as Mr Samuel's motion to admit women as Members of Parliament, to allow women strangers to sit in the Strangers' Gallery as well as the Ladies' Gallery;[11] but the Distinguished Strangers' Gallery was still denied them. No ladies, not even the secretaries of ministers and members of the Opposition front bench, could be entertained in the Strangers' Dining Room, but had to be taken to the more expensive Harcourt Room. Now a lady *member* was arriving who would be able to go everywhere at will—even into the Smoking Room—only the honourable gentlemen's cloakrooms (now there were to be two kinds, labelled 'Members' and 'Lady Members' respectively), would be safe from her. In addition a room, overlooking the terrace and lately occupied by the Under-Secretary for Air, was assigned to Lady Astor as a Lady Member's Room. It was really a partitioned-off part of a larger room, the other half of which was a Ladies' Tea Room where male members were also allowed to bring guests. These two rooms were where the Strangers' Cafeteria is today.

The historic introduction took place before a crowded House soon after 3 p.m. at the end of Question Time.

The galleries were full. Lord Astor was there, of course, and some of their children. (One of them—David, aged seven—told T. P. O'Connor : 'Mother told me if I got too excited to recite poetry to myself.')[12] In the Press Gallery there was another sensation : two women reporters sat there for the first time. At the given moment the first woman member was seen to be advancing down the floor of the House towards the Speaker's Chair. On her right hand was

David Lloyd George, Prime Minister of His Majesty's Government, and on her left A. J. Balfour, President of the Council and Leader of the Conservative Party. She was wearing a dark tailor-made costume and a tricorne hat and looked charming and attractive, quite unlike the grim suffragette termagant that many fearful members may have envisaged as the first woman M.P. She seemed by far the most self-possessed of the trio, for Lloyd George and Balfour showed, said *The Times* correspondent, 'all the ingenuous shyness of boys at their first dance . . . which does them credit'.[13] According to some accounts Lloyd George made a false start and forgot one of the three bows so that she had to prompt him with 'George, you forgot your bow.' This caused a Labour backbencher to shout out, 'George, you will be losing your job',[14] and Jack Jones, another Labour member, called out 'Take off your hat, Austen'[15] for both Austen Chamberlain and that diehard reactionary, Sir Frederick Banbury, kept up the old custom of sitting covered in the Chamber.

It was observed that Mr Speaker did not alter custom by rising to shake hands with the new member, but remained seated. She was led to a corner seat in the second row below the gangway to the left of the Speaker. This seat was not to be hers for long, for when Sir William Joynson-Hicks returned from a trip abroad he claimed that it was his and not without some argument she moved up to sit next to him.

It had all gone off well; the lady member's first appearance had been a success. Even though it was 'nothing less than the capitulation of a fortress that had been exclusively masculine for over 600 years' no difference could be detected in the House of Commons except, as *The Times* gallantly remarked, 'an improvement in its appearance'.[16] But perhaps some members would have been less reassured if they could have foreseen that the new presence was going to be anything but mute and would indeed add to the liveliness and controversy of the House.

On that particular afternoon the business before it was a motion introduced by Horatio Bottomley, editor of *John Bull*, concerning Victory (or premium) Bonds. Lady Astor voted with the Government against it. Although it was reported at the time that she seemed at ease at once she disclosed towards the end of her life in a television interview with Kenneth Harris that she had been terrified and sat in the House 'for five hours without moving'.[17] She rounded off the day by giving a dinner party attended by Lloyd George and his

ministers, the Leader of the Opposition and several other members.
That in itself was unusual for a member of either sex.

On the whole the House received 'the noble lady' well, although
many members had reservations about her, and a powerful group is
said to have campaigned for her to stand down at the next election.
'Men whom I had known for years,' she is reported to have said,
'would not speak to me if they passed me in the corridors. They said
I would not last six months. But I stuck it out.'[18] Winston Churchill,
who had often been her guest, was one who ignored her. One day
she challenged him about this and he replied that he found a
woman's intrusion into the House of Commons as embarrassing as
if she had burst upon him in his bathroom when he had nothing
to defend himself with but a sponge. 'Nonsense, Winston,' she
retorted. 'You are not good-looking enough to have fears of this
sort.'

She was at once extremely busy both inside and outside the House
and from an early stage employed three secretaries to deal with her
very heavy correspondence. Much of it came from women and as
early as 10 January the *Pall Mall Gazette* was reporting, 'Her post-
bag is enormous and it has been absolutely impossible for her to
cope with a quarter of the letters from women with a grievance, suggestions and desires from all over the world.'

A few days after her introduction she had so far recovered her
nerve as to intervene when the Secretary of State for India was dealing with women's franchise in that country,[19] and on 23 December
she asked the Food Controller about the price of milk, a commodity
that particularly interested her.[20]

Her maiden speech was awaited with eagerness. She had been
advised against speaking too soon and certainly not on the night of
her introduction ('only Irish members do that', according to the
Press). She made her maiden speech on 24 February 1920 on a subject dear to her heart: Sir John Rees was introducing a motion
to abolish the Liquor Control Board that had been set up during the
war in the interests of national efficiency. The Government decided
to oppose it because it wanted to bring in a bill of its own embodying
some lesser degree of control and Lady Astor decided to speak in
support of the Government. Again the House was crowded and
the galleries were full. Lady Astor's reputation as a wit had preceded her and this subject was the sort that always allowed the
House some hilarity. Sir John Rees anticipated her speech when he
said good-humouredly that he knew what was coming from the

next speaker. 'Not only will I submit to chastisement with resignation, but I shall be ready to kiss the rod,' he said.[21]

She began, as recorded in Hansard, by saying : 'I know it is very difficult for some members to receive the first lady member of Parliament into the House' (hon. members cried gallantly, 'Not at all.') and went on to pay a tribute to her constituency, 'The world will not forget that it was the fighting men of Devon who dared to send the first woman to represent women in the Mother of Parliaments. . . .' Her voice was a little hoarse from nervousness but soon became clear. ('It was the clearest I ever heard in the House,' wrote one correspondent.) She elaborated her argument for the continuance of control by saying : 'How I wish I were really an orator. I would like to tell you about drink . . .' and went on to draw a graphic picture of the horrors of drink as it affected women and children, recalling a scene outside a public house in Plymouth when she saw a drunken mother come reeling out, terrifying the five-year-old child who had been waiting outside for her, so that it ran away screaming.

It is perhaps difficult for us today to imagine a time when drink was cheap enough and poverty bitter enough to make drunkenness in men and women a social problem. Now it impinges on us only as it leads to motoring accidents. Rereading Lady Astor's maiden speech those forgotten conditions come back with something of a shock for her phrasing was vivid and her sincerity undoubted. She said she was not pressing for prohibition ('I am far too intelligent for that'), though she thought it would come. Gesturing freely with a white-gloved hand she made some very acute observations such as : 'If you care enough about people, they will listen to the truth from you.' She ended on a note which commanded attention and respect :

> I do ask hon. members not to misread the spirit of the times. Do not go round saying that you want England a country fit for heroes to live in, do not talk about it unless you mean to do it. I do not want to rob the hon. member opposite of anything that has given him pleasure. I do not really want to take the joy out of the world; . . . but you know and I know, that drink really promises everything and gives you nothing. . . .
>
> I do not want you to look on your lady member as a fanatic or a lunatic. I am simply trying to speak for hundreds of women and children throughout the country who cannot speak for themselves. . . .[22]

The speech was well received. The next speaker, Sir Donald Maclean, Chairman of the Parliamentary Liberal Party (and father

of the Donald Maclean who defected to Russia in 1951), always a
champion of women's rights, conveyed the congratulations of the
whole house: 'It was a very brave speech. It was thoroughly informed. It was distinguished by diction, which I think we might at
all times very properly endeavour to emulate.' The motion was subsequently defeated. Afterwards Lloyd George warmly congratulated
Lady Astor saying, as she reported later, 'your voice is your fortune'.[23]

Again letters arrived in quantities and the Press, with the exception of the liquor trade journals, was flattering. *The Times* found
that 'Lady Astor proved that women have much of value to give
to the debates of the House. Her speech was good enough to make
any estimate of its quality that is different in standard from what
one would apply to the speech of a man the worst form of impolite-
ness.'[24]

From the beginning Lady Astor's career was lively and controversial. As she had said during the by-election campaign she saw her
role in Parliament as a dual one: that of representing the Sutton
division of Plymouth and of acting as spokeswoman for the women
and children in the whole country. Her interests were clear: equal
franchise, pensions, better education and working conditions, reform
of the property and marriage laws, and legislation to protect young
children. In addition she had her pet causes of temperance, better
milk supplies and measures to discourage gambling. To further any
of these causes she was not afraid to go against her own party. Her
impact on the House was immediate and not entirely due to her
sex. She had an uncomfortable way of getting under the skin of
members with her arguments and could needle her enemies to fury.
Her speeches were a blend of the commonplace and common sense
spiced by flashes of remarkable insight and wit. Even if she did not
speak during a debate she made her presence felt by what were
often maddeningly irritating interruptions (Bernard Shaw said her
interruptions were better than her speeches).[25] She never succeeded
in mastering the rules of debate and frequently had to be called to
order by the Speaker (or the Chairman if the House were in committee). At an early date he had to remind her that, 'We do not
say "you, you," across the floor of this House.' With a wave of a
white-gloved hand she would fervently agree with him, excusing
herself perhaps as she did on this early occasion by saying, 'It is very
upsetting to have to speak when you know there are members behind you who are longing for you to sit down.'[26]

She was never a good committee woman and, although she tried hard to scrutinize bills and play her part in committee, and spoke from carefully drafted speeches prepared by her secretaries, she was always at her happiest and most effective when speaking extempore. She was careful never to embarrass members outside the Chamber. She never went into the Smoking Room or other public rooms and seldom ate in the Members' Dining Room. At all times she was soberly but becomingly dressed.

Two or three days after her maiden speech Lady Astor spoke again in support of a private member's bill to amend the 1918 Representation of the People Act. In introducing his bill Mr Grundy generously declared that 'her presence adds grace and charm to this assembly. If the number of lady members is to be increased I am sure none of us has anything to fear.'[27] The purpose of the bill was to give women the vote at twenty-one and its supporters spoke so flatteringly of women's political capabilities that Lady Astor said to the enjoyment of the House : 'I feel that someone ought to take up the cudgels on behalf of the men since we have so many gallant defenders of our sex.' She went on to allay members' fears that women in the House would combine into a sort of sex party—a possibility still feared by many. 'We could not do it', she said. 'We women disagree just as much as the men.' She also advanced an argument often used by advocates of women's participation in political life : the moral value of the presence of women. 'Women bring into public and private life a sort of moral courage which men need.' But, as she was to do so often in the future, she softened the astringency of her remarks by an ingenuous rider : 'I am so fond of men and that is why I want more women to have the vote.'[28] The bill passed its second reading with a large majority but was subsequently blocked by the Government on the grounds that it proposed to introduce a more comprehensive bill of its own along these lines.

In the spring of 1920 Lady Astor first experienced the unpleasant side of public life. In her particular circumstances she was probably ill-advised to speak in opposition to a private member's bill to reform the divorce laws. She held that though men would benefit from an easing of the law it would be detrimental to women and children. 'You will never get real morality anywhere so long as you recognize a double standard for men and women',[29] she said. This view was very unpopular with many women and she now received a heavy mail saying she had no right to speak in this way for women as a whole. A Labour Party women's conference also passed a resolution to this

effect. But worse was to come. A fellow member, Horatio Bottomley, unearthed the facts about her earlier marriage and divorce and
published an article in his newspaper *John Bull* accusing her of
hypocrisy. It was advertised in large letters on placards all over London : 'Lady Astor's Divorce'. This gave the uninformed public the
impression that she was seeking a divorce from Lord Astor and
created a sensation. At the time Lady Astor was in France visiting
the battlefields. On her return to Westminster she experienced what
she was to call 'the dauntless decency'[30] of members : as she entered
the Chamber she received an ovation because they felt that Bottomley
had acted like a cad. The Plymouth Conservatives passed a resolution of confidence in her, but a great deal of lasting harm was done
to her reputation, for many people who did not know the complete
facts continued to think of her as a hypocrite.

During this year Lady Astor put in a very full attendance in the
Chamber and spoke in debates on the Finance Bill, the Emergency
Powers Bill, the naval estimates where they concerned Plymouth,
early closing, drink, marriage and welfare, and the employment
of women and children. She supported a bill to give free milk to
children and widowed mothers and on 19 May 1920 she took part in
a memorable debate on a motion moved by Major Hills, the Conservative member for Durham; 'that it is expedient that women
should have equal opportunity of employment with men in all
branches of the Civil Service within the United Kingdom and under
all local authorities and should also receive equal pay.' She said that
she was becoming disillusioned with the Government's promises
about what they were prepared to do for women and she thought
women in the country were too. Those that had managed to enter
new fields 'have found the same old asses browsing around them'.[31]
The motion—no doubt with an eye on women electors—was agreed
to without a division; but Lady Astor's suspicions were justified, for
nothing was done about equal pay, as we shall see, for another
thirty-five years.

Lady Astor was very active at Question Time and was always on
the alert to see that women were adequately represented on any
appropriate bodies; she herself served on four committees including
one concerned with women police. Not all she saw of the House
pleased her. She was inclined to endorse the remark attributed to
Stanley Baldwin that her own party included some 'hard-faced men
who looked as if they had done well out of the war', and she and
certain members soon developed a mutual antipathy which in time

became almost legendary. Sir Frederick Banbury, the Conservative member for the City of London, and a consistent opponent of women's suffrage, was foremost among these members, In June he deliberately talked out a private bill to reduce shop hours which Lady Astor supported since it would have improved the conditions of women shop-assistants. She was outraged at this and vainly tried to move the closure of the debate before 4 p.m. so that the bill could be put to the vote.[32] This marked the beginning of her private war with Sir Frederick.

She was much in demand as a speaker at meetings throughout the country. She continued to entertain at Cliveden and at 4 St James's Square (now the office of the Arts Council of Great Britain), the Astors' London house. She even found time to keep up her golf and was to be seen practising her strokes on the terrace of the House. No doubt her excellent, well-trained domestic staff helped to make this possible and she herself admitted that she could not have undertaken so much without three secretaries. Even so she was a woman of formidable energy. Everything she did in those early days had news value, yet she disliked personal publicity and rarely gave interviews. This probably accounts for the wealth of undocumented and probably apocryphal stories about her. Possibly no other Member of Parliament except Sir Winston Churchill has given rise to so many anecdotes.

1921 Another First Lady

IN 1921 Lady Astor was as busy as ever. Among other things she seconded the Guardianship of Infants Bill, a private bill to give mothers equal rights with fathers over their children;[1] she asked the first of what was to be a series of questions stretching over the years about women police;[2] and she spoke amid much jocular repartee against the Government's bill to abolish the war-time Liquor Control Board and ease restrictions on the sale of alcohol.[3] By November Lady Astor was able to report to her constituents in Plymouth: 'I do not know whether I have become a force in the House of Commons as much as a nuisance. . . .' She was also said to have remarked at this time, 'the toast used to be—"the Ladies, God bless 'em." Now women have the vote it should be—"the Gentlemen, God help 'em".'[4]

By this month her lonely tenure of the Lady Members' Room overlooking the terrace had come to an end. Earlier in the year Mr Tom Wintringham, the Liberal member for Louth in Lincolnshire, had collapsed and died in the Smoking Room of the House. He had been very popular with all parties, and the Prime Minister, Sir Donald Maclean and other influential Liberals combined to persuade his widow to fight the ensuing by-election. Margaret Wintringham was well-known in Louth for her immense amount of public work and was very popular. She was a magistrate; she had been chairman of the women's war agricultural committee at Louth; and she was a member of the county agricultural committee for Lincolnshire as well as of the Grimsby Education Committee. A tall, well-built woman of forty-two with a high complexion and bright brown eyes she was a good platform speaker and had spoken during many of her husband's campaigns, but throughout the by-election campaign, in deference to her bereavement, she sat silent on the platform in her widow's weeds while eminent Liberals came to speak on her behalf. She did not expect to win, for her husband had held the seat by a mere 2,505 votes at the last election. But to her own

and everyone else's surprise she topped the poll on 23 September
with a majority of 791 in a three-cornered fight.

Under a headline 'Louth Reduces Sex Prejudice' *The Times* correspondent said that Mrs Wintringham's ability and charm had
triumphed over prejudice, and reported her as having said with dis-
arming frankness, 'I never anticipated winning because of the split-
ting of the progressive vote' (between herself and the Labour candidate). She was worried, he said, about her capacity for the job
but 'would do her best'. He went on to try to suggest some connection between the candidate and the women's vote, asking: 'Is sex a
help or hindrance?'[5]

Mrs Wintringham was widely hailed by the Press as the first
British-born woman M.P. Her constituents were jubilant, Lady
Astor sent her a telegram 'Rejoicing over victory, shall welcome you
in the House of Commons', and the Women's Freedom League
decorated its office in High Holborn with flags.

She was well received in the House to which she was introduced
on 18 October by Mr Asquith and Sir Donald Maclean and took
her seat on the corner of the fourth bench above the gangway on the
Opposition side, two benches above Lady Astor's usual seat. The
Daily News[6] reported 'warm applause' from the House when on 2
November she asked her first question, on the number of unemployed
agricultural workers.[7] In fact she became, as Mary Stocks has
pointed out in her biography of Eleanor Rathbone, one of those few
M.P.s, like James Maxton and Josiah Wedgwood, 'whom the House,
irrespective of party, takes to its heart with a kind of paternal affection'.[8] At a London dinner of the Lincolnshire Society soon afterwards she could say, rather ungratefully perhaps, quoting St Paul,
' "the barbarians did give me welcome". They [the Commons] have
certainly made up their minds to give women a chance to take
part in the legislature of the country.'[9]

With Lady Astor she was immediately *en rapport*. They had many
interests in common including education, better milk supplies and
temperance—for Mrs Wintringham was the vice-president of the
Lincolnshire Total Abstinence Association. Lady Astor insisted that
the new lady member should use the Lady Members' Room as an
office and install her secretary there, since she herself had an office
in her London house. The two members could not have been more
unlike in appearance and manner: Lady Astor small, vivacious and
volatile; Mrs Wintringham tall, stately and businesslike. Years later
she was to describe Lady Astor as a 'young prancing pony' with her-

self as 'a slow old carthorse trotting beside'.[10] While Lady Astor provoked and stimulated the House, Mrs Wintringham calmed and soothed it; perhaps that was why it liked her so much. She was probably not as placid as she looked but her unruffled manner has been said to have been the greatest asset to the women's movement.

Mrs Wintringham took her full share of parliamentary work. She made her maiden speech on 9 November during the second reading of the Consolidated Fund Bill in which she put in a plea for good national housekeeping on behalf of women 'to whom', she said, 'economy appeals very much'.[11] In March 1922 she and Lady Astor intervened in a debate on the police to plead for the retention of the patrols of auxiliary policewomen who during and since the war had been patrolling the parks and other parts of London in order to protect and warn young women who seemed to be in moral danger. Mrs Wintringham made a well reasoned case for keeping the patrols while Lady Astor interjected admiring Hear, hears and Listen to thats! and, when the Home Secretary, Mr Short, refused to give way, shook her fist at him.[12]

In June Mrs Wintringham fired the first shot in a campaign that was to last forty years by asking the Government to introduce at an early stage a bill to amend the Sex Disqualification (Removal) Act to enable peeresses in their own right to sit in the House of Lords.[13] The background to this question was interesting. The Act had been passed in 1919 as the natural sequel to the Representation of the People and Parliament (Qualification of Women) Acts, making it law that 'a person shall not be disqualified by sex or marriage from the exercise of any public function.' It was thought at the time that these terms were wide enough to allow peeresses in their own right to take their seats in the House of Lords without further legislation. But when the Viscountess Rhondda had sought to receive the writ earlier that year, the Committee of Privileges of the House of Lords had first found in her favour, but they later reversed the decision on the grounds that the Sex Disqualification (Removal) Act only removed disqualifications; it did not confer rights that had not previously existed.[14] At the same time the Lords made it clear that they had no intention of passing a measure to allow peeresses to sit with them. Accordingly Sir Austen Chamberlain answered Mrs Wintringham's question in the negative, since he said he saw no point in introducing a bill which had no chance of becoming law.

Other subjects which Mrs Wintringham spoke on this year were ex-servicemen's pensions, beer distilling, criminal law amendments

as they affected women and children, and education. Like Lady
Astor she kept a watchful eye on public bodies to see that women
were adequately represented on them. She sat on a parliamentary
committee for agriculture and her words on this subject of which
she had extensive knowledge were always listened to with attention
by the House.

1922-1923 Two Becomes Three

WHILE MRS WINTRINGHAM was settling down to her first
parliamentary session in 1922, Lady Astor paid her first visit to her
mother country as a Member of Parliament, at a time when Anglo-
American relations were strained as a result of differences over the
Treaty of Versailles. Her speech to the Women's Pan-American
Conference in Baltimore on 28 April made a great impact and it is
likely that this and other speeches which she made during her tour
and which were included in her book *My Two Countries*, published
in 1923, did contribute towards better Anglo-American relations.
She was to play the part of mediator many times during her annual
trips to the United States. On this first occasion she gave her
audiences her impressions of parliamentary life. In Washington she
said that the members of the House of Commons were 'a lot of
grown-up schoolboys' and added, 'Don't make too much fun of
women in politics. I know it's a tremendous temptation. We are
funny, but so are you. Make fun of me, if you like, I'm used to it
and have got a sense of humour. But some of these women are sensitive and it will scare them off.'[1]

The question of the control of the sale of intoxicating liquor was
still very much in her mind and before she left for the United States,
backed by J. H. Thomas, the Labour leader, and Mrs Wintringham,
she had drafted and circulated a private bill, the Local Option Bill,
to give local authorities power to opt for partial or total prohibition
in their areas if they wished. This aroused a good deal of opposition
among many sections of the public, including some women's organizations and particularly in Plymouth where such a measure did not
commend itself to the Navy. As a result a Dr Wansey Bayley announced his intention of standing as an Independent Conservative
candidate for Sutton at the next election to fight on this very issue.
He was alleged to be receiving powerful support from the breweries.
As for Lady Astor's bill, it did not receive a second reading.

The shadow of a forthcoming general election stretched over the
whole of this year. The Coalition Government was coming to an

end; the Conservatives were making no secret of the fact that they wanted to break away. On 19 October at a meeting at the Carlton Club under the leadership of Bonar Law they decided on this course and as a result Lloyd George had to appeal to the country. A general election took place on 15 November 1922.

In the four years since the election of 1918 potential women candidates had had time to look around for seats, and organizations such as the Women's Election Committee (a non-party body under the presidency of Dr Christine Murrell, which was founded about 1921 to promote the candidature of women), and former suffrage societies such as the Women's Freedom League and the National Union of Societies for Equal Citizenship had rallied to support them. In 1920 two Labour women, Miss Susan Lawrence and Miss Margaret Bondfield, had fought by-elections unsuccessfully at Camberwell North and Northampton respectively. In 1922 thirty-three women, almost double the previous number, were nominated as candidates. They were made up as follows:

	CONSERVATIVE	LABOUR	LIBERAL	INDEPENDENT	TOTAL
1922	5	10	16	2	33
1918	*1*	*4*	*4*	*8*	*17*

It will be seen that the Labour and Liberal parties maintained their considerable lead over the Conservatives in adopting women candidates, and that the number of Independents standing had dropped considerably. Only two women, both to become well-known, stood without party backing: Miss Eleanor Rathbone stood as an Independent candidate for the East Toxteth division of Liverpool, with the support of the Liverpool Women's Citizenship Association and the help of the East Toxteth Liberals; in Brentford and Chiswick Mrs Ray Strachey again faced her former adversary, this time in a straight fight.

Four of the five Conservative candidates had honours or titles. One of them was Dame Helen Gwynne-Vaughan (Camberwell N.W.), a distinguished woman who was Professor of Botany at London University and during the Great War had been successively Chief Controller of Queen Mary's Army Auxiliary Corps attached to the British Army in France, and Commander of the Women's Royal Air Force. The Labour candidates included Margaret Bondfield (Northampton) and Susan Lawrence (East Ham North). Five Liberal candidates were titled and others included Commandant Mary Allen (St George's, Westminster), co-founder and head of the

London auxiliary women police, and Mrs Burnett Smith (Glasgow, Maryhill), better known as the novelist Annie S. Swan whose books were said to be awarded as school prizes more often than those of any other writer.

When the results were declared it was found that the Conservatives had an overall majority of seventy-nine, though both they and the Liberals had lost seats to the Labour Party which had nearly doubled its representation. The women candidates were all defeated with the exception of the two former members, Lady Astor and Mrs Wintringham.

Lady Astor had had a lively campaign fighting against Dr Bayley, the Independent Conservative, and a Labour candidate. Neither of the opposition candidates had had any luck in recruiting prominent women to their aid. The Countess of Selborne wrote to Dr Bayley; 'I certainly could not speak for you at Plymouth because if I had a vote in that borough I should give it to Lady Astor.' Mrs Philip Snowden had turned down an invitation to stand against her as the Labour candidate saying: 'I would not in any circumstances stand against Lady Astor. I am a Labour woman, but the work which Lady Astor is doing for women and children both in Parliament and the country makes her services invaluable.'[2] It was a remarkable display of feminine solidarity.

Although Lady Astor found it prudent to play down the temperance issue at this election her majority dropped by 2,000 votes to 3,093, but she triumphed over Bayley and the brewers to the tune of some 10,000 votes. In thanking her supporters she said: 'I have made mistakes and very likely shall make more, but I don't think I have ever done anything of which Plymouth need be ashamed.'[3]

In a tough fight and with a swing against the Liberals Mrs Wintringham increased her majority by a few votes to 883.

The results in the other constituencies were a sharp blow to feminist hopes and some newspapers drew the conclusion that neither men nor women voters were yet free from prejudice against women candidates. To blame either the electorate or the candidates, however, was hardly justifiable for the majority of women were fighting unwinnable seats (and, as most of them were standing for the first time, this was only to be expected). At least ten stood for seats not contested by their party at the previous election. Nevertheless eleven of the others increased the votes for their parties and two women fought to a very close finish: Dame Helen Gwynne-Vaughan and

Lady Cooper, who as Conservative candidate at Walsall was defeated by the Liberal candidate by only 325 votes. Eleanor Rathbone, although soundly beaten, polled over 9,000 votes at East Toxteth, and Ray Strachey polled 7,804, reducing the Conservative majority from 6,457 to 2,346—quite a remarkable feat for an Independent.

As a footnote to this election it is interesting to notice in passing that Winston Churchill lost his seat in Dundee to a rabid prohibitionist named Scrymgeour who announced that the miracle of his election was due to God's wish for prohibition and that England would go dry in a year. He made Lady Astor's views seem quite moderate.

Early in the new session of Parliament Lady Astor fell foul of her own party by telling an annual Conservative Conference : 'People who live in two houses do not realize what it is like to live in two rooms. That's what is wrong with the Conservatives.' Press reports of the meeting record 'disorder, uproar and pandemonium' following these words. A fellow M.P. at this time called Lady Astor 'the cheekiest little sparrow that ever sat on a doorstep' while another declared that 'she hadn't the manners of a street corner cat'.[4] None of these criticisms appeared to worry her and she was delighted when she won third place in the ballot for private bills. She had one ready, needless to say, concerning intoxicating liquors. But this bill, which the Government promised to back, was a comparatively mild and sensible measure to prohibit the sale of such liquor to young persons under eighteen. It was known as the Intoxicating Liquor (Sale to Persons under 18) Bill and seemed assured of support from both sides of the House. Its passage however was marked by incident. In her speech at its second reading on 9 March[5] its promoter was at pains to discourage the idea that it was 'Lady Astor's Bill' or some private whim of her own. She had received scores of letters from schoolteachers and medical women, she said, urging the need for such a measure. 'I am simply the godmother and I hope a fairy one.' In her own irresistible fashion she appealed to the House to support the bill, saying : 'Boys up to eighteen are children. You are all children in a way. We women love you because you are children.' Mrs Wintringham made a calm, sensible speech dealing with the welfare aspects of the bill, but, if Lady Astor was the fairy godmother, Sir Frederick Banbury was certainly the wicked uncle. His case rested on the fact that at Winchester he had always had beer at dinner and supper ('Look at the result !' shouted an hon. member) and did not think that as a result he exhibited any serious incapacity. (Lady Astor: 'Oh, yes you do.') The bill passed the second reading with a good majority but was drastically amended in Committee, one of the most important amendments being the insertion of the word 'knowingly' to apply to barmen who served drinks to young people (it was felt that they might otherwise often be unjustly penalized). These amendments annoyed Lady Astor who had to be asked by the Chairman to withdraw her words after she had called Mr Remer, the Conservative member for Macclesfield, 'a village donkey'.

The third reading of the bill took place at the end of June and there the enmity between Lady Astor and Sir Frederick Banbury flared to a climax.[6] Lady Astor had been in the House from 11 a.m. to 4 p.m.—'on a boiled egg and a glass of water' as she told her constituents afterwards; just before 4 p.m. she saw Sir Frederick Banbury rise to move an amendment. 'I went up to Sir Frederick and said quite jokingly, "I have tried kindness, I have tried rudeness, now I shall try force. I shall hold on to your coat-tails and you shall not rise. . . ." '[7] She clung on to them but Banbury was too strong for her and with maddening imperturbability rose majestically and talked out the bill. Some Press reports made the most of the incident describing Lady Astor as 'pummelling' Sir Frederick, but this was an exaggeration. Nevertheless this obstruction caused the bill to wait another fortnight for its third reading; but on 13 July it was passed by a majority of 247 with only ten votes cast against it.[8] It was piloted through the Upper House by Lord Astor. This was the first private bill moved by a woman to become law; it is still in force.

Later in the year Lady Astor was in trouble with her own party again when she wrote an article in the *Pall Mall Gazette*—which was owned by Lord Astor—urging Conservatives to adopt more progressive policies. Among those she advocated were town planning, more houses, revision of the Poor Law, improved welfare services, raising the school-leaving age from fourteen to sixteen and reform of the penal system.[9] These ideas were well ahead of their time and annoyed the right-wing of the party; in Plymouth some Conservatives threatened to put up another candidate at the next election.

In April 1923 Mrs Wintringham boldly attacked Mr Baldwin's Budget as 'a man-made Budget', castigating him for reducing the tax on beer while leaving that on tea and sugar intact. 'The . . .

housewife', she declared, 'is one of the most heavily burdened and taxed people in the country . . . for in homes where the weekly wage is only 25s a tax of 8d on tea is a large item.'[10]

Soon after Mr Baldwin had succeeded Bonar Law as Prime Minister in May 1923, another woman took her seat in the House. Like Lady Astor and Mrs Wintringham she had inherited the seat from her husband, but in rather unusual circumstances, and she herself was an unusual candidate, for Mrs Mabel Hilton Philipson was already well-known to the public as Mabel Russell, a musical comedy actress, who had charmed audiences at Daly's, the Prince of Wales, and the Gaiety Theatres. She had taken the part of Fifi in the original production of *The Merry Widow* and a leading role in *The Dollar Princess*. Later she went into straight plays and became Gerald du Maurier's leading lady in *London Pride*. During the war she had married as her second husband (her first, a nephew of Cecil Rhodes, was killed in a motoring accident) Captain Hilton Philipson. They now had three small children and ran a model farm in Esher. In 1922 Hilton Philipson had been returned as the National Liberal member for Berwick-on-Tweed but he was unseated in April 1923 by petition because of the fraudulent practices (unknown to him) of his agent. As a result he was banned from standing in the division for seven years. At a meeting to select his successor an old farmer was said to have first suggested that Mrs Hilton Philipson should stand. She was already admired in the division for the work she had done there and for her easy, friendly manner. She had a ready wit and a genuine sympathy for human problems, for she herself had built up a career from small beginnings. She was also genuinely interested in farming and rural life. When the proposal was put to her, she said she would stand on one condition—that she stood as a Conservative. This was a bold decision in a traditionally Liberal constituency, once held by Sir Edward Grey, particularly as she made no secret of the fact that she intended to keep the seat warm for her husband's eventual return. However the Conservatives (who had not contested the seat in the previous general election) adopted her as their candidate on 6 May. Her husband helped in her campaign and no doubt swung over a good deal of support from Lloyd George's National Liberals who did not put up a candidate, although an Independent Liberal and a Labour candidate stood against her. When the votes were counted it was found that Mabel Philipson had polled 12,000 in a three-cornered contest, rather more than her husband had achieved in a straight fight, and had a majority of over

6,000. It was a great triumph and heartened the Conservatives who had under-estimated her vote by some 2,000. The Press reported wild scenes of enthusiasm in Berwick when the figures were announced. The winning candidate had difficulty in reaching her hotel through the crush of well wishers and suffered a black eye by coming rather sharply into contact with a policeman's elbow.

Mrs Wintringham was attending an inquiry into domestic service when the result came through and explained her pleasure to *The Daily Telegraph* reporter in this way : 'It is not a case of whether a woman is of my party or not. It is a case of whether she is going to help in our work, particularly in women's and children's questions and then, of course, the question of peace'.[11] Women members were still women first and party politicians second.

Mrs Philipson took her seat on 7 June. A photograph in the Press on the following day showed her arrival at the House, looking demure and not at all actressy in dark, inconspicuous clothes. With the glamour of the stage and her political triumph behind her, as well as being at thirty-six the youngest woman to take her seat, she had filled the galleries and the benches which hummed with anticipation. She was reported to be 'rather nervous' and to have had some coaching beforehand in her new part. Her sponsors were Colonel Leslie Wilson, the Government Chief Whip, and Sir Thomas Inskip, President of the Board of Trade. They made their bows amid the cheers and counter-cheers of the House. 'Nothing', reported *The Times* '[could be] more stately than the entrance of this little woman who charmed the British public in a previous public career', while *The Daily Telegraph* found her reception 'as cordial as she ever received before the footlights'.[12]

In one of the last debates of the 1923 Parliament Mrs Philipson made her maiden speech in support of the Government which was resisting a vote of censure on the unemployment situation moved by Ramsay MacDonald. She spoke for five minutes and made the House laugh when she said of the Labour leader, 'He wants us to assert our position in Europe by a moral gesture. Have you ever tried to stop a dog fight by a moral gesture? You will get your fingers badly bitten if you do.'[13]

Thus when Parliament was dissolved[14] three women members, two Conservatives and one Liberal, returned to their constituencies to defend their seats which they had inherited in different ways from their husbands.

Not everyone was pleased with them, however. Sir Henry Craik, a Conservative member who had hotly opposed women's suffrage, wrote to *The Times* in July saying that in his opinion women were still out of place in the House on the grounds that 'our attitude towards women used to be that of homage and I fear that fits in badly with political contentions.'[15] In other words, in becoming practical politicians women had stepped down from the pedestal.

1923-1924 'See How They Grow!'

THE 1923 General Election campaign took place in damp, foggy weather. Polling day was on Saturday, 6 December. In the twelve months since the last election the number of women candidates had risen by one to make a total of thirty-four. Of these, twelve (including the three former members) had stood before. Their party affiliations were as follows:

	CONSERVATIVE	LABOUR	LIBERAL	INDEPENDENT	TOTAL
1923	7	14	12	1	34
1922	*5*	*10*	*16*	*2*	*33*

Only Mrs Ray Strachey stood this time as an Independent candidate, making a third and last vain attempt to unseat the Conservative member for Brentford and Chiswick. Both the Conservative and the Labour parties put forward a slightly increased number of women, but the Liberals had reduced their number. As before, the candidates were standing for electorates scattered throughout England, Scotland and Wales, though fourteen were in the southern half of England. As before, the majority were contesting urban seats.

The election results announced on 8 December revealed an unprecedented state of affairs: no party had an overall majority. Baldwin, far from having strengthened his position, found that the Conservatives had only 258 seats (a loss of 89 seats), while the Liberals had increased their numbers by 33 to 151 and the Labour Party by 49 to 191. With this electoral swing to the left eight women had been elected, including all the former members, so that three Conservative, three Labour, and two Liberal women took their seats in the House. Moreover four of the five new members had won seats on their own account instead of 'inheriting' them. It was a moment of triumph widely acclaimed by the Press. *The Times,*[1] which at this time made a feature of publishing a separate list of women candidates after nomination day, commented soberly: 'A year ago the general impression was that male voters were generally disinclined to vote for women candidates, but the heavy polls recorded on this occasion suggest that the prejudice is disappearing.' The feminist societies were jubilant. One of them immediately put in hand a pamphlet about the new women M.P.s, and the Women's Election Committee which had given active help to ten candidates put out some triumphant leaflets. One was entitled 'See How They Grow!' and reminded the public that '83 women had so far appealed to the electorate,[2] polling 1,057,425 votes between them.' Another leaflet inaccurately attributed to Miss Dorothy Jewson, one of the new M.P.s, the highest number of votes and the largest majority 'recorded at the last election'. In fact Miss Jewson's Labour colleague in the two-member constituency at Norwich had polled over 20,000 votes to her 19,000. 'PLEASE', concluded the leaflet, 'BRING THESE FACTS TO THE ATTENTION OF THE LOCAL CHAIRMAN OF YOUR PARTY when the selection of a candidate is under consideration.'

But were these successes in fact due to the disappearance of sex prejudice? In the light of today there is nothing in the figures to suggest it. It seems that women benefited or suffered at the polls along with male candidates in so far as the electoral swing affected their party. None of the unsuccessful candidates could have been expected to triumph in the circumstances. One of the most interesting of these was Frances ('Daisy'), Countess of Warwick, standing as the Labour candidate for her home constituency of Warwick and Leamington against a young Conservative named Anthony Eden who was related by marriage to her son, Lord Brooke. The Countess had been a noted beauty and in the 1890s was King Edward VII's mistress. She became converted to Socialism in 1895 and since then had worked hard for the Labour Party, campaigning and contributing to its funds. She now had high hopes that her record of social work and her local standing in Warwick might lead to victory but, alas, when the results were declared she was bottom of the poll.

Lady Astor in a straight fight with Labour (no Independent Conservative stood against her after all) retained her seat with a reduced majority. She was in excellent form during the campaign. 'Say, missus', shouted one joker, 'how many toes are there on a pig's foot?' 'Take off your boot, man, and count for yourself' was the lightning reply.[3]

Mrs Hilton Philipson polled over 10,000 votes but her majority declined to 1,869; Mrs Wintringham in Louth was able to take advantage of the swing to increase her marginal majority to 1,101 in a tough fight.

A new Conservative member, Katherine (Kitty), Duchess of Atholl, did well to recapture by a bare 150 votes the seat of Perth and Kinross (which had been represented by her husband until 1917), since it had not been contested by the Conservatives at the previous election. She was the first woman member of Parliament for Scotland—and belonged to what Mary Agnes Hamilton was to call the 'O.B.E. type . . . the sort of woman "who did good work in the war".'[4] In fact she had been created a D.B.E. in 1918 following much good work, which included turning Blair Castle into a hospital. The daughter of a scholarly baronet, the Duchess herself inclined to intellectual pursuits (she had edited a *Military History of Perthshire* with painstaking attention to detail); she was also an accomplished pianist who had studied at the Royal College of Music. Dedicated to good works and particularly interested in education she has been described as 'a Tory bred in the Whig tradition', but strangely enough she had opposed women's suffrage. She was small and rather hawk-like, high-principled and very sincere, but did not have much sense of humour.

The idea that she should stand for Parliament was first suggested to her by Lloyd George who wanted to see more women of all parties in the House. She consulted King George V during one of his visits to Blair Castle and His Majesty expressed doubts whether, although she had no children, she could combine her social duties with life at Westminster.[5] But the Duchess had no worries on that score because of the 'wonderful domestic gifts' of 'Bardie' (her husband); he was the sort of man who remembered to place a Koran at the bedside of King Feisal of Iraq when he visited the castle. Furthermore, hearing that a good many Conservative M.P.s were not yet reconciled to the presence of women in the House, 'If I could do anything towards smoothing over matters', she says in her memoirs, 'I felt it my duty to try.'[6]

Following her election she made a speech at a women's luncheon in Edinburgh which was much quoted at the time. In the course of it she said :

> I think we have still to make the House of Commons and the nation realize what women can contribute to the work of Parliament and to do this, it seems to me, we have to use many of the qualities we find needed in our domestic life. Forty years ago, the ideal wife was one who said 'Amen' to her husband whenever he opened his mouth.

Today that idea has been abandoned and we have instead an ideal of comradeship, of partnership in life's happiness and difficulties alike which we recognize as much better.[7]

Lady Terrington, wife of the second Baron Terrington, without benefit of inheritance, won at her second attempt a notable victory in the Wycombe division for the Liberals. In a three-cornered fight she ousted the sitting member, Colonel du Pré, from a seat held by the Conservative Party almost continuously since 1886. There was particular jubilation among the feminist societies because Colonel du Pré's attitude to women's questions had been far from satisfactory. Lady Terrington herself said after her election, 'I really think the women put me into Parliament' although she also disclosed that during the campaign she had been 'kissed by dozens of men'.[8] Perhaps this was not surprising as she was a tall, elegant woman of thirty-five who, the *Daily Mail*[9] said, looked twenty-five and was enthusiastic enough for eighteen. On 3 December the *Daily Express* had published an article about her under the headlines 'The Best Dressed Woman M.P. Lady Terrington's Aim If Elected—Furs and Pearls'. 'If I am returned to Westminster,' she was quoted as saying, 'I intend to wear my best clothes when I go there. I don't believe in a woman politician wearing a dull little frock with a Quakerish collar and keeping her nice clothes for her social appointments. It is all humbug.' Lady Terrington sued the newspaper for libel, claiming that this report was untrue and defamatory, but her action failed.

Furs and pearls as maybe, Lady Terrington was very much an open-air type who campaigned on horseback, and her main interests, as befitted a rural seat, were concerned with agriculture and the welfare of animals. She was in favour of credit facilities for the farmer and co-operative farming schemes as well as legal and economic equality between the sexes, declaring that she would like to introduce a private bill to give women the vote at twenty-one. She was associated with many worthy causes and also had the distinction of being the first woman president of the Marlow Football Club.

But the real interest in this election lies in the arrival in Parliament for the first time of three Labour women members. They were not only the first single women to take their seats in the House of Commons, but they were quite a new type of woman M.P.: they had all worked professionally in the women's trade union movement and brought a highly trained expertise to bear on employment and kindred questions.

The honour of being the first Labour woman elected fell to Miss (Arabella) Susan Lawrence in that her results in East Ham North, where she had a narrow majority of 416, were announced before the others. She was also the first woman to be returned in the London area. Susan Lawrence was the daughter of a solicitor and had been brought up in affluent surroundings. She showed early intellectual promise and went up to Newnham College, Cambridge, where she took the mathematical tripos. She had led an active social life, and had mixed in circles that included her fellow M.P., the Duchess of Atholl. She became interested in local government and, in addition to all her other 'firsts', had been the first woman member for West Marylebone elected to the L.C.C. in 1910. She was then a Conservative but when she carried out an inquiry into the circumstances of charwomen employed by the L.C.C., she was so horrified to find how poorly they were paid that she resigned her seat in 1912 and joined the Labour Party. This brought her into contact with Mary Macarthur with whom she worked for several years in the National Federation of Women Workers. She became a member of the Fabian Society and was re-elected to the L.C.C. as Labour representative for Poplar where she lived. She also served on the Poplar Borough Council and in 1921 went to prison with the other Poplar Guardians, led by the Mayor and future Labour leader, George Lansbury, for failing to collect the poor rate. A friend who visited her in Holloway at the time found her with sparkling eyes exclaiming jubilantly, 'What a lark! What a lark!'[10] She spent her six weeks there writing a pamphlet on taxation. She had fought a by-election unsuccessfully in Camberwell in 1920. She was extremely well-liked in her present constituency where she was known as 'our Susan'. (It is worth noting in passing that many successful women Members of Parliament have been referred to in this affectionate way by their constituents. There was even some attempt to call Lady Astor 'our Nancy' in the early days in Plymouth but she discouraged it.)

Looking at Susan Lawrence with her cropped hair and brusque manner the hon. gentlemen may have thought at first that their worst fears that the Chamber would be invaded by formidable blue-stockings had been confirmed, but they came to respect Susan for her knowledge and powerful intellect, for she had the faculty of being able to explain complicated detail with clarity and precision enlivened with a fierce and biting wit. She was the only woman M.P. to give her age in *Who's Who* (she was fifty-two at the time of this election). Her interests, besides local government organization and finance, were 'parties, Tolstoy, rowdy meetings, mountaineering, and reading Government Blue Books.'

Miss Margaret Bondfield ('our Maggie' to her constituents) had won Northampton at her third attempt, tipping over a 5,000 Conservative majority to one of 4,036 in her favour. When she asked Bernard Shaw to speak for her during her unsuccessful campaign of 1922 he wrote: '. . . why Northampton? You are the best man of the lot, and they shove you off to a place where the water is too cold for their dainty feet . . . and keep the safe seats for their now quite numerous imbeciles.'[11] This time unemployment in the local boot and shoe trade had made the water warmer and 'our Maggie' was well-known and much esteemed in the division. She herself had known poverty and unemployment. The daughter of a lacemaker, Margaret was born in Chard and was a shop assistant at fourteen. When she was twenty she came to London with five pounds in her pocket and trudged the length of Oxford Street until she found another shop assistant's job, living in and working a sixty-five-hour week for a salary that rose from £15 to £25 a year. She first read about a Shop Assistants' Union in a newspaper that had wrapped up a supper of chips; she joined the Union and eventually became its assistant secretary. Later she became assistant to Mary Macarthur in the National Federation of Women Workers and took over as organizing secretary at Mary's death. At the time of her election she was not only Chief Woman Officer of the Women's Section of the National Union of General and Municipal Workers (with which the National Federation of Women Workers had merged) but Chairman for 1923 of the General Council of the T.U.C.

Margaret Bondfield was a small dumpy woman of fifty with a round, amiable face that made her look like a country woman long after she had left Somerset. If she had not the intellectual capacity of Susan Lawrence she combined shrewd political sense with great organizing ability. She had firm religious convictions and a powerful platform manner. Bernard Shaw is said to have put many of her qualities into the Postmistress General in *The Apple Cart*. She fought a gruelling campaign in Northampton, touring the constituency in a borrowed red Ford car, speaking as many as six times a day, and helping Labour candidates in other constituencies, sustaining herself on what she called 'the ideal candidate's supper' of onions stewed in milk. Ramsay MacDonald came to speak for her. By the end of the campaign she was said to have completely overcome the antipathy that had at first been shown by the male trade unionists—often the most conservative of people—to a woman candidate.

She took such a high moral stand in her election address and speeches, asking the voters 'to lift controversy above party wrangling and consider that they were deciding the destinies of the country', that some of her supporters feared she was talking above the heads of her audience. One of them questioned an unskilled labourer:

'Have you been listening to Miss Bondfield?'

'Yus.'

'And could you understand what she was talking about when she said the country was in chaos?'

'Why, yus. She meant it was in a bloody mess.'[12]

In any event there was no doubt about the result—even some of the spoiled ballot papers had 'God bless her' scrawled across them. After the poll was declared 'our Maggie' was hauled round the constituency by her electors for more than two hours in a big, rope-drawn charabanc.

Miss Dorothy Jewson, at thirty-nine the youngest of the Labour Members, had had a notable victory in her home town of Norwich even if she had not achieved quite all that the Women's Election Committee claimed for her. She, like Susan Lawrence, came of a middle-class professional family and was a graduate of Girton College, Cambridge. She had been an active suffragette and had also worked with Mary Macarthur in the National Federation of Women Workers. At one time she worked as a housemaid in a hotel for six weeks in order to study conditions there.

As the excitement of the election results died down the parties were confronted with a difficult situation for none of them had an absolute majority. The Liberals held the key to the situation but they were riven by the feud between Asquith and Lloyd George and it was uncertain whether they would swing behind the Tories or the Labour Party. The Labour Party itself was uncertain whether it wanted to take up the reins of government for it had no experience in office and would be committed to an expensive programme of social measures and nationalization in a worsening economic climate. At a meeting in the Albert Hall Margaret Bondfield roused the Labour audience to a high pitch of enthusiasm by demanding that if it had the opportunity the Party should seize office with both hands.

At the State opening of Parliament the Duchess of Atholl savoured the unusual position of standing in her ordinary clothes with the other members behind the bar instead of sitting in state in full regalia with her husband to hear the King's Speech. She and Susan Lawrence did not wait long to make their maiden speeches; both spoke during the debate on the King's Speech. On 16 January 1924 in a speech which in its profound knowledge of local affairs and finance showed the House what to expect from her in the future Susan deplored the Government's failure to make any mention of an extension of school meals.[13] Two days later in a rather more rambling speech the Duchess, who had been coached by her husband the night before, touched on unemployment among young people, the legitimacy of children born out of wedlock, and the property of the Church of Scotland; she also welcomed Government plans for naval shipbuilding.[14] She was cheered and afterwards Lloyd George, always a champion of women members, congratulated her as did Lady Astor and Sir Austen Chamberlain.

In the meantime the Liberal Party had decided to back the censure motion of J. R. Clynes 'that the political advisers of His Majesty have not the confidence of this House'; this made the downfall of Stanley Baldwin's Government certain. Margaret Bondfield managed to squeeze her maiden speech into this important debate, speaking after Sir John Simon. After apologizing for intervening in a battle of giants she spoke sensibly and from first-hand knowledge of unemployment among women; a quarter of a million of them, she pointed out, had been unemployed for over three years.[15] It was a competent speech but she herself felt it to be a failure for she found, as so many new members have discovered, that speaking in the intimate atmosphere of the House of Commons is a very different matter from declaiming on a public platform. A Press correspondent, however, described it as 'the first intellectual speech by a woman the House had ever heard'.[16] That was Margaret Bondfield's first and last speech as a backbencher for some time.

Following the carrying of the vote of censure Mr Baldwin resigned on 21 January 1924 and the next day Ramsay MacDonald accepted office. The day after that Margaret Bondfield was called from a T.U.C. meeting by the newly appointed Minister of Labour, Mr Tom Shaw, who asked her to be his Under-Secretary of State. With remarkable sangfroid Margaret stayed until the end of the Council meeting. That evening she entered her office at Montagu House for the first time: a 'beautiful room with a most elaborately painted ceiling, but no cloakroom accommodation whatsoever'.[17] The first woman minister had been appointed. A few days later she was representing the British Government at a meeting of the International Labour Office in Geneva and on 18 February standing at the dispatch box, she answered her first question—on the cost of this Office.[18]

It was a sudden and dramatic triumph for women politicians but at least one person was not satisfied. Speaking at a reception she gave for the new women members Lady Astor declared that Margaret Bondfield should have had a place in the Cabinet: 'Some people say that she was not admitted because she had no parliamentary experience.' But, she added darkly, 'I know the Cabinet pretty well and there are some men in it whose parliamentary experience is not to their credit.'[19]

As the new session got under way the Whips ensured that women members were often heard in the Chamber. In February it was announced that Mr Charles (later Sir Charles) Trevelyan, the President of the Board of Education, had appointed Susan Lawrence as his Parliamentary Private Secretary; she was the first woman to occupy this honorary post which is often the first step to ministerial position.

On Leap Year day (which some newspapers regarded as significant) Dorothy Jewson made her maiden speech seconding a motion by Mr W. M. Adamson, to amend the 1918 Representation of the People Act to give women the vote at the age of twenty-one. She accused the Coalition Government of 1918 of not honouring its election promises. Most of the other women members spoke in this extremely lively debate.[20] The Duchess of Atholl tried to block the motion with an amendment to set up a conference to consider the matter. As it stood she did not favour the bill because it would give the franchise to tinkers and people who wandered about and lived in caravans (hon. members: 'Why not?'). She also denied that the average housewife and mother wanted the vote; mothers with large families had no time for political meetings. An extension of this kind looked, she thought, like taking advantage of the heroic sacrifices of the men who had been killed in the war. This last remark was interrupted by cries of dissent.

Mrs Wintringham disagreed entirely with the Duchess. As for women not wanting the vote, probably agricultural workers had not

wanted it either but the country had been the better for the agricultural vote; it would be the better for the women's vote. She went
on to assure the Government benches that not all women had voted
Conservative at the last election, but that, since women had been
able to vote, more humane legislation than ever before had been
introduced. Lord Hugh Cecil made the honourable ladies gasp
when he opposed the bill saying that since they entered the House
while members might have gained in efficiency 'they had lost in
dignity'. Lady Astor was to be seen throughout the afternoon desperately trying to catch the Speaker's eye and when she did she
spoke vehemently. 'We are not asking for any revolution,' she said.
'Have women since they got the vote ever pressed for anything that
has not been for the good of the country, and has it not in every
way added to the purity of national life?'

For the first time women acted as Tellers: Miss Jewson for the
ayes and the Duchess of Atholl for the noes. The ayes had it by
288 to 72. But the bill got no further in this short Parliament.

In March Mrs Wintringham made another attempt to alter the
position in the Upper House by seconding a motion introduced by
Mr Briant, the Liberal member for North Lambeth, 'that leave be
given to bring in a bill to enable peeresses in their own right to sit
and vote in the House of Lords'.[21] The House voted overwhelmingly
in favour of the motion (313 to 45). The Government however
refused to give time for the bill.

An opportunity for several women to speak came in April when
Mrs Wintringham moved the second reading of the Government's
Guardianship of Infants Bill. Both she and Mabel Philipson had
been members of a Joint Select Committee to consider provisions
for this bill during the previous Parliament. She outlined the injustice
suffered by mothers who, unless they were in the unfortunate position
of being divorced or unmarried, had absolutely no rights over their
children. 'I do not want to legislate for happy marriage,' she said,
'but I want to legislate for unhappy marriages and unhappy
homes.'[22] The bill was committed to a Standing Committee and
eventually reached the Statute Book in July 1925 during the next
Parliament.

Lady Astor was pursuing her usual interests, and references to her
recorded utterances, including short interruptions, fill four columns
of the index to the 1923–4 Hansard. In a vivid and spirited speech
she supported a bill to restrain drinking in Wales,[23] and championed
the under-privileged in a debate on the Finance Bill, telling the

Government with some insight to 'tax the rich as long as it does not ruin the poor.'[24] During an adjournment debate on Government policies in February she had welcomed its social reforms in terms which made one Labour member shout 'Your place is over here.'[25] In the House she was relieved of the presence of one of her enemies; Sir Frederick Banbury, translated to the Upper House by the New Year Honours, had departed to irritate her husband. The *Daily News* summed up his qualifications for this honour as 'a Tory of Tories, but fond of dogs.'[26]

Among the other backbenchers Mrs Hilton Philipson's interests continued to lie with matters affecting her constituents: agriculture, fishing, Summer Time, pensions, unemployment. She sat on a number of committees including the Agriculture and Kitchen Committees and was the only woman member of a parliamentary delegation that visited Italy where she met both the Pope and Mussolini. On the Government benches Susan Lawrence displayed impressive knowledge during the debates on the Local Authorities (Emergency Provisions) Bill.[27] She also showed a great interest in events in Russia,[28] an interest that was deepened by her visit there later in the year. Dorothy Jewson was particularly concerned with health and housing and advocated making advice on birth control available to the poorer classes.[29] Vera Terrington, after a maiden speech on old age pensions,[30] did not speak as often as the other women but seems to have put in a good attendance; during a debate on the Traffic Bill the Press reported that she was the only woman to sit until the House rose at 4 a.m.

On the front bench Margaret Bondfield was having an arduous and testing time, for the Labour Government, committed to their expensive programme of social advance, had neither the power nor the resources to implement it and knew their tenure of office must end fairly shortly in another general election. Moreover all the Labour ministers were untried in office and some like Margaret even lacked experience in Parliament. Unemployment figures were rising steadily as the post-war boom petered out and she found herself plunged into controversies concerning unemployment insurance and training schemes for women and young people.

Outside the House all the women were in demand and constantly in the eye of the Press. Dorothy Jewson hit the headlines in January during a rail strike when she hitchhiked the seventy-two miles back to her Norwich constituency to avoid riding on a 'blackleg' train;[31] another time she told a reporter that what impressed her most about the House of Commons was 'its frightful waste of time and want of proportion'. Vera Terrington acted as a mannequin at a charity fashion show at the Hotel Cecil and on another occasion told the Press that 'being in Parliament was one of the most delightful duties any woman could take up.'[32] In July Mrs Wintringham made history by broadcasting from 2LO on 'The Work of a Woman Member of Parliament'. The Duchess of Atholl wrote an article in *The Spectator* of 15 March repudiating Christabel Pankhurst's proposal for a Woman's Party; she told the Press Club that a woman M.P. found herself in a dilemma in that she was elected to Parliament by both sexes 'but when you get there, the women of the country have a charming habit of thinking that it is they who have sent you there and that you are only responsible to them.'[33] Susan Lawrence objected to being called 'a woman M.P.' 'Why don't you call Churchill a man M.P.?' she was apt to demand.

There is one other event to record about this session of Parliament and that is the affair of the painting showing Lady Astor's intro-duction into the House of Commons. Charles Simms A.R.A. had been commissioned some time earlier by Lord Astor to immortalize this historic scene and Lloyd George, Balfour and Lady Astor had posed for it. When it was completed Lord Astor offered the painting to the Commissioner of Works in Baldwin's Government who, after taking official soundings, accepted it as a gift to the Commons. When it was hung on the public staircase leading up to the committee rooms in 1924 some members complained that they had not been consulted and that the picture offended against a rule that paintings of living persons should not be shown. Lord Astor then removed the picture, but the affair rumbled on for weeks in the newspapers to which several prominent people wrote letters of protest against the removal. In 1925 Lord and Lady Astor lent the picture to Bedford College for Women. In her speech at the ceremony Lady Astor wondered what women a hundred years hence would say about the first woman M.P., and Dame Edith Lyttelton foresaw the day when women M.P.s would claim the picture back.

That day has not yet arrived. During the war Bedford College handed the painting over to the Government for safekeeping and it is now in the custody of the National Portrait Gallery.

1924-1929 'Orphans of the Storm'

DURING the summer recess of 1924 Margaret Bondfield led a delegation to Canada to confer on problems affecting British immigrants, and Susan Lawrence flew to the Soviet Union—the first woman M.P. to visit the Soviet Union[1]—to convey the fraternal greetings of the British Labour Party to the Moscow City Soviet where she spoke to an audience of 3,000 people. She returned to decorate the walls of her flat in Sidney and Beatrice Webb's house in Grosvenor Road, Westminster, with the hammer and sickle and from this time on was apt to address her friends as 'comrade'. This was brave of her because distrust and fear of the 'Reds' were widespread and exacerbated by the curious affair of Mr Campbell, the editor of the *Workers' Weekly* (forerunner of the *Daily Worker*) who had been put on trial after publishing an appeal to the Armed Forces not to assist in crushing industrial disputes. When the prosecution's case against him was suddenly and mysteriously withdrawn many people saw in it the hand of the Government, and the Conservatives combined with the Liberals in the House of Commons to carry an amendment which was tantamount to a vote of no confidence in the Government. Mr Ramsay MacDonald as a leader of a minority Government decided to dissolve Parliament and a general election, the third in three years, was announced for 29 October.

In this election the Labour Party put up 514 candidates (there were 615 seats), and the Conservatives a full quota, but the Liberals fielded only 333, 110 fewer than in 1923. These figures were reflected in the party distribution of the 41 women candidates nominated.

	CONSERVATIVE	LABOUR	LIBERAL	OTHERS	TOTAL
1924	12	22	6	1	41
1923	*7*	*14*	*12*	*1*	*34*

Miss Mary Richardson, the suffragette who slashed the *Rokeby Venus* in the National Gallery in 1914 and who contested Acton in 1922 as a Labour candidate, who now fighting this seat as an

Independent. Of the forty-one women standing, half had fought before.

Four days before polling day the *Daily Mail* published the text of the Zinoviev letter (the subject of continuous and particularly of recent controversy in 1966), which increased distrust of the Labour Party and swung the electorate behind the Conservatives with the result that Stanley Baldwin gained a majority of 223 over all others. The Labour Party lost 40 seats (although it increased its vote in the country) and the Liberals returned only 40 members.

Only four women were returned, three Conservatives and one new Labour representative, Miss Ellen Wilkinson. All the Conservative women members returned to the House with increased majorities. Lady Astor's went up from 2,676 to 5,079; the Duchess of Atholl's shot from 150 to 8,279 and Mrs Hilton Philipson's from 1,869 to 3,965. But Mrs Wintringham and all the new members of 1923 lost their seats. Mrs Wintringham lost Louth to the Conservatives by 1,344 votes, a narrow margin that was a tribute to her popularity there. Although she was to fight several more elections and was a candidate up to the time of the Second World War she was not returned to Westminster again; her party affiliation was against her. She was a loss to the House where she was popular and had done much diligent and useful work, although there is some evidence that she occasionally found the activity there frustrating,[2] for she was a committee woman rather than a parliamentarian. She continued her public work on many bodies outside Parliament. She died in 1955.

There was considerable disappointment in feminist circles at the reversal of feminine fortunes. The high hopes of an increasing flow of women into the House, which the results of ten months before had seemed to indicate, were dashed and Mrs Eva Hubback, parliamentary secretary to the National Union of Societies for Equal Citizenship, wrote to *The Times* in November[3] expressing the hope that constituencies would not be deterred from adopting women. She pointed out that the reason for the results lay not so much in the sex of the candidate as the fact that of the thirty-three new candidates the great majority were fighting hopeless seats, at least eight of which had not been contested by their parties for a year or more. She also pointed out that the majority of candidates had received an encouraging increase in the number of votes polled. There seems no reason now to dispute her findings; women candidates suffered no worse than the men in the electoral swing.

Naturally attention was focused on the new woman member, Ellen Wilkinson, the only female representative on the Opposition benches. 'Our Ellen's' victorious campaign at Middlesbrough, which she won by only 927 votes, had been termed a 'real women's election' for she was helped by members of the Women's Freedom League of which she was a member. This small, dynamic person, only five feet high, who at thirty-three was the youngest woman so far to enter the House, had auburn hair that suited her temperament. She was born in one of the small mean streets of Manchester, the daughter of a cotton operative turned insurance agent. Scholarships took her to Manchester University where she was taught by Frederick Marquis, later Lord Woolton. Her nicknames 'Red Ellen' and 'the Fiery Particle' were not entirely due to her colouring for, a member of the I.L.P., she was on the extreme left of her party, and in 1920 she joined the Communist Party and visited Russia the following year.

After the Zinoviev affair she resigned from the Communist Party because she was annoyed by the Soviet attitude towards the Labour Party. She had been a journalist and a trade union organizer, becoming woman organizer of the National Union of Distributive and Allied Workers during the war. In 1923 she was elected to the Manchester City Council.

Ellen Wilkinson was one of the women M.P.s destined to make a considerable impact on the House. Although never a first-class speaker—she was said to write better than she spoke—she was a shrewd politician with a quick brain, a good administrator and an excellent debater. Tough and ambitious, she was perhaps, as Lady Astor said, 'a revolutionary rather than a reformer',[4] but she was intensely loyal to people and causes which she supported, and hated any form of injustice.

On the other side of the House there had been a fluttering in the feminist dovecote about Mr Baldwin's ministerial appointments. If the Labour Government had given a junior post to Margaret Bondfield, the Conservative Government must keep abreast of the times and appoint a woman too. Mr Baldwin's dilemma was that there were really only two women to choose from : Lady Astor with six years of parliamentary experience but rather unreliable views, and the Duchess of Atholl, a loyal party supporter, but only ten months in the House. Many people felt that Lady Astor should be given office but some did not. Lady Rhondda wrote in *Time and Tide* : 'I trust that Lady Astor will not under any circumstances allow herself to be persuaded into committing the blunder of accepting minor office.' In the event Mr Baldwin played safe and on 6 November— her fiftieth birthday—the Duchess received a letter from him asking her to accept the post of Under-Secretary of State to the Board of Education under Lord Eustace Percy. In the Conservative victory rally at the Albert Hall a few days later she found herself walking up the hall to the platform in the procession of newly appointed ministers, escorted by Lord Curzon who, as a former opponent of women's suffrage, had perhaps mixed feelings about the honour. Lady Astor took the appointment well; in fact she was reported in the Press as saying a few days before it was made that she hoped the Duchess of Atholl would get office.[5] Probably she herself was happy to remain on the back benches, unmuzzled.

In the meantime the three remaining backbenchers were also hard at work. Ellen Wilkinson lost no time in making herself felt at Westminster. On 10 December she made her maiden speech in the debate on the King's Speech, deploring that no mention had been made of extending the franchise to younger women; she made the House laugh by referring to the four women M.P.s as 'orphans of the storm'. She also introduced a sharply partisan note into this speech by criticizing the Government's industrial and economic policies.[6]

Ellen Wilkinson stirred the House in other ways. At the reassembly of Parliament after the Christmas recess there was a gasp of astonishment at Ellen's entry in a vivid green dress. 'Since the late Keir Hardie startled the House with a yellow tussore suit and a cummerbund', reported *The Daily Telegraph*,[7] 'there has been no such sartorial effort at brightening the House of Commons.' A few days later the *Westminster Gazette*[8] carried a photograph of Ellen as 'the shingled M.P.'. The question of hats came up too. Ellen did not always wear one and when she rose to ask a question on 11 February, Colonel Applin, a Conservative member, to cries of 'There's a gentleman!' and 'What a snob!' from the Labour benches, asked the Speaker whether she was in order in addressing the Chair uncovered. The Speaker held that she was.[9]

The return of a Government with a substantial majority brought to an end the period of annual general elections and the Conservative administration settled down to a programme of long overdue legislation to deal with post-war conditions and the economic situation which was giving cause for anxiety. Much of this legislation concerned matters of close interest to the women backbenchers. All three of them spoke in the debates on the Contributory Pensions Bill[10] introduced in 1925 by Mr Neville Chamberlain, the Minister of Health.

Lady Astor was in a particularly militant mood early in this session. During the second reading of the Adoption of Children Bill in April 1925 she ran into trouble with Mr Hayday, a Labour member. He interrupted her to ask whether there was a working mother on a certain committee, at which she protested: 'I hate the assumption that a working woman mother is any different from any other mother. A mother is the same in all walks of life.'

> *Mr Hayday:* The noble lady might read about those society people who spend their time petting little puppy dogs when they might be paying a little more attention to human beings.
> *Lady Astor:* If I told all I knew about the hon. member I would give the House something to think of today. I might go into some of the company that the hon. member has kept that would not reflect credit on him nor on his party.[11]

Mr Hayday, the father of eighteen children, was outraged, and the Speaker asked Lady Astor to withdraw, murmuring: 'If the noble lady will accept my advice, often given to her, she will not entangle herself in such discussions. She should address me personally and avoid all this.' Lady Astor agreed to withdraw and later sent a written apology, but since it was signed by her secretary, Mr Hayday was not satisfied; he raised the matter again in the Chamber and three days later she had to make another public apology.[12]

Another lively interlude came during the debates in June 1926 on the Chancellor of the Exchequer's (Mr Churchill) betting tax on bookmakers. Gambling was almost as provoking as strong liquor to Lady Astor and she felt that by bringing in this bill the Government were in effect condoning betting. 'Of all the . . . ugly duck-lings this is the ugliest of the lot and I see no chance of it ever getting handsomer as it grows older', she said of the bill, claiming that the moral welfare of women and children was at stake.[13] In his reply Mr Churchill echoed the opinions of members who thought her objections inconsistent, particularly as Lord Astor was the owner of bloodstock and had just had a notable success on the turf. He went on to recall that she had given advice 'from a public platform to a large number of persons (Lady Astor: I never did!) as to the horse on which they had better, if they were so tempted, repose their faith and their stakes. But . . . she only gave that advice in order to sicken them of a bad habit. The horse which she advised them to back did not run first; it ran last.'[14]

There were plenty of interruptions after that.

In the same month Lady Astor introduced a private bill—the Public Places (Order) Bill—'to repeal certain laws relating to prostitutes and to amend the law relating to order on the streets or public places'[15] but this bill did not progress. In the same month the Legitimacy Bill to regulate the position of illegitimate children was given its second reading and was supported by Lady Astor and the other women members.[16] It was during this Parliament too that a visit to a nursery school in south London pioneered by Margaret McMillan aroused her life-long interest in these schools which did so much for children in crowded urban areas.

Mabel Hilton Philipson introduced a successful private bill, the terms of which had been approved by a Select Committee of the House, to license nursing homes—The Nursing Homes (Registration) Bill.[17] This was a much needed measure to exercise control over private establishments, many of which left a great deal to be desired. It had an easy passage through Parliament and is still on the Statute Book.

In 1924–5 Ellen Wilkinson spoke and asked questions on education, young people, trade boards, rating and valuation, food prices, and relations with Russia. In those days it was unusual for a woman member to speak during economic debates, but, during the third reading of the bill in May 1925 to bring Britain back on to the gold standard, she intervened to forecast widespread unemployment as a result, telling the Chancellor of the Exchequer that he was 'paying a high price for the smiles of the financiers of America'.[18] She, as well as Lady Astor, wanted to see more women police and in December 1925 introduced a private bill to amend the Municipal Corporation Act of 1882 in order to allow more women to join the police forces[19] (by then the number in uniform outside the London area was only eighty-five and the authorities were very reluctant to appoint women) but the bill did not reach a third reading.

In June 1925 'Miss Perky', as a Conservative member called her, asked the Home Secretary a question on a personal matter which attracted wide attention. She wanted to know why two police officers 'disguised as waiters' had attended a dinner-party in a private room of the Boulogne Restaurant, Soho, at which she was a guest. Sir William Joynson-Hicks refused to give much information beyond saying that the men in question had not been disguised as waiters, but had dined in the public restaurant. 'Is it the policy of the Government to exercise surveillance over their political opponents?' Ellen demanded. The Home Secretary then excused the affair by saying that the officers would not have been sent if it had been known Miss Wilkinson was there and promised that such a thing would not happen again.[20]

The unrest in the mining industry culminated in May 1926 in the General Strike. Party acrimony increased and Ellen was often in the thick of battles on the floor of the House. During a debate on the Economy Bill in March she had put in a passionate plea for the unemployed.[21] In the same month she introduced the second reading of a private bill, the Factories Bill, to tighten up regulations to prevent industrial accidents, reminding the House that there had been no legislation on this matter for twenty-five years.[22] This bill did not reach the Statute Book but it anticipated later Government legislation.

During the second reading of the Coal Mines Bill she answered an allegation made by a Conservative member that she had used a faked photograph of a naked Somerset miner harnessed to a tub to illustrate an article which she had written for a Socialist paper. Dramatically Ellen waved aloft in the Chamber a rope and chain harness like the one shown in the photograph, which she said had been worn recently by a miner and she also produced pay checks to prove her statements about low wages. 'Therefore I stand by that article,' she said, 'and I can only say if anything I have done has in any way called public attention to the conditions under which these men are working, I am thankful for what I have written. . . . In this staple industry men are working in conditions which in many cases are fit only for beasts. . . .'[23]

By the time of the General Strike (May 1926) Susan Lawrence had joined Ellen Wilkinson on the Opposition benches. In a by-election in May caused by the death of the Conservative member for East Ham North she regained the seat by 1,627 votes. She was very active during all the stages of the Boards of Guardians Bill that Neville Chamberlain had introduced in order to curb local government expenditure, following the West Ham Board of Guardians' failure to keep within the prescribed spending limits of Poor Law relief.[24] With her unrivalled knowledge of the subject and area Susan was a formidable critic who can hardly have endeared herself to the Minister of Health.

It was during the debates on the Local Government Bill and

the Rating and Valuation Bills in 1928 that she really established her reputation. Together with Arthur Greenwood she subjected these bills to an intensive scrutiny and after her closely reasoned speech on the second reading of the Local Government Bill in November 1928[25] she gained what the *Daily News*[26] termed 'the greatest debating triumph ever achieved by a woman in the House of Commons'. The correspondent went on to say : 'I am not quite sure whether Miss Lawrence will be pleased or womankind flattered by the surprise and pleasure that was expressed. "A wonderful speech for a woman" seems to be the general comment—but after all Miss Lawrence was educated at Newnham. . . . Let us drop the qualification and say it was a good speech.'

At the beginning of 1929 Susan Lawrence performed a useful service by introducing a private bill, the Bastardy (Witness Process) Bill, to enable magistrates to compel attendance of witnesses in affiliation cases.[27] This stopped a loophole in the existing law about which several women magistrates had complained to her. The Home Secretary gave the bill his blessing and his office drafted its proposals. It passed unamended through the House and came into law in July.

Margaret Bondfield also returned to the House in the summer of 1926, bringing the number of women up to six, three on each side of the House. On the recommendation of the Labour Chief Whip, Arthur Henderson, she had been adopted to fight the by-election at Wallsend caused by the retirement of the Labour member, Sir Patrick Hastings, who had been Attorney General during the Campbell case. The theme of her election appeal was that Tory government was favouring the rich at the expense of the poor; the electorate returned her with a handsome majority of over 9,000. Out of Parliament she had been a member of the Blanesburgh Commission which had been considering what alterations were necessary to the unemployment insurance system. Margaret had made herself unpopular by signing the Commission's unanimous proposals together with Conservative and Liberal members. She did this, as she explained to her critics, because although she was not satisfied with all their recommendations she felt that much had been gained by the fundamental proposal that the fund should be administered on insurance principles, and the unemployed person compensated according to the damage suffered and not according to the amount of his contributions.

Returned to the House she often spoke on employment problems, particularly concerning women and children. Her major concern however in 1928 was the Unemployment Insurance Bill.[28] During the debates on unemployment, in spite of opposition from her own party, she advocated domestic training for unemployed women, for she held the view that domestic work need not be degrading but could become a worthwhile calling.[29]

In March 1929 Margaret Bondfield, Susan Lawrence and Lady Astor supported Ellen Wilkinson's Aliens Bill to amend the law so that women who married foreigners need not lose their British nationality, and to make it less easy for a foreign woman married to a British subject to acquire British nationality.[30] As the law stood a foreign woman automatically acquired British nationality on marrying a British subject, a state of affairs that led to many abuses and was widely resented. But this measure did not succeed, on the Government's plea that a committee of experts at a forthcoming Imperial Conference would consider the whole matter.

In November 1927 a new woman member had appeared in the House as a result of a by-election at Southend-on-Sea. She was the Countess of Iveagh who inherited this safe Conservative seat from her husband on his succession to the earldom. The *Manchester Guardian*[31] commented: 'It is curious how Conservative *voters* prefer to accept a woman representative only if she is . . . stepping into the discarded shoes of her husband . . .' and added that only Labour *voters* seemed to have the courage to elect straightforward examples of what old lawyers called a '*feme sole*'. I have italicized the words 'voters' because it is interesting that in these early days commentators often confused the wishes of the party selection committees with those of the electorate. Lady Iveagh came of a family of strong political traditions—she was the daughter of the fourth Earl of Onslow and three of her ancestors had been Speakers of the House of Commons—and in her own right she had done much work for her party. She was in fact the first Conservative woman M.P. to have had active political experience before election. She had been chairman of the Conservative women's organization since 1925 and vice-chairman of the Women's Advisory Committee of the Conservative Central Office since its formation in 1918 when women voted for the first time. One of her by-election opponents was an Independent Conservative who declared himself against extending the franchise and went to the polls under a 'no votes for flappers' slogan. This caused the National Union of Societies for Equal Franchise to send a letter to the Press asking for support for Lady Iveagh and reminding the public of some of the measures for which women M.P.s had pressed.

Lady Iveagh made her maiden speech in support of an unsuccessful ecclesiastical measure to introduce a new Church of England Prayer Book.[32] It was a shrewd and competent contribution. Ellen Wilkinson in a series of 'Bo-peeps on Politicians' that she wrote for the *Evening Standard*[33] was to say of the Countess that she had not 'the reforming zeal of Lady Astor' but that she had a combination of shrewdness and common sense that might have made a good businesswoman. Be that as it may the Countess, as recorded by Hansard, does not seem to have contributed to debates as often as the other women members.

Another woman who spoke in support of the Prayer Book measure, which was again moved and left to a free vote (and again defeated) in 1928, was the Duchess of Atholl, although she made herself unpopular with some of the clergy in her Scottish constituency by doing so.[34] She had not been having a particularly easy time at the Board of Education. As a delegate to Geneva in 1925 she had been dubbed the 'Duchess of Not-atoll' for her strict interpretation of the Government's wish for financial economy and in the House of Commons she came under Opposition fire for the reduction in expenditure which her department was having to effect. She acquitted herself well at the dispatch box when she wound up an education debate in December 1925,[35] and over one important matter she influenced Government policy: she threatened to resign if the educational grants to local authorities were included in the general block grants proposed by the Local Government Bill. She won her point and the education grants were excluded.[36] She attended many school prize-givings and presided over several educational conferences including the 1927 Imperial Education Conference in London, and she chaired a committee on examinations for part-time students which produced the Atholl Report. With all these ministerial occupations and constant travelling between London and Scotland and other places at home and abroad, the Duchess found time to accept the invitation of an N.S.P.C.C. inspector to visit some canal-boat children and from her investigations she was disturbed to discover how little schooling these children were getting. Her efforts on their behalf were to continue for the rest of her time in Parliament.

The Duchess did enjoy some compensations. In 1926 the University of Oxford conferred an honorary degree on her, and her relations with the Prime Minister were always most cordial. Mr and Mrs Baldwin were her guests at Blair Castle and she spent part of one summer holiday with them in Switzerland. The Prime Minister liked listening to her playing Beethoven on the piano.

One of the questions on which the Duchess disagreed with her woman colleagues during this Parliament was that of extending the franchise to women on the same terms as men. As Ellen Wilkinson had reminded the House in her maiden speech at the 1924 election, the Government had given a pledge to do this. Shortly afterwards, in February 1925, yet another private bill to amend the 1918 Representation of the People Act along these lines was given a second reading. Sir William Joynson-Hicks, the colourful Home Secretary who was known to be well disposed towards women's suffrage, had a rough passage with Lady Astor and Ellen Wilkinson when he endeavoured to uphold the Government's policy of playing for time. Referring to the pledge he said :

'The Prime Minister adheres to his statement. It will be carried out. (hon. members : When?) It will be carried out by this Parliament.'

Lady Astor : Votes at twenty-one?

Joynson-Hicks : Equal rights for men and women.

The Speaker : The noble lady I know hopes to catch my eye later on and I suggest that she should not attempt now to make that speech in jerks.

Lady Astor : May I suggest that more important than catching your eye is to ask just this question which is of vital importance— does the right hon. gentleman mean equal votes at twenty-one?

Joynson-Hicks : It [*sic*] means exactly what it says (hon. members : Answer !) . . . The Prime Minister's pledge is for equal rights at the next election. I will say quite definitely that means that no difference will take place in the ages at which men and women will go to the polls at the next election. (hon. members : At what age?)

Ellen Wilkinson : Are you going to take the vote from some of the men?

Joynson-Hicks : It would be extremely difficult to take away anything that the men have at the present time. . . .[37]

I have given this passage almost in full as recorded in Hansard because political memoirs have since disclosed that 'Jix' under the relentless questioning of Lady Astor and Ellen Wilkinson was pushed into giving an undertaking that was news to Mr Baldwin and his other colleagues on the front bench. They had been thinking unrealistically of making the voting age for both men and women twenty-five. In the Cabinet the next day there was a good deal of acrimony but Mr Baldwin was shrewd enough to realize that a pledge of this sort would have to be honoured or things might go badly with his party at the next election. Against a great deal of opposition he persuaded the Cabinet to his way of thinking. 'The Cabinet went mad yesterday and decided to give votes to women at the age of twenty-one', wrote Lord Birkenhead to the Viceroy of India, Lord Irwin (later Lord Halifax).[38] Therefore two women backbenchers can be said to have had some hand in pushing forward this final stage in the enfranchisement of women. It was not however until March 1928 that the Government at last brought forward the Representation of the People (Equal Franchise) Bill which among other provisions proposed to give women the vote on the same terms as men. In reply to an earlier question the Home Secretary had disclosed that the number of voters on the new register would be 12,250,000 men and 14,500,000 women.[39]

Although there was little opposition to it the bill had, as might be expected, a fairly lively passage through the House. During the second reading a few Tory diehards had their say. When Colonel Applin envisaged the frightening prospect of a woman Chancellor of the Exchequer, Ellen Wilkinson cried 'Why not?' and she made short work of his objections to equal franchise on the grounds that the Moslem subjects of His Majesty would not care for it. Margaret Bondfield answered doubts about women's attitude to foreign affairs : 'In my experience of international affairs, there is no sex barrier in the way of an intelligent understanding of international questions, even questions of peace and war.' Lady Astor declaimed : 'Progress comes in spite of faint-hearted men. . . . One of the remarkable features concerning the party to which I have the honour to belong is that we should be able to go forward in spite of such albatrosses about our necks.' As another member, Major Kindersley, said 'the noble lady always adds to the gaiety of this House and on this occasion she has not been wanting.' Mr Baldwin wound up the debate after which only ten members were found to vote against the bill.[40] It received the Royal Assent in July.

The battle that had lasted nearly seventy years was over : women now had the franchise on equal terms with men.

It is a coincidence that this should have come about in the year in which the great suffrage campaigner, Mrs Emmeline Pankhurst, died. At the time of her death she still had political aspirations for, although she was over seventy, she had been adopted as prospective Conservative candidate for Whitechapel. The following year another great campaigner, Dame Millicent Fawcett, died after seeing the fulfilment of her hopes.

Another striking example of feminine solidarity in the House was the private bill put forward in December 1928 by Margaret Bondfield and all the women backbenchers to provide footwear for children in the distressed areas. Margaret Bondfield in asking leave of the House to bring in the bill gave some revealing statistics of children in her own constituency who were away from school for lack of boots. 'Some of us,' she said, '. . . cannot look at these [Christmas] shop-windows without seeing behind them the ghosts of these little ones who will get no Christmas and who have to go to school in rotten boots. . . .'[41] But the Government was not prepared to give facilities for the bill, pleading that it intended to bring in special measures of its own to deal with the distressed mining areas.

Various domestic matters affecting women M.P.s were also dealt with during this Parliament. At the end of 1928 Ellen Wilkinson scored what the Press called her 'New Victory' by raising the matter of the Strangers' Dining Room, pointing out the anomaly whereby male secretaries of ministers and Opposition leaders could eat in this cheaper dining room where a meal could be obtained for two shillings and sixpence, while female secretaries, including Miss Rosenberg, secretary to Mr Ramsay MacDonald, had to eat in the more expensive Harcourt Room. The Speaker ruled that lady guests could in future be entertained to dinner but not to lunch in the Strangers' Dining Room. 'Do not women need luncheon, too?' demanded Lady Astor, but the Speaker pleaded shortage of accommodation.[42] To celebrate her victory Ellen Wilkinson entertained a party of women guests, which included Miss Rosenberg, to dinner in the Strangers' Dining Room a few evenings later. According to the *Daily News*[43] 'the unwonted sight of lady guests in the Strangers' Dining Room caused one member, the Rev. Herbert Dunnico, to pause on the threshold exclaiming, 'God bless my soul!' It should also be added that the celebration dinner was both vegetarian and non-alcoholic.

Mr Pethick Lawrence raised the matter of the galleries with the Speaker, asking whether ladies must still be confined to the Ladies' Gallery, and was told that in the Speaker's opinion the time had not yet come to make a change in the regulations.[44] The perennial question of hats came up again too when early in 1929, in order to

(a) Constance Markievicz in the uniform of the Irish Citizen Army, 1914.

(b) The moment of triumph. Lady Astor hears her by-election result announced in Plymouth, November 1919.

(c) The first woman Cabinet Minister at her desk in the Ministry of Labour, June 1929: the Rt Hon. Margaret Bondfield.

Women M.P.s on the terrace of the House of Commons, January 1924. Left to right : Miss Dorothy Jewson, Miss Susan Lawrence, Lady Astor, Mrs Wintringham, Duchess of Atholl, Mrs Hilton Philipson, Lady Terrington, Miss Margaret Bondfield.

speak after a division had been called, Susan Lawrence put an order paper over her head and looked, as one member said, as if she were 'playing bo-peep with Sir Kingsley Wood'. Mr Speaker Fitzroy ruled that women could in future remain uncovered on these occasions.[45] An inveterate smoker, Susan Lawrence was also reported in 1926 to be demanding a women's smoking room, for there was then, as there is still today, a kind of unwritten *apartheid* that keeps most women out of the members' Smoking Room unless invited there by a male colleague.

In the last eighteen months of this Parliament three more women entered the House as a result of by-elections. By a curious coincidence two of them, Mrs Walter Runciman and Mrs Hugh Dalton, joined their husbands in the House, to become the first married couples to sit in the Commons together and they did so for the same reason —to keep a more attractive seat warm for their husbands. In March 1928 Mrs Hilda Runciman was adopted as Liberal candidate for the St Ives by-election, a seat for which her husband (later Viscount Runciman), who was not altogether happy representing Swansea, had been adopted to fight at the next general election. Mrs Runciman had taken first class honours in the History Tripos at Cambridge; she was a member of the Northumberland County Education Committee and one of the earliest women magistrates; she had for many years been a bulwark of the temperance movement. She made a splendid impression during the by-election campaign which she won by 763 votes. Although it was hinted that she did not have the support of Lloyd George and received no message from him, Sir Herbert Samuel (later Viscount Samuel) spoke on her behalf. In the House her particular interests were local government questions, education and housing. She made her maiden speech in May 1928 on overcrowded housing conditions.[46] It was well received.

The other victor of a 'warming pan' election, Mrs Ruth Dalton, was returned for the Labour seat of Bishop Auckland in the by-election of February 1929, following the death of the Labour member. Her husband was Member for Peckham, but had been selected earlier to fight the safer Bishop Auckland seat at the next general election. Rather than cause two by-elections by transferring from Peckham or let Bishop Auckland go by default, he persuaded his wife, a gifted woman with a B.Sc. degree from the London School of Economics and a member of the L.C.C., to stand in for him. She sat for the remaining months of Parliament and made her maiden speech on the Lord Mayor's Fund for the distressed areas;[47] *The*

D

Times[48] described it as 'composed and compact'. But she was quite content to hand over her seat to her husband at the general election. When Ramsay MacDonald asked her to tea soon after she took her seat and said he hoped she would stand again somewhere else, she replied with more honesty than tact that she found the L.C.C. more congenial than the House. 'There wo *do* things', she said. 'Here it seems to be all talk.'[49]

The last woman to enter this Parliament did so in March, three months before the dissolution, bringing the number of Labour women M.P.s up to five and, with the four Conservatives and one Liberal, the total of women in the House to the record number of ten. She was Miss Jennie Lee, the daughter of a Fifeshire miner and at twenty-four the youngest woman who has ever so far entered the House. She had won a notable victory in North Lanark, reversing a Conservative majority of 2,000 to a Labour one of over 6,000. This caused a tremendous sensation because, as the *Manchester Guardian*[50] commented: 'It is amusing to reflect that no girl of her own age had a chance of voting for the youngest woman M.P.' A flapper had entered the House before flappers had the vote. Not that Miss Lee was aptly described by a name that conjures up the giddy bright young thing. She had by dint of grants and awards taken a law degree at the University of Edinburgh. She was a school-teacher, and had been very active in left-wing I.L.P. political circles. During the election she campaigned hotly against the Government's failure to deal with economic distress and to cure the unemployment situation. The Conservative candidate, Lord Scone, had rather a wretched time for not only did he acquire a black eye as the result of an accident during the campaign, but he was between two feminine fires, since the Liberal candidate was a lively girl called Elizabeth Mitchell. When she heard he was an Oxford graduate she shouted: 'Tell Lord Scone I got a first in Greats at Oxford. It will frighten him off.'[51] She polled 2,488 votes.

When the results were announced 'good old Jennie' was mobbed outside the County Buildings in Glasgow. She told the crowd that her victory was a vote of confidence in the coming of a Labour Government and 'should be taken as a declaration of war on poverty'. It also showed, she said, that electors were no longer pre-judiced against women candidates. The Lanarkshire Bookmakers' Association felt that her success was in great part due to their support which they had given as a protest against the Government's betting tax.[52]

Jennie Lee made her maiden speech during the Budget debate in April. It was unusual for its strongly partisan appeal. She did not look upon the present House as a place of inspiration, she said, and she saw herself as 'a chip of the next Parliament which has made rather a precipitate arrival rather than as one belonging to the present House'; she found Mr Churchill's Budget 'a mixture of cant, corruption and incompetence'. In spite of its controversial nature the speech in its freshness and conviction pleased the House, and the next speaker, Sir Frank Meyer, a Conservative member, went so far as to say that he had never heard a maiden speech 'showing greater gifts of oratory, command over the House and sincerity. . . .'[53]

In November 1928, Mabel Hilton Philipson met her constituency executive to tell them that she would not stand again, explaining that her husband's political aspirations had faded because of financial difficulties and 'the reason why I have held the seat has ceased to exist.'[54] She now wanted to spend more time with her children who were still young. Her decision was greeted with a good deal of regret in Berwick where she was always much liked. Mabel Philipson was not a first-class parliamentary performer but in a limited way did some useful work and left on the Statute Book the Nursing Homes Act. After the dissolution she returned to her other career, appearing on the stage in 1929 as Mrs Tilling in *Other People's Lives* at the Wyndham Theatre. She died in 1951.

Her retirement made people realize for the first time that the difficulty of getting more women into the House of Commons was not going to be entirely due to sex prejudice : women themselves might not always be keen to go there. This provided much food for thought and the *Evening Standard*, after commenting that 'a Parliamentary career is not as appealing to women as one might have expected', said that for this reason alone their number in the House, even with 'the flapper vote' at the next election, might not increase at the rate that had at first been prophesied. Perhaps one of the most interesting reactions came from the Prime Minister's wife, Mrs Baldwin. According to the same newspaper she held that the House of Commons was no place for a woman for 'it is essentially a man's institution evolved through centuries by men to deal with men's affairs in a man's way.' What was wanted, she was reported as saying, was a 'Women's Council', a sort of second-class Parliament where women could devote themselves exclusively to the affairs of women and children. She went into considerable detail as to how the Council members should be elected and how they would enact legislation. The idea did not commend itself to the feminist societies or to the women M.P.s.[55]

And so we come to the end of the first ten years in which women members had sat in Parliament. So far thirteen women had reached Westminster and the highest number to sit there at one time was ten (achieved in 1929). Eight of them were married or widowed, and of these seven had come into Parliament in place of their husbands. Their average age was forty and most of them had upper- or middle-class backgrounds. Their interventions in the House had so far been largely on domestic and social issues, but at least one, Susan Lawrence, had shown herself to have a first-class grasp of finance and to be of outstanding calibre, and some of them, notably the Duchess of Atholl, Ellen Wilkinson and Margaret Bondfield, were women of first-class ability.

With the emancipation of 'the flapper vote' hopes ran high among the feminists that the time had now come for a great leap forward that would carry a much larger number of women into the House of Commons.

PART TWO
1929-1945
On the Swing of the Pendulum

1929 The Flapper Election and Its Results

DESPITE the surprise caused by Mrs Hilton Philipson's retirement, interest in the women candidates preparing to fight the 1929 election ran high. There had been plenty of time for them to look for seats and the feminist societies had been active on their behalf. Moreover the addition of some six to eight million women voters to the electoral registers was thought by many to favour their chances.

The Press took the temperature of the situation at regular intervals. In October 1928 the *Manchester Guardian*[1] reported 'only 49 adopted so far'. Labour's list was the longest and the Conservative and Liberal Parties were making a poor showing. 'An interesting point . . .', reported the paper, 'is that the Labour Party has recognized the value to a candidate of previous election experience and has not, like the other two parties, let most of the former women candidates drop out.' All the former members, except Mabel Philipson and Ruth Dalton, were standing again. While Mrs Walter Runciman was still member for St Ives, which she handed over to her husband at this election, she was invited by the Tavistock Liberals to be their candidate (they had been very impressed by her success in the St Ives by-election, particularly as about the same time they had lost one to the Conservatives by a narrow margin); but Liberal Headquarters took exception to her adoption because she was not a supporter of Lloyd George. Sir Herbert Samuel sent for the party elders and is reported to have told them that Mrs Runciman's adoption would be 'a bombshell in the ranks of the Party'; they retorted that if she were not adopted 'it would be a bombshell to Tavistock', and there the matter rested.[2] In Wales another Liberal woman had been assiduously courted by constituency parties: in the end Miss Megan Lloyd George accepted the invitation of Anglesey, a Liberal-held seat, and was busy practising her speeches in secret, refusing any help from her father. Miss Eleanor Rathbone of Liverpool, the President of the National Union of Societies for Equal Citizenship, had been adopted to contest the

Combined English Universities as an Independent candidate, and for the first time three women were standing as Communists.

The really noteworthy thing about the new candidates was that at least eleven of them were young—in their twenties or thirties—'girl candidates' or 'flappers' according to the Press. The young Liberal candidates included Megan Lloyd George, Miss Helen Schilizzi (Northampton)—a British niece of the Greek Premier, Mr Venizelos, and Dr Betty Morgan (Sunderland), aged only twenty-three; Lady Cynthia Mosley (Stoke), daughter of Lord Curzon of Kedleston, and Miss Jennie Lee (North Lanark) were youthful Labour candidates; and Miss M. G. Williams (Pontypridd) was a young Conservative contender. Although women of twenty-one and over had been able to stand for Parliament since 1918, this was the first election at which young women had stood in any number. No doubt it was felt that they would make a special appeal to the newly enfranchised women voters.

The Labour Party had been reported to be devising schemes to increase their number of women candidates but nothing came of them. For example it was suggested by the women's section of the Party Conference in 1927 that every constituency party should make a yearly contribution to a national fund for the support of women candidates; but this was not popular with the party generally.[3] Early in 1929 too there was talk of plans to get more working women into Parliament but nothing more was heard of them.[4]

The feminist societies however had laid their plans well in advance. The Women's Election Committee was again active and in 1926 the National Union of Societies for Equal Citizenship (NUSEC) announced plans to help several women candidates, including Mrs Wintringham, Lady Astor and Susan Lawrence, as well as its President, Miss Rathbone. In 1928 at a conference of feminist societies organized by the Women's Freedom League, the NUSEC carried a resolution that women should be put on constituency selection committees and the conference passed other resolutions pressing for more women to be nominated by all parties and asking that a fair proportion of them should be offered constituencies where they had a reasonable chance of success.[5]

As well as campaigning on behalf of the candidates, the societies were hard at work endeavouring to prepare the new women voters for their responsibilities. Deputations waited on the party leaders and the societies organized all-party meetings for women in constituencies up and down the country. Reports varied on feminine reactions to these campaigns : some spoke of crowded meetings and battalions of 'flappers' active everywhere in support of candidates of their choice, while others said that, though young married women and older women were showing interest, the single under-thirties were indifferent. How would these women vote? '[They] have revealed their knees but not their minds', grumbled the Press. A body of opinion still felt that the additional women's votes would help women candidates and Mr Shaw Desmond writing in the *Sunday Pictorial* in 1927[6] went so far as to forecast a matriarchal state by 1947 saying that the 'little band of women sitting today in Westminster are but single spies for the battalions to come.' Other commentators felt that the Conservative Party would stand to gain by the women's vote and Conservative leaders were busy reassuring nervous Tory audiences throughout the country that this progressive franchise measure would work in their favour. Some cynics had it that the new electorate would be swayed by the good looks of a candidate, but the *Manchester Guardian*[7] soberly concluded that the new voter was likely to be 'the old voter writ fair'. The extent of public curiosity as to how these young women would vote (which seems to have far exceeded that shown in the affiliations of the women who were enfranchised in 1918), is revealed by a question which the Conservative member for Chelmsford, Colonel Howard Bury, asked the Home Secretary in June 1928.[8] He wanted to know whether Jix would consider using different coloured ballot papers as the German Government had done to distinguish the sex of the voter. This suggestion was not taken up, but a correspondence in *The Times* in 1930[9] revealed that in at least one constituency during the 1929 election the returning officer organized separate rooms for men and women voters, to obviate, he maintained, the danger of any interference by one married partner with the other.

After all the preparations and conjectures, when nomination day arrived on Whit Monday, 20 May, the number of women candidates was found to total sixty-nine of whom twenty-seven had fought before. Their party affiliations, compared with those of 1924, were as follows :

	CONSERVATIVE	LABOUR	LIBERAL	OTHERS	TOTAL
1929	10	30	25	4	69
1924	12	22	6	1	41

Thus the number of women candidates had risen by one-third since the 1924 election and this increase was due to the comparatively large number of Labour and Liberal candidates. But the increase was not nearly as great as had been hoped for by feminist circles.

The campaign turned out to be quiet and unexciting. The Conservative posters showing Mr Baldwin over a caption of 'Safety First' failed to make the desired appeal to many people who were worried about the growing unemployment figures, and the Liberals under Lloyd George were still suffering from the odium attached to the unfulfilled promises of the 'coupon' election of 1918. Polling was on 30 May. When the returns came in Labour was found to have 287 seats, the Conservatives 260, the Liberals 59, and others 9. Mr Baldwin resigned and Mr Ramsay MacDonald took up office, although once again Labour did not have an absolute majority.

Among the victorious candidates were fourteen women (nine Labour, three Conservatives, one Liberal and one Independent), an increase, it is true, of only four over 1924, but proportionately an improvement. In 1924 only 10 per cent of women candidates were successful, whereas 20 per cent were returned in 1929. All the former members retained their seats except Mrs Runciman, who after a gallant fight lost Tavistock by 62 votes. The three Conservative noble ladies were returned with reduced majorities. (Lady Astor touched her lowest ebb at Plymouth with a majority of 211 compared with one of over 5,000 in 1924.) For Labour, Susan Lawrence and Ellen Wilkinson were returned with increased majorities, and Margaret Bondfield, after a four-cornered contest in which a Communist candidate had attempted to discredit her because of her part in the Blanesburgh Report, was returned at Wallsend with a slightly reduced majority. Jennie Lee in a straight fight retained North Lanark but with a reduced majority. In addition five new Labour women had been brought into the House by the swing to the left: Dr Ethel Bentham, who turned a Conservative majority of 3,894 into a Labour one of 1,558 in East Islington; Dr Marion Phillips who topped the poll in the two-member seat of Sunderland; Mrs Mary Agnes Hamilton who was the first of two Labour members returned for Blackburn; Miss Edith Picton-Turbervill who captured the Wrekin; Lady Cynthia Mosley who won a notable 7,850 majority over the Liberal at Stoke. Miss Megan Lloyd George retained Anglesey for the Liberals with a majority of over 5,000, and Miss Eleanor Rathbone was returned for the Combined English Universities to become the first Independent woman member of Parliament. In the proportional system of voting used for the university seats she had come top in first preferences for the two seats, but on the counting of second preferences she came second to Sir Martin Conway, the Conservative candidate. The universities they represented were Durham, Manchester, Liverpool, Leeds, Sheffield, Birmingham, Bristol, and Reading. Among the unsuccessful candidates Mrs Barbara Ayrton Gould (Labour) just failed to win Northwich by four votes.

These results did not altogether satisfy the Press and feminist societies. Disappointment was expressed that Mrs Wintringham had failed to capture Louth by 439 votes and that Mrs Corbett Ashby had not succeeded in her fifth attempt to get into Parliament. In an interview the secretary of the NUSEC declared herself delighted at the return of Eleanor Rathbone but said she was disappointed with the results generally and she complained once again that none of the parties had given more than a few women a fair chance of success. She added more significantly, 'I think it is very interesting to see that the women's vote has not changed the balance of the parties.'[10] Indeed, although the women's vote was often held from this time forward to be responsible for this or that electoral swing, it was impossible, looking at these results, to say whether the 'flapper vote' had given Labour a victory or prevented its victory from being a landslide.

In any event there was great rejoicing in the train bringing many victorious Labour candidates down from the north to King's Cross, among them Margaret Bondfield, Ellen Wilkinson, Mary Hamilton and Cynthia Mosley. When on 5 June Mr Ramsay MacDonald agreed to form a Government, Mr Arthur Henderson pressed, 'as a matter of principle' for one woman to be in the Cabinet. There was apparently some opposition to this among the Labour leaders but Ramsay MacDonald was in favour and 'Uncle Arthur' got his way although no particular name was mentioned.[11] In the event the choice for this honour inevitably fell on Margaret Bondfield. Although not as brilliant as Susan Lawrence she was an extremely able administrator, she had seen long service in the trade union branch of the Labour movement, and was of politically correct 'working class' origins.

On her return from Brighton where she had gone for a short rest after the election campaign Margaret Bondfield was handed a telegram at Victoria Station summoning her to the Prime Minister. He offered her the post of Minister of Labour and a seat in the Cabinet, which she accepted. Immediately her appointment was known congratulations poured in on her from all over the world, as she describes in her memoirs *A Life's Work*: 'from China to Peru, from Europe, Asia, Africa and from all the Americas . . .',[12] from colleagues and opponents and all the women's societies at home. Once again the newspapers were busy with questions of dress. What should she wear at Court levees and ceremonial occasions? As she herself recalled:

> June 8 (Saturday). Rose at 5.30 a.m., tidied the flat and went to early communion; back at 9 a.m. to dress for Windsor. A simple matter, as I had little time for new clothes. The coat and hat I had worn through the election campaign was pressed and brushed and I had a new white silk shirt and new gloves. I was neat and tidy and not conspicuous. Sir Maurice Hankey had kindly consulted 'an authority' at Buckingham Palace, who thought I should wear a hat during the ceremony. To this I could not agree and later my hat-lessness was approved as being more suitable to the occasion.[13]

With the rest of the Cabinet she went down on the special train to Windsor to kiss hands and when her turn came King George V broke the customary silence to say: 'I am pleased to be the one to whom has come the opportunity to receive the first woman Privy Councillor.'[14] Margaret appointed Mr Jack Lawson as her Parliamentary Secretary and later appointed Mr Tom Williams (the Labour Minister of Agriculture after the Second World War) as her Parliamentary Private Secretary. On 10 June she attended her first Cabinet meeting at 10 Downing Street. Before it began photographs were taken in the garden in which the right honourable lady looked small and demure among the packed ranks of her male colleagues; then, for the historical record, a short documentary film was made in which Mr Ramsay MacDonald introduced his ministers in turn, coming at the end to Margaret Bondfield:

'Last, but most unique, is our friend, Margaret Bondfield. She is a double first—the first woman who has been admitted to the Privy Council, so that she is now the Right Honourable Margaret Bondfield; she is also the first woman to have taken a seat in the Cabinet. In the name of the whole country we greet her in the new position she is to fill.'[15]

In the middle of all the excitement, as she tidied up her trade union and domestic affairs, Margaret was beset with a feeling of depression at the magnitude of her task. Looking back on the appointment today it may strike us as odd that this particular Cabinet post, now generally reserved for a strong man in a governing party, should have been the first to be held by a woman. But

Margaret's task, for which she was well qualified, was really confined to administering unemployment relief. The wider question of solving the unemployment problem and finding ways of creating more jobs was to be the care of a triumvirate composed of the Lord Privy Seal, Mr J. H. Thomas, the First Commissioner of Works, Mr George Lansbury, and the Chancellor of the Duchy of Lancaster, Sir Oswald Mosley. Even so the new Minister of Labour's assignment was formidable enough. As she herself wrote later : 'Immediately upon taking up the threads at the Ministry I was plunged into labours which needed for their proper performance all the experience I had acquired in thirty years of work.'[16] Certain very great difficulties had arisen in administering the employment acts, the chief of which concerned the clause allowing relief to be paid only to those who could give proof that 'they were genuinely seeking work.' The Courts of Referees were having some difficulty in interpreting this condition. Moreover more money would rapidly have to be provided, since at the time Margaret assumed office the unemployment fund was overdrawn almost to the statutory limit of £40 million.

In minor ways the arrival of a female minister also posed problems for the Ministry : was she to be referred to as 'her' or 'she' in official documents? On 21 June the Solicitor to the Ministry, Sir Berham O. Bircham, thought it necessary to sign a 'memo on the gender of the minister'[17] in which he said 'that, as at present advised, the intention of Parliamentary counsel was to use the masculine gender with reference to the Minister of Labour, in all Acts of Parliament', and that 'it would be better, unless the minister expressed a decided wish' to apply the same principle to Orders, Special Orders, and Regulations. He thought there was no harm in using the feminine gender in recitals to documents, but it was really unnecessary to use any gender at all and perhaps this was the best course for 'it would obviously be excessively inconvenient to have the feminine in your recitals and the masculine in the operative part of the order and in as much as the operative part of the order should be properly in the masculine, the recitals should also be in the masculine. If, however, all gender in recitals were omitted, the masculine in an operative part could always be used. . . .' The red tape was getting very tangled indeed.

A few days after Margaret Bondfield's appointment Susan Lawrence was made Parliamentary Secretary to the Ministry of Health. This, as *The Times*[18] recalled, was a tribute to her work in connection with the former Government's Local Government Acts, of which she and Mr Arthur Greenwood (now her minister) had been the only really effective critics on the Labour benches. Susan appointed Ellen Wilkinson as her Parliamentary Private Secretary.

While the new ministers were taking the measure of their departments, the new women members were getting accustomed to Westminster. Lady Astor entertained some of them to lunch and, according to Mary Agnes Hamilton, expressed the hope that they would 'function as a woman's party' on women's questions, an idea that they did not receive with any enthusiasm.[19]

They were an interesting group this new intake of women M.P.'s, all but one of whom could be said to have won their way to Westminster without benefit of family inheritance. The exception was Miss Megan Lloyd George whose adoption for the safe Liberal seat of Anglesey cannot have been unconnected with the eminence of her father. She was, however, at twenty-seven an able performer on the platform with a gift for witty repartee in English and Welsh, and was expected to have an outstanding career in the House. Her brother Gwilym (later Viscount Tenby) was also returned at this election, giving Mr Lloyd George the unique distinction of sitting in the Commons with his son and his daughter. Even Mr Baldwin was pleased at this feat though his only recorded comment was the cryptic aside : 'I like Gwilym; he takes after his mother.'[20]

Dr Ethel Bentham at sixty-eight was the oldest of the new women M.P.s. She came of the Quaker family that Jeremy Bentham had made famous. After taking her medical degrees in Dublin she specialized in the care of mothers and children. She had established a baby clinic in North Kensington that was the first of its kind. She was one of the first women magistrates and was a member of the Kensington Borough Council and the Metropolitan Asylums Board. As might have been expected, her main interests concerned health questions and her maiden speech dealt with the causes of industrial accidents and nystagmus, an eye disease prevalent among miners.[21]

Mrs Mary Agnes (Molly) Hamilton was quite a different kind of person. The daughter of the late Robert Adamson who had held the Chair of Logic at Glasgow University, she graduated from Newnham College, Cambridge, with a first class degree in economics. She married early and unhappily and turned to journalism, becoming one of the group of pacifist intellectuals which included the Woolfs, the Huxleys, D. H. Lawrence and Lytton Strachey. Mary was the biographer of the party, writing books on MacDonald, Margaret

Bondfield and Mary Macarthur, and she was successively a member of the staff of the *Economist* and assistant editor of *Common Sense* and the *New Leader*. She owed the last appointment to her allegiance to Ramsay MacDonald whom she knew well and admired. When the split between left and right developed within the I.L.P. she took his side and was made assistant editor to try to curb the left-wing tendencies of H. N. Brailsford, the editor, but the experiment was not a success and did not last long. In 1924 MacDonald appointed her to the Balfour Commission on trade and industry, on which she signed the minority report. She had contested Rochester and Chatham in 1923 and Blackburn in 1924 before reaching the House at the age of forty-five.

She took to parliamentary life at once, finding in it 'an equality as between man and woman that I have not met elsewhere except in the newspaper world.'[22] But even before she had made her maiden speech she received an uncomfortable reminder of the overriding majesty of Parliament. In November she gave the first talk ever broadcast by the B.B.C. in the Week in Westminster series, and Mr Remer, the Conservative member for Macclesfield (whom Lady Astor had once called 'a village donkey'), raised the fact of her having given an account of the proceedings at Westminster as a matter of privilege. Mary explained to the House that she, the Duchess of Atholl and Eleanor Rathbone had all been invited to give these talks in turn; they were chiefly addressed to women and were broadcast in the morning.[23] Her explanation was accepted.

Mary Hamilton's main interests were industry and finance, and when she made her maiden speech it was to move an amendment to an Opposition motion urging economy in State and local government expenditure.[24] She was not one of those members disposed to represent the women's point of view and she told an audience later that she 'could not give any picture of Parliament that was specifically a woman's picture.'[25] Hugh Dalton thought her the ablest of the Labour women M.P.s and she was soon given special jobs. The Foreign Secretary, Arthur Henderson, 'always on the lookout for going one better than the Tories',[26] decided that two women should represent Britain at the Assembly of the League of Nations at Geneva in the summer of 1929 and Mary Hamilton became one of them (the other, Mrs Swanwick, was outside the House). She was a great success at Geneva both in committee and socially and became a warm admirer of Arthur Henderson. In June 1930, on becoming Chancellor of the Duchy of Lancaster, Major C. R. Attlee appointed her his Parliamentary Private Secretary and thereafter she spent much of her time at Westminster in his cell-like office below stairs, remaining with him when he became Postmaster General.

A very different kind of woman again was Lady Cynthia Mosley. At thirty-one she was not only a beauty but also one of the wealthiest women in the county, having inherited a large fortune from her grandfather, a Chicago millionaire. She had early shown her independence by taking a job during the war at the War Office at a salary of thirty shillings a week. She is said to have met her future husband, Sir Oswald (Tom) Mosley, when they were both campaigning for Lady Astor in Plymouth; the King and Queen attended their wedding. Sir Oswald was then Tory M.P. for Harrow, but when he changed his politics Cynthia too joined the I.L.P. and she and her husband became very friendly with Ramsay MacDonald. Now Sir Oswald was the Labour member for Smethwick and together, 'a pair of magnificent cuckoos in the Labour Party nest', they made up the third husband-and-wife team to sit in the Commons. To celebrate her victory at Stoke-on-Trent Sir Oswald gave his wife a diamond brooch in the shape of the House of Commons with the figures of her majority—7,850—set across it in rubies. Lady Cynthia, as the mother of two young children, was chiefly interested in education and child welfare. With Lady Iveagh and Ellen Wilkinson she became a member of the Kitchen Committee. Although having an attractive voice she was never a good debater, for she had a lifeless, conversational style of delivery far removed from the oratory of her father, Lord Curzon. She was warmly regarded by her own party, many of whom did not care so much for her husband.

Miss Edith Picton-Turbervill also came of Conservative stock; her Glamorganshire family claimed to be descended from one of William the Conqueror's knights. At fifty-seven she was a tall commanding-looking woman who resembled, some people thought, a cross between a mediaeval abbess and a female sergeant. Not as formidable as she looked, she was a kind, fair-minded woman who sometimes found it difficult to take party politics seriously, and frankly admitted she was a pink rather than a bright-red Socialist. A supporter of the suffrage movement she had come into politics by way of social service, first working among the railway navvies in Glamorganshire and then doing welfare work in Shoreditch. She too was a friend of Ramsay MacDonald, and largely because of his influence and that of other Labour friends she was persuaded to stand for Islington North in 1922. She stood again unsuccessfully

for Stroud in 1924 before being adopted by the Wrekin division of
the Labour Party in 1925. She built up a great deal of goodwill in
her constituency by her work for the miners during the General
Strike, and several of her family's friends in the area cut her for
standing as a Labour candidate.

Edith Picton-Turbervill's main preoccupation was with ecclesiastical affairs and she was soon appointed the first woman member of
the Joint Parliamentary Ecclesiastical Committee. After its initial
meeting she noted in her diary : 'My first Ecclesiastical Committee
in the Lords. I, the only woman. Lord Clarendon in the chair suggested passing the Pluralities Measure without comment. Greatly
daring, I asked if it did not interfere with the right of appeal to the
Privy Council. A noble lord said it did and it was not passed.'[27] It
often fell to Edith to present measures from the Church Assembly
which had been passed by her committee, to the House of Commons
before they received the Royal Assent. It was not a very arduous
task since they had been thrashed out elsewhere and were seldom
debated for long in the Commons, but she had the ear of the Prime
Minister when it came to making Church appointments, although
she maintained in her autobiography that her influence here was
negligible. Another of her interests was agriculture and she sat on an
inter-departmental committee dealing with agricultural tied cottages.

Poor Edith Picton-Turbervill was absent-minded and tended to
get into rather bizarre situations. She once annoyed a Tory member
in hot weather by using a fan in the Chamber. He demanded of the
Speaker whether this was fair, since gentlemen were no longer able
to wear swords. During an all-night sitting she stretched out full
length, undetected, on a bench in a dim corner to read a book. In
the Members' Dining Room she once sat down by mistake among
a party of Tories (such a thing was apparently not often 'done') and
thoroughly enjoyed the experience. More unfortunately, she once
found herself voting in the Opposition lobby by mistake.[28] It is to
Edith Picton-Turbervill that we owe some interesting sidelights on
the life of women M.P.s at this period.

The women members were still using the little room on the terrace
allocated to Lady Astor in 1919. It was small and when one member
used the telephone it disturbed others dealing with their correspondence. Incidentally Edith records in her autobiography that she dealt
with much of her correspondence by hand; she could not afford a
secretary because 'much of my M.P.s salary went back to my constituency and political work in one way and another'.[29] This 'boudoir

or underground dungeon' had other annoying disadvantages: there
was no annunciator to tell inmates who was speaking in the Chamber, and no changing room. It was Edith Picton-Turbervill who,
wanting to dress for an evening function, dared to ask the barber in
charge of the bathrooms, hitherto used only by male members, to
reserve one for her. He rose to the occasion nobly, going so far as
to place a box of face-powder on a shelf for her. Even so the experiment was not altogether a success for the bathroom was small and
the lady was large; there was nowhere to put clothes and they kept
slipping into the bath. The upshot was that in October 1931 Edith
went to see Lord Londonderry, then National Government Commissioner of Works, to ask him to provide a dressing-room for women
members similar to those already provided for men. Probably as a
result of her efforts such a room was provided in the next Parliament.[30]

It is also worth recording that early in this Parliament thirteen of
the fourteen women members signed a letter to the Speaker protesting that the Distinguished Strangers' Gallery was still sacred to men.[31]
The only woman who did not sign was the Duchess of Atholl, who
explained in a letter to the *Women's Leader*[32] that she felt that while
women strangers had thirty-six seats reserved for them in the Ladies'
Gallery and fourteen in the Speaker's Wife's Gallery they had no
cause for complaint. 'If we are to have sex equality in this matter,'
she wrote, 'let it be a real one.' The Speaker took her point of view
and refused the request. In 1931 however women strangers gained
a further concession by being able to lunch as well as dine in the
Strangers' Dining Room.

To return to the new women members of this Parliament, the
fourth woman on the Government benches was Dr Marion Phillips,
the victor of Sunderland. Of Jewish descent, she had come to
Britain from Australia with a research studentship to study at
the London School of Economics. She became a Fabian, and at
the suggestion of Beatrice and Sidney Webb a special investigator for
the Poor Law Commission. She too was from the Mary Macarthur
stable for she was the organizer for the Women's Trade Union
League before she became Chief Woman Officer of the Labour
Party and editor of *Labour Woman*. She was a member of the Kensington Borough Council and one of the first women J.P.s. Although
she could be tough and cynical she was very popular in the Labour
Party to whom she was affectionately known as 'Maid Marion'. She
spoke first during the debate on the King's Speech when she referred

to the distressed conditions in Sunderland and, from her knowledge of Australia, maintained that Imperial Preference would not ease the economic position.[33] She was naturally interested in all matters affecting working conditions and during this Parliament seconded a private member's bill to improve the employment regulations for children and young persons.[34] But she was not very often heard in the House for much of her work was still done within the party organization.

Of all the women entering Parliament for the first time in 1929 the one destined to make the most impact upon it was Miss Eleanor Rathbone, the Independent Member for the Combined English Universities. She was the daughter of a wealthy Liverpool family and her father had been Liberal M.P. for the city. Eleanor early showed intellectual promise and went up to Somerville College, Oxford, to read Greats. She campaigned for the vote as a member of Mrs Fawcett's National Union of Women's Suffrage Societies, became a member of its executive committee, and eventually succeeded Mrs Fawcett (later Dame Millicent Fawcett) as president of what became the NUSEC. She was also a member of the Liverpool City Council. She entered the political arena at Westminster with two main causes to further: family allowances and the improvement of the condition and status of women in India. In 1924 she had expounded her case for family allowances in a book called *The Disinherited Family* which caused considerable controversy. She swung the NUSEC behind this campaign, to the disapproval of Dame Millicent Fawcett. As for India, according to her biographer, Mary Stocks, it is doubtful whether Eleanor would have ever again attempted to get into Parliament after her defeat at East Toxteth in 1922 if she had not been profoundly moved by a book called *Mother India* written by Katherine Mayo, an American social worker.[35] It described in horrifying detail the suffering of Indian widows and child brides. After investigation Eleanor was fired with the desire to do something to right these wrongs, and although she had already been active in surveying the conditions of Indian women within the NUSEC she felt that this campaign could only be successfully carried through from inside Parliament.

As an Independent Eleanor sat behind the Liberals in the House. She at once felt at home in Parliament, but to many members, with her air of earnest dedication, her unfashionable clothes that seemed to date from the previous century, and her large brief-case that bulged untidily, she seemed a formidable blue-stocking spinster (of whom her biographer writes that not even 'the minutest record of her . . . career [can] offer any suggestion of susceptibility to male attraction').[36]

An excellent speaker, indefatigable in research and forcible in exposition, marshalling her facts and presenting them in such a way as to build up an impressive case, she was admired but never popular in the House. After her death Harold Nicolson was to recall:

> Again and again I have observed ministers or under-secretaries wince in terror when they observed that familiar figure advancing towards them along the corridors; they would make sudden gestures indicating that they had left some vital document behind them, swing round on their feet, and scurry back to their rooms or equally suddenly they would engage some passing colleague in passionate conversation, placing a confiding or retentive hand upon his startled shoulder, waiting in trepidation until she had passed by. . . .[37]

Eleanor's maiden speech, made in July 1929, was on the bill introduced by Arthur Greenwood, the Minister of Health, to maintain the housing subsidy which would otherwise have lapsed in the following September.[38] With Sir Ernest Simon (later Lord Simon of Wythenshawe) she put up a fight against a flat-rate subsidy and to amend the bill so that it related to the needs of the tenant rather than to the nature of the house. The amendment was lost, but Mr Greenwood did accept a permissive clause to allow local authorities to charge differential rents based on family needs. During the next ten years no fewer than 419 local authorities were to operate the clause.[39] Thus at an early date Eleanor was able to make some slight headway towards her goal of complete family endowment. An experienced and formidable campaigner, she always believed that every small concession, every tiny crack in the opposition, was worth taking advantage of, and she likened this process to picking away at the walls of Jericho, brick by brick.

1929-1931 A Double First in Difficulties

THE GREAT problem before the House of Commons during this short, uneasy Parliament was the economic and industrial situation. The catastrophic slump had begun in the United States and was already making itself felt in Britain. In May 1929 when the Labour Government took office the number of unemployed stood at a million and with trade dropping and works closing this total began to rise steadily. While Thomas, Lansbury and Mosley tried without much success to find ways of bringing people back into employment, Margaret Bondfield as Minister of Labour had the difficult task of administering the unemployment fund. In the 1929–30 index of Hansard there are no less than forty-six columns under her name, for she was continually at the dispatch box bringing in successive bills to cope with the rising tide of claims for unemployment relief.

In November 1929 she introduced the Unemployment (No 2) Bill to remedy certain defects in existing legislation.[1] She had to fight throughout on two fronts: first against the Conservative Opposition led by Winston Churchill who maintained that the new concessions went too far towards easing the lot of the unemployed; secondly against her own backbenchers, in particular those I.L.P. members who came from Clydeside. They kept the House sitting all night and accused her of not fulfilling the party's pledge to raise the scale of relief and of failing to remove the much hated 'not genuinely seeking work' clause. During the committee stage of the bill, between 2 and 10 December, they divided the House five times. Ellen Wilkinson and Jennie Lee were among the Labour critics who tried to get the benefit raised from two shillings to five in respect of each child of the unemployed. In refusing to accept this amendment the minister said sadly: 'The position I am in is simply that my shoulders have to bow a little lower.'[2]

On 28 March 1930, with the unemployment figures approaching 1,700,000, she brought in a motion that the limit of borrowing for the unemployment fund should be raised from £40 million to £50 million.[3] Mr Churchill again led the attack against this proposal, claiming that the Government was in effect encouraging unscrupulous people to exploit the scheme. On this occasion his attack was so virulent that the Chancellor of the Exchequer, Philip Snowden, felt called upon to wind up for the Government.

Although Margaret Bondfield had no direct responsibility for the failure to get the unemployed back into work, she had to face severe criticism over the working of the unemployment grants, the delay in starting public work schemes, and the fact that agricultural workers remained outside the Insurance Acts. The distressed condition of the cotton industry was also a subject of special concern to the House.

Several women took part in the debates that tossed backwards and forwards over the floor of the Commons. Lady Astor wanted to see unemployed women encouraged to enter domestic service, an idea that was not popular with the other side of the House, not only because a certain body of opinion found such service degrading but because women would thereby lose their insurance benefits.[4] Ellen Wilkinson, whose constituency of East Middlesbrough was particularly hard hit, advocated increased trade with Russia which she felt would create more work at home.[5]

However the arguments might run, unemployment figures rose steadily to two million, and to the Minister of Labour the strain and anxiety must have been great. There was a strange lack of direction from the top. Something had gone wrong with Ramsay MacDonald; 'Our leader did not lead', she recalls.[6] He was in fact 'the boneless wonder' of Churchill's classic taunt. The nightmare task of keeping the Unemployment Insurance Fund solvent went on. In July 1930 the borrowing powers had to be raised to £60 million, in December to £70 million; and in February 1931, with the unemployment figures approaching two and a half million, to £90 million.[7]

The first British woman Cabinet Minister certainly had no easy baptism. Probably the only really pleasant things that happened to her at this period were the award of the honorary degree of Doctor of Laws in 1929 from the hands of her sternest critic, Winston Churchill, Chancellor of Bristol University, and the gift of the Freedom of Chard, her native town, in 1930.

Susan Lawrence had a less harassing but equally busy time at the Ministry of Health. She was apparently held in some awe in her department, for her rather grim demeanour and caustic wit scared several of her assistants. Her lack of any of the usual feminine graces also set her apart. There is a story that her method of choosing a new dress was to get a Ministry secretary to ring up Barkers and instruct them to send round six inexpensive dresses. When they arrived she would look up from her papers long enough to tap the one of her choice with her pencil and that was that.[8] Her performance in the House remained first-class. When she rose to speak every neck was craned to hear her for her speeches were full of a dry wit and delivered in a flat monotone that if anything enhanced the effect. She was however somewhat difficult to hear. When she had occasion to castigate the Opposition she had the uncomfortable habit of fixing her eye on one unfortunate member as if all his party's wrongdoing was vested in him until he squirmed in his seat. On one occasion she told Lady Astor who had evidently neglected to read the Ministry of Health bill which was under discussion : 'Theologians inform us that it is possible to rise to Heaven on the arms of invincible ignorance—the noble lady's seat *there* is safe.'[9]

She helped to pilot through the House the Widows, Orphans and Old Age Pensions Bill, which was of the greatest interest to women members. Several of them took part in the debates, pressing the claims of various classes of needy people.[10] Other bills which Susan Lawrence helped to pilot through the preliminary stages concerned housing, mental treatment, and national health insurance. In 1930 she went as a delegate with Mary Hamilton to the League of Nations Assembly at Geneva.

Outside the great unemployment and economic issues some useful work was done by women members during this short Parliament. The Duchess of Atholl, pursuing her concern for canal-boat children was able, with Mr Baldwin's permission, to support a Labour Member's bill to organize their education, a measure which Ellen Wilkinson also supported, although it did not succeed.[11] In November 1929 the Duchess successfully introduced the Illegitimate Children (Scotland) Bill, similar to the one already passed for England and Wales, to give unmarried mothers the right to better financial allowances.[12]

The Duchess had also become much concerned about the welfare of women in Kenya, particularly in relation to the barbaric practice of enforced circumcision. In 1929 at her instigation an all-party Committee for the Protection of Coloured Women was set up under the chairmanship of Josiah Wedgwood, the Labour M.P., and with a young Conservative member named R. A. Butler as secretary. Among members of the committee were Eleanor Rathbone, Edith Picton-Turbervill and Ethel Bentham. On 11 December 1929, when the Colonial Office Estimates were being debated, the Duchess courageously raised the question of circumcision, describing it in all its horrifying aspects which, as she recalled later, for a person of her upbringing and temperament in a more modest age 'was not easy'.[13] As a result the Secretary of State for the Colonies asked colonial governors to report on this subject. One of the people whom the Duchess met and questioned at this time was a Kikuyu leader, Jomo Kenyatta, of whom she said, 'there was something very unsympathetic about him'.[14] Other matters covered by her committee were the status and condition of women in India, particularly the evil of child marriages and the practice of *mui-tsai*, or child slavery, in Hong Kong and Malaya.

Eleanor Rathbone was also asking many questions in the first half of 1930 concerning the position of women in the Colonies, the training of women medical officers in Tanganyika, educational and medical services in Kenya, education of native girls in Nigeria, the education of Moslems in Northern Nigeria, marriage rites of native women and so on. The famous Rathbone hammer technique had full play here, and the Under-Secretary of State for the Colonies felt its continuous impact.

Eleanor took her responsibility towards her constituents far more seriously than most university members. She sent them regular news letters and travelled all over the country to speak to her scattered electorate. In defence of her type of seat she made a persuasive speech on 3 February 1931 during the second reading of the Government's Representation of the People Bill, which among other provisions sought to do away with university representation. And she pulled no punches. 'Is not some of the enthusiasm with which the abolition of university representation has been received by some of the members opposite,' she demanded, 'a sign of the kind of jealousy some of them feel towards those who have enjoyed educational privileges?'[15] The university clause was subsequently squashed in committee and the danger to her constituency averted for the time being.

When Eleanor secured a place in the ballot for private members' bills in 1931 she lost no time in introducing the Wills and Intestacies (Family Inheritance) Bill to safeguard the position of spouses and children who might be disinherited by capricious property owners, and she made a speech during the second reading which showed her firm grasp of the very complicated legal issues involved.[16] The bill was carried by 149 votes to 28 and the Government agreed to set up a Select Committee. In spite of the sympathetic reaction in the Press the legal experts, many of whom were Conservative, set their faces against the measure and secured its rejection by the Committee. But this matter was to be taken up again by other members as well as Eleanor later in the thirties.

In 1931 Ellen Wilkinson tried to bring in a bill to safeguard customers under hire purchase agreements, the first attempt to legislate for this comparatively new form of deferred payment. As she pointed out, under the existing law a customer could buy £80 worth of goods, pay off £60 and then if he fell into arrears to the tune of £10 could have the goods removed and still be prosecuted for the £10 he owed.[17] The Government did not allow time for the bill and she had to wait until 1938 to get a similar one on to the Statute Book. She was supported in this first attempt by a new woman member, Lady Noel-Buxton who was returned to the House in July 1930 by a narrow majority of 170 at a by-election in North Norfolk caused by the elevation of her husband to the peerage.

Lucy Noel-Buxton made up the number of women M.P.s to fifteen and was the twenty-first woman elected in twelve years. She was also the first Labour peeress to sit in the Commons. Educated at Westfield College and the mother of six children, not surprisingly her interests included child welfare and horticulture. She made her maiden speech during a debate on unemployment insurance, urging the Minister, Margaret Bondfield, to bring agricultural workers into the scheme,[18] a speech which the *Women's Leader*[19] found 'brief and neat in manner, well informed and generous in content'.

In February 1931, under the ten minute rule, Edith Picton-Turbervill successfully introduced a private bill, the Sentence of Death (Expectant Mothers) Bill,[20] to abolish the passing of the death penalty on expectant mothers. In a speech which commanded the silent attention of the House she described the terrible effect on an expectant mother of seeing the judge don his black cap and pronounce sentence even though it were later commuted to life imprisonment. The Government, in spite of its crowded programme, gave this bill its blessing and the Lord Chancellor himself moved the bill in the Lords. After it had received the Royal Assent he wrote to tell Edith that 'judges will be grateful to you for removing an abomination from the Statute Book.'[21]

Another woman, Dr Ethel Bentham, was concerned with capital punishment too as a member of a Select Committee sitting to consider its abolition. In November 1930 she also introduced an unsuccessful private bill on the nationality of women.[22] It was one of her last preoccupations for in January 1931 after a relapse following an attack of influenza she died, the first sitting woman M.P. to do so. Her death necessitated a by-election in East Islington in which two notable women took part : Mrs Leah Manning for Labour, and Miss Thelma Cazalet, sister of the member for Chippenham, for the Conservatives. A Liberal, and a brigadier-general fighting under the banner of Lord Beaverbrook's Empire Crusaders also contested the seat. Mrs Manning was returned with a 2,277 majority. A teacher and President of the National Union of Teachers for that year, she had been born in the United States. She was also a member of the Women's Freedom League which had found a by-election involving two feminists rather a tricky one into which to throw its support. Leah was a favourite in the constituency where she was generally known as 'dearie' or 'gal' and was reported to have emerged from the battle looking 'as fresh as paint'.[23] Naturally one of her interests was education and, as the first 'working class' mother to sit in the House, she was also an advocate of family allowances. She was later appointed to the Select Committee considering the hours and conditions of employment of shop assistants.

Lady Astor spent July 1931 visiting the Soviet Union. The visit caused surprise and controversy both in Russia and Britain because she and her husband were members of a party led by their friend George Bernard Shaw. The Russians were nonplussed when Shaw, a Fabian, turned up with a party of Conservatives and capitalists, including the Astors and the Marquess of Lothian; at home this visit got a very unfavourable press. Winston Churchill criticized Lady Astor in the *Sunday Pictorial*[24] and 'A gentleman of Plymouth' advertized in the Press for 'a gentleman willing to oppose her as an Independent Conservative' but the Conservative executive committee of the Sutton division countered this by passing a vote of continued confidence in her.[25]

As the economic situation had worsened and the unemployment figures rose to two and a half million, within the Government Party itself strains and stresses were becoming evident. In May 1930 Sir Oswald Mosley with much pomposity had resigned from his post as Chancellor of the Duchy of Lancaster. ('Poor MacDonald has had to resign and Mosley has sent for the King', ran a witticism of the time.) He later left the Labour Party and formed his New Party which attracted temporary support from John Strachey, Harold Nicolson and Harold Macmillan among others. His wife Cynthia followed him and early in 1931 was reported to be in trouble with her constituency party in Stoke. In March she too resigned from the Labour Party and sent her former friend, the Prime Minister, a letter in which she wrote *inter alia*:

'Ever since I have sat in the House of Commons I have been forced to the conclusion that the present Labour Government differs little from preceding Tory and Liberal Governments.... Every effort to make the Government take more drastic action, every attempt to make the Front Bench face up to the situation and put through an adequate policy to deal with the unemployment problem has met with complete failure.'[26]

While her husband was ill with influenza Cynthia Mosley, with John Strachey and others, addressed meetings of the New Party up and down the country. She had a rough reception. Mary Agnes Hamilton recalls how sorry the other members of the Labour Party felt for her in all the successive phases of the Mosley fiasco: 'She showed unvarying dignity. . . . She went in his place to meetings that were expected to be nasty; she stood by him inside the House and outside. We all liked her; most of us were desperately sorry for her. We kept our sympathy to ourselves; she would have fiercely resented anything of the kind.'[27]

From the extreme left Jennie Lee had also grown more and more critical of the Government. In the debate on the Loyal Address in October 1930 she had said: 'It would be far better for us to be defeated in this House of Commons even if that defeat meant that for a temporary period we were out of office, provided that we clearly carried on our distinctive socialist education.'[28] She was an attractive figure making these inflammatory speeches with her high colour and curly black hair which she had a habit of tossing back as she spoke. (Edith Picton-Turbervill found that after Lady Astor, Jennie was the most quickly recognized of all the women M.P.s outside the House.) In the Chamber she loved to roll out long words and vague phrases in her soft voice and, like Susan Lawrence, she had the uncomfortable habit of addressing her attacks to one particular member on the benches opposite. In spite of the advice of her future husband, Aneurin Bevan, the member for Ebbw Vale and a rebel himself but a more circumspect one, she voted several times against the Government, particularly in the divisions on the bills that Margaret Bondfield introduced in 1931.

In June of that year the Minister of Labour had been obliged to raise the borrowing powers of the Unemployment Insurance Fund from £90 million to £115 million in order to meet the demands for relief. She defended herself by saying : 'I am not supporting the idea of further borrowing because I believe that it is right, or because I believe that it is a good principle. I say that in the world situation in which we find ourselves it is the only possible course. . . .'[29] Critics on both sides of the House advanced all the old familiar arguments and she had the wearisome task of answering them once more. In July she brought in the last Unemployment Insurance Bill she was to pilot through the House, a measure designed to save the Exchequer some £5 million a year in anomalous benefits paid to casual and seasonal workers and married women.[30] She was complimented by Major Walter Elliot, the leading Opposition spokesman, for her 'admirable, clear and lucid statement' in introducing the measure and the real opposition came from the implacable I.L.P. members, Jennie Lee among them. On 15 July twelve of them spoke in relays throughout an all-night sitting and until ten in the morning and forced thirty-two divisions, extracting a few minor concessions from the exhausted minister who was to write rather wryly in her autobiography : 'Future women ministers need not worry about imposing all-night sittings on the House of Commons. . . .'[31] Although she never succeeded in charming the House, Margaret Bondfield won its respect for her competence and patience. She knew her brief thoroughly and had a complete mastery of her subject. A Press report of the time describes her at the dispatch box, speaking clearly and rapidly with a trace of west country accent, and dealing with interruptions with unruffled calm 'leaning over the counter of the Commons with an air of "and the next thing, please" which makes him, the interrupter, sorry to have spoken.'[32]

The third reading of the Unemployed Insurance (No. 3) Bill was taken on 21 July only ten days before Parliament rose for the recess.[33] Both Cynthia Mosley and Jennie Lee voted against it. As members dispersed they were handed copies of the May report telling its grim tale of national insolvency. There were crisis Cabinet meetings, often sitting late into the night, throughout August. Philip Snowden supported by the Prime Minister wanted to introduce 10 per cent cuts in insurance benefits but the majority of the Cabinet including Margaret Bondfield would not agree and finally the Labour Government decided to resign. On 25 August Mr Ramsay MacDonald became Prime Minister of a National Government with Mr Stanley Baldwin as Lord President of the Council and Sir Herbert Samuel as Home Secretary. But most of the Parliamentary Labour Party, including all its women members, remained outside the National Government under the leadership of Arthur Henderson. And so the first woman Cabinet Minister's term of office came to an abrupt end when overnight the Labour Party found itself dispossessed of power. Edith Picton-Turbervill recalls that when the House met again on 8 September everyone seemed to be in the wrong place; the atmosphere was electric and personal relations were strained. She herself was torn by loyalty to her friends Ramsay MacDonald and Jimmy Thomas and in the first division, regarded as a vote of confidence in the new Government, abstained from voting in spite of the efforts of George Lansbury and Ellen Wilkinson to persuade her into the Labour lobby. 'Just like you middle-class people', exclaimed Ellen furiously as she flounced off.[34] The next day Edith was invited to the Prime Minister's room with several others, including his son Malcolm, for a harassing and painful interview during which Ramsay MacDonald said, 'If I die, I shall die of a broken heart.' Nevertheless Edith decided to remain with the Labour Party.

No woman was appointed to office in the National Government, but both Mary Hamilton and Ellen Wilkinson were elected to the Parliamentary Labour Party executive which acted as a Shadow Cabinet. Margaret Bondfield was away ill with what the Press described as 'fatigue poisoning'. Mary Hamilton, disillusioned with Ramsay MacDonald and appalled at the unemployment figures in her constituency of Blackburn, sat for 'a few miserable weeks' on the front bench and wound up the debate on the Budget for the Opposition,[35] finding it 'easier to speak from the box, but a horrifying experience' in the circumstances.[36]

Mary's responsibilities did not last long for on 7 October Parliament was dissolved and a general election was announced for the 27th. Most of the Labour Members left for their constituencies with the uneasy feeling that they would not come back to Westminster. And so it turned out. Every one of the nine Labour women lost her seat, and only Ellen Wilkinson and, after an even longer interval, Jennie Lee, Leah Manning, and Lucy Noël-Buxton were later able to re-enter the House.

Of those who then passed for ever from the parliamentary scene there were at least three women of first-class ability, a match for any who have so far succeeded them: Margaret Bondfield, Susan Lawrence and Mary Agnes Hamilton. In retrospect Margaret Bondfield has been subjected to a good deal of faint praise if not criticism;

many of her own party including Harold Laski inferred in the Press[37] that she was not up to the job, but Herbert Morrison, a Cabinet colleague, disagreed, saying :

> [she was] a fine and able woman with a good record as a trade union official, but in my opinion MacDonald should never have persuaded her to accept the post. . . . She found herself in great difficulties. The unemployment figure were rising and departmentally she was accountable for the fact—and by implication responsible for it. This was unfair to her, but it was a cross she had to carry. Not only was it her first ministerial office, but it was unjustly assumed in a number of quarters that, being a woman, she was almost bound to make a mess of the job. . . .[38]

Margaret who was already unpopular because she signed the Blanesburgh Report (see page 59) now suffered the general odium of a Government that failed. She still however had political aspirations and at the outbreak of the Second World War she was prospective Labour candidate for Reading. During the war she did valuable work lecturing on the British war effort in the United States and was created a Companion of Honour in 1948, but she never seems to have regained much influence in the Labour Party. She died in 1953.

Susan Lawrence, on the other hand, although she never returned to Parliament, remained on the National Executive Committee of the Labour Party until 1941 and her work for Poplar is commemorated there by a school named after her. She died in 1947.

Mary Agnes Hamilton would undoubtedly have retained her place on the front bench if her time in Parliament had been longer. But outside Parliament she had a long and successful career. She was the author of several books, and after ceasing to be an alderman of the County of London in 1940 she entered the Civil Service, eventually becoming head of the American Division in the Ministry of Information, for which she was rewarded with a C.B.E. She remained in the Civil Service until 1962 and died in 1966.

Of the backbenchers, Edith Picton-Turbervill, as a member of a commission to inquire into child slavery in Hong Kong and Malaya in 1936, signed a minority report which, most unusually, the Conservative Government accepted in preference to the majority one. She campaigned for the ordination of women in the Church and herself preached from the pulpit on occasion (her friends felt that she would have made an admirable bishop). She died in 1960.

Both Dr Marion Phillips and Lady Cynthia Mosley met early deaths. Marion Phillips died in 1932. She was a woman of considerable ability who never reached her full potential in Parliament. Cynthia Mosley did not contest the next election because she was pregnant and her husband took her place as the New Party candidate for Stoke where he came bottom of the poll but with over 10,000 votes. After the birth of the baby, Cynthia was never really well. She attended a Fascist rally in Rome in the spring of 1933 where she stood with her husband giving the Fascist salute, for by that time the New Party had become the British Union of Fascists. A month later, at the age of thirty-four, she died in the London Clinic of peritonitis. Her friends doubted whether she ever really believed in Fascism,[39] but her loyalty to her husband was unquestioned. Churchill, Lloyd George, Lansbury and MacDonald issued a public appeal for a memorial fund which, with help from the L.C.C. and the Lambeth Borough Council, resulted in the building of the Cynthia Mosley Day Nursery at Kennington. She was buried in a magnificent tomb designed by Edwin Lutyens at Savehay Farm, Denham, which was then the Mosley home.

During this Parliament women had not only achieved new positions of power in the Government; they were also more active than ever before on the back benches and most of them had had considerable political experience outside or inside the House. The only two who did not often make themselves heard in the Chamber were, first, Lady Iveagh, who may at this time have had considerable responsibilities outside Parliament since in July 1930 she became first woman Vice-Chairman of the Conservative Party Organization; and, secondly, Megan Lloyd George, who after a competent maiden speech on housing[40] spoke on only three other occasions and always on agriculture or housing topics relating to her constituency.

It is nevertheless interesting that at this time of achievement with the first woman in the Cabinet and a second as junior minister, Press and public comment should have tended to become disenchanted. Women politicians still had first-class news value and no item was too trivial to be reported about them, but the honeymoon period was over; a note of criticism had crept in. In 1930 Mr Shepherd, Labour M.P. for Darlington, found it necessary to take Lord Newman to task in the *Daily Herald*[41] for saying 'women M.P.s were no good'. In May 1931 a letter to *The Daily Telegraph*[42] criticized women M.P.s for not protesting at the treatment of women and children during the Indian riots. In the same month a lady at the Manchester Conference of the National Union of Teachers had harsh words to say about women M.P.s : they did not take sufficient interest in the question of uncertificated teachers. There was a danger, she maintained, that they were devoting themselves exclusively to feminine interests;[43] in fact she posed once again the question that had already become familiar : ought women in Parliament to represent women as a whole as well as their constituents?

Miss Eleanor Rathbone M.P.

(a) Labour women M.P.s on the terrace of the House of Commons, June 1929. Back row, left to right: Dr Marion Phillips, Miss Edith Picton-Turbervill, Dr Ethel Bentham, Mrs Mary Agnes Hamilton. Front row: Lady Cynthia Mosley, Miss Susan Lawrence, the Rt Hon. Margaret Bondfield, Miss Ellen Wilkinson, Miss Jennie Lee.

(b) Conservative women M.P.s on the terrace of the House of Commons, November 1931. Standing, left to right: Lady Astor, Mrs Helen Shaw, Mrs Mavis Tate, Miss Thelma Cazalet, Mrs Sarah Ward, Mrs Ida Copeland, Miss Florence Horsbrugh. Seated: Mrs Norah Runge, Lady Iveagh, Duchess of Atholl, Miss Irene Ward, Hon. Mary Pickford.

1931-1935 'Where are the Women M.P.s?'

THE GENERAL ELECTION of 1931, in spite of the unusual and
hurried circumstances of its coming about, was one of the quietest
and most orderly for years. Broadcasting was used on a greater scale
than ever before by both Government and Opposition parties. Mr
MacDonald, in order to demonstrate the dangers of inflation, made
a feature of waving a German 1000-mark note at his audiences,
telling them in dramatic tones how little it would buy in Germany.

There had been little time for candidates and constituencies to
prepare and the number of women candidates was found to be only
sixty-two, seven fewer than in 1929. Of these, thirty-seven, well over
half, had stood before. All the former members except Lady Cynthia
Mosley were defending their seats. The candidates were disposed
as follows.

	CONSERVATIVE	LABOUR	LIBERAL	OTHERS	TOTAL
1931	16	36	6	4	62
1929	*10*	*30*	*25*	*4*	*69*

'Others' consisted of Miss Eleanor Rathbone, Independent; two
Communist candidates, Mrs Duncan and Mrs Crawford in Green-
wich and Aberdeen North respectively; and Miss Elma Campbell, a schoolmistress who fought St Rollox, Glasgow, for the National
Party of Scotland. There were two all-women contests: at East
Islington where Mrs Leah Manning was defending her seat against
her former adversary, Miss Thelma Cazalet; and at Wallsend where
Miss Bondfield was fighting Miss Irene Ward. The feminist societies
too had been caught unawares; NUSEC did not have time even to
distribute a questionnaire but it sent help impartially to Lady Astor
and to Edith Picton-Turbervill at the Wrekin. (Edith herself refused
for reasons of feminist solidarity invitations to speak against Lady
Astor.)

When the results began to come in on the night of polling day, 27
October, they revealed an unprecedented landslide away from the
Labour Party. Arthur Henderson and all his Shadow Cabinet except

George Lansbury had been defeated, but Ramsay MacDonald and
J. H. Thomas had been returned with comfortable majorities. The
Conservatives gained 208 seats without losing one, while the Labour
Party lost 213 and returned to the House only 50 members—but
not one woman. The titled Conservative women were all returned
to the House with increased majorities; Lady Astor's rocketed to
10,204, the Duchess of Atholl's rose to 5,695, and Lady Iveagh's of
38,323 at Southend-on-Sea was one of the largest in the country.
In addition ten new Conservative women candidates had been
swept into the House. Miss Rathbone who was supporting the
National Government topped the final poll for the Combined English
Universities, this time with 5,096 votes. Her runner-up and fellow
member was Sir Reginald Craddock who had been a distinguished
member of the Indian Civil Service. Miss Megan Lloyd George as
an Independent Liberal—she did not support the National Government—retained Anglesey with only a slightly reduced majority.
There were thus fifteen women returned to the House : thirteen
Conservatives, one Liberal, and one Independent.

Since there were 15,600,000 women on the electoral register compared with 13,500,000 men, women were again blamed for the
swing-over of votes. 'The very gentleman who in October suggested
to me that I owed my defeat to women', recalled Mary Agnes
Hamilton in an article in the *Political Quarterly* the following April,
'[had] said to me in May 1929 that the votes of my own sex had
got me in.'[1]

The newly elected Conservative women were the first of their
party to win seats on their own account without inheriting them
from husbands. But for the phenomenal swing in the Conservatives'
favour the majority of them would never have reached Westminster,
and some at least must have been surprised to find themselves there.
Both Thelma Cazalet (now Mrs Cazalet-Keir) and Irene (now Dame
Irene) Ward recall that when they were adopted as candidates there
was virtually no competition since both East Islington and Wallsend
were regarded by the Conservatives as forlorn hopes. As for Florence
Horsbrugh, her arrival in Westminster was more than unexpected.
She had done valuable war work in Scotland for which she was
awarded the M.B.E. and more recently she had worked with Lady
Haig in the British Legion; she also spoke on occasion for the Scottish Unionist (Conservative) Central Office. She was adopted to fight
the two-member division of Dundee without the formality of a
selection committee because the Conservatives there had been im-

pressed with her handling of an unruly meeting. The first thing she
saw in the Conservative office was a notice recording the fact that
the Tories had fought Dundee for a hundred years and never got a
candidate in; she turned the notice to the wall and set about campaigning. When the results were announced she found that she was
runner-up to Dingle Foot, the Liberal, having polled 48,000 votes,
and was a Member of Parliament for Dundee.

The majority of the other new women M.P.s had very much the
same sort of voluntary social work or party political background as
Florence Horsbrugh; they were nearly all, as Mary Agnes Hamilton
wrote, 'the O.B.E. type; the sort of woman "who did good work in
the war" ',[2] and their biographies, though worthy, make rather
monotonous reading. Thelma Cazalet, who at her second attempt
after the by-election in East Islington (which was becoming something of a female stronghold) had ousted Mrs Manning by a majority
of 14,110, was a strong feminist and had decided at an early age on
a political career. On Mrs Pankhurst's advice she became a parish
councillor at the age of twenty, and five years later was elected to
the L.C.C. By the time of this election she was an alderman of the
County of London and chairman of the sub-committee on elementary education. Together with her brother Victor, the member for
Chippenham, she made up the second brother-and-sister team after
the Lloyd Georges to sit in the Commons.

Mrs Ida Copeland, who had triumphed over her Socialist
opponent and Sir Oswald Mosley at Stoke with a majority of over
6,000, was of Anglo-Italian parentage and had inherited something
of the Italian temperament, being given to great enthusiasms. As the
wife of the head of the Copeland-Spode pottery works she had done
a great deal of social work in Staffordshire. Mrs Norah Runge who
had won Rotherhithe with a slender 130 majority had done welfare
work for the services during the war and had been a tireless party
worker. Mrs Helen Shaw, a war widow aged fifty-one, won Bothwell
with a 2,148 majority after contesting it in 1924 and 1929. She had
done a great deal of welfare work for ex-servicemen for which she
had been awarded the M.B.E.; she was also a member of the Lanarkshire Education Committee.

Mrs Mavis Tate, who had ejected the former Assistant Postmaster
General, Mr Sam Viant, from West Willesden by turning a Labour
majority of 7,804 into a Conservative one of 8,360, was at thirty-
eight a rather younger and more sophisticated type of woman. Her
striking appearance as well as her wit and vivacity and splendid

speaking powers are still remembered by some of the older residents in Willesden today. She had married as her second husband (an earlier marriage had been dissolved) a member of the Tate sugar family and had first become interested in politics when helping her cousin, Sir Douglas Hogg (later the first Lord Hailsham), fight an election in St Marylebone. She was a keen motorist and held an air pilot's licence; on her entry into Parliament her chief interests centred on trade and commerce.

Miss Irene Ward, 'the only blonde in the House' according to the Press, had defeated Margaret Bondfield at Wallsend with a majority of 7,606. She had done a great deal of voluntary work for the Conservative organization, had stood for Morpeth in the 1924 and 1929 General Elections and for her political services had been awarded the C.B.E. She was keenly interested in industrial questions, particularly the coal industry of which she had a detailed knowledge, since she had been secretary to a northern industrialist with coal, steel and gas interests. Her namesake, Mrs Sarah Ward who won Cannock with a 4,665 majority, had also had a long career in local party politics in her constituency. In addition she had a good knowledge of agriculture.

The two new members who were unlike the others in that they had had professional careers were Miss Marjorie Graves who had defeated Herbert Morrison, the former Minister of Transport, at Hackney South at her first election, and the Hon. Mary Pickford who won over Hammersmith North. Marjorie Graves had worked in the Foreign Office during the First World War and had attended the Peace Conference in 1919. She had then been employed in the Intelligence Department of the Home Office. She came of a political family and was a member of the Holborn Borough Council. As might be expected her chief interest lay in foreign affairs.

Mary Pickford, the daughter of Lord Sterndale, Master of the Rolls, was a graduate of Lady Margaret Hall, Oxford, and had had an exceptionally varied and distinguished career. During the war she had gained valuable knowledge of industrial working conditions as a temporary factory inspector. She had helped to compile the official Naval History of the Great War and in 1927 had become Technical Adviser to the Government delegation to the International Labour Conference at Geneva. In the same year she was appointed a member of the Malcolm Committee inquiring into education in relation to industry. In 1929 she contested Farnworth and in the same year was awarded the C.B.E. Now aged forty-seven she had much to offer Parliament although she was never an outstanding speaker. She had, however, a gift for repartee which came in useful on the hustings.

And so when the new members gathered at Westminster on 3 November to re-elect Mr Speaker Fitzroy and be sworn in, there were many new faces and some of them wore very nervous expressions. Coming down on the night sleeper from the north Florence Horsbrugh was appalled at her unpreparedness. She knew little of London and had never been inside the Houses of Parliament. She managed to waylay another Scottish M.P. on the platform in London. 'Please,' she said, 'can you tell me—do I go through the big gates and just walk in?' He took pity on her and escorted her in, but she needed some time to get used to Westminster. Mr Baldwin had arranged that the many new Conservative M.P.s should each be looked after by a senior colleague; when Florence's mentor said to her : 'Now, do let me know if there is anything I can do for you', her reply was, 'How do I apply for the Chiltern Hundreds?'

The Press continued to find every small detail about women M.P.s of the greatest interest, particularly their clothes. It was reported that some of the new members did not favour Lady Astor's style of dress, but were more fashion conscious. Lady Iveagh and Mrs Mavis Tate were said to be very well-dressed but Eleanor Rathbone continued to look like 'an Edwardian fashion-plate', or, as Ellen Wilkinson once aptly described her, continued 'looking what she is, a great public institution'.[3]

Thanks to Edith Picton-Turbervill the women found a new Lady Members' Room awaiting them. It had formerly been a Smoking Room known as 'The Terrace Night Club' or 'The Red Room' since it had been much used by Labour members in the last Parliament. It had the advantage of having a small changing room attached to it, but it had no annunciator and there were complaints that there were not enough mirrors. It is still in use.

During the debate on the King's Speech some of the old members found occasion to ride their particular hobby-horses. Lady Astor demanded to know whether a woman was to be given a post in the Government. In replying, the Prime Minister, already becoming known for his incoherence, excelled himself, this time by design. He said :

> I should be very glad not only to have one in the administration but half a dozen and if my noble friend will find that there are not quite so many, or even worse than that, I, having made that state-

ment to her and given her that assurance, am perfectly certain she will not blame me for the result.

Lady Astor : Arising out of that answer, may I say I cannot understand it?

Mr MacDonald : I plead guilty. I do not mean that the noble lady should understand it. But I promise her this, that what I have said this afternoon will enlighten her tomorrow morning when she looks up her newspaper.[4]

No woman was appointed.

The Duchess of Atholl, as chairman of a Conservative sub-committee on Russian trade, was at this time much concerned about reports of starvation in the Soviet Union (one of which had been given to her by a young journalist named Malcolm Muggeridge, newly back from the Ukraine). She raised the question of the dumping in Britain of surplus Russian foodstuffs which she felt would be better employed in the land of their origin.[5] Eleanor Rathbone made another plea for proportional representation adding weight to her case by referring to the disappearance of so many former members : 'the storm arose and in one night they were swept before it like autumn leaves are swept before the western wind.'[6] Thelma Cazalet spoke for the first time on the social services and the need for more council housing.[7]

The fact that so many of the new members came from industrial constituencies was well illustrated by their maiden speeches. Ida Copeland and Mavis Tate spoke during the debate on the Import Duties Act in May 1932. Ida advanced the claims of the pottery industry,[8] and Mavis, in a speech which captured the attention of the House, pleaded for greater protection for the cotton trade.[9] *The Daily Telegraph* was full of praise and said that her 'voice was pleasant to the ear and [her] appearance to the eye'. Florence Horsbrugh spoke for the first time during a debate on the Abnormal Importations (Customs Duties) Bill;[10] Mary Pickford, from her expert knowledge of the working conditions of women and young people, on the Expiring Laws Bill;[11] Irene Ward in her maiden speech during the second reading of the Coal Mines Bill in May 1932, dealt with the surplus tonnage and the closing of uneconomic mines, and at this early stage showed her independence by deploring the fact that the Government had not seen fit to guarantee miners' wages.[12] Sarah Ward also made her maiden speech during a coal-mining debate.[13]

Helen Shaw spoke on education[14] and Norah Runge pleaded for the Sunday opening of cinemas,[15] while Marjorie Graves waited until July 1932 to speak during a debate on foreign affairs and more particularly the Lausanne conference, when she appealed for strong British leadership in Europe. The next speaker, Josiah Wedgwood, paid her a handsome compliment by saying 'we have just listened to a speech for which the House has been waiting 25 years.'[16]

The Government and Parliament settled down to a long period of administration in which the restoration of the economic situation was the first priority. Cuts were introduced in unemployment benefits and salaries, and protective trade measures were introduced. The unemployment figures rose to about three million but after 1933 the position gradually improved. There were several domestic measures before the House in which the women members were interested, such as the bill to regulate the protective laws for children and young persons (Children and Young Persons Bill)—criticised by Lady Astor for failing to cover cases of indecent assault against children.[17] Several women members intervened in the debates on the National Health and Contributory Pensions Bill. Eleanor Rathbone fought hard for better rates for unmarried women, saying that the State's attitude to them under the proposed pension scheme seemed to be a case of 'heads we win, tails you lose. . . .'[18]

She was hotly critical too of the Government's proposed 10 per cent cuts in unemployment benefit, saying that it would have been better to increase taxation on higher incomes and luxury spending, and engaged in a long battle during all the stages of the Unemployment Insurance Bill on the scales of relief payable by the National Employment Assistance Board. Another bill which interested her was the Milk Bill of 1934 and while it was being debated both Lady Astor and the Duchess of Atholl spoke along familiar lines. 'The noble lady,' said Lady Astor, 'has got Soviet Russia on the brain and cannot get away from it, just as I have got beer on the brain and cannot get away from it.'[19]

If the period 1931 to 1935 saw the gradual easing of economic strains, it also saw clouds massing on overseas horizons. A matter that preoccupied the Government and both Houses of Parliament for much of the time was the new constitution being planned for India. During the previous Parliament a Round Table Conference had been sitting and in December 1931 its second session closed after deciding to set up, among others, a Franchise Committee under Lord Lothian. The position of women in India was already a matter of concern to the Duchess of Atholl and Eleanor Rathbone. It was in fact confidently expected by the women's organizations that Eleanor would be appointed a member of the Lothian Committee, but the choice—equally well merited—fell on Mary Pickford. Eleanor however also went to India on a visit of investigation at the same time that the Lothian Committee was there.

The Committee's suggested ratio of one woman to four men voters for the Indian women's franchise was less than Eleanor hoped for, but she was prepared to accept it. However the White Paper published in March 1933 proposed a ratio of one to seven for the provinces and one to twenty for the centre, which she considered quite unacceptable. On 28 March she made a powerful speech, one of her best, on the motion to set up a Joint Committee. Her qualification for speaking on the position of women under the new constitution, she said, was that 'for the last four years I have lived almost night and day with this question. There has hardly been a day and certainly not a week, which I have not spent partly in pondering it.' She went on to show that the proposals were 'wholly inadequate' and outlined some of the special problems of Indian women: illiteracy, purdah, marriage customs (particularly the practice of child marriage), and maternal mortality.[20]

That was her first shot in another of her protracted campaigns. In April 1933 she became chairman of the British Committee for Indian Women's Franchise, a joint body consisting of representatives of various women's organizations. It produced a closely printed memorandum and some of its members gave evidence before the Joint Select Committee, while Eleanor herself bombarded it with special evidence throughout its eighteen months' sitting. As a result the findings of the Joint Select Committee were a definite improvement on those of the White Paper in regard to women's franchise, even if they still fell short of those of the Lothian Committee, for the ratio of women to men voters was raised to roughly one to five and certain other concessions were made.

Although the Duchess of Atholl had never visited India, she was also worried about the proposed constitution from a wider standpoint. She felt that India with its Moslem-Hindu tensions was not yet ready for a further transference of powers. When the Round Table Conference proposals were debated in December 1931 she abstained from voting and by May 1932 she had come to the conclusion that she could not support the Government's policy. By the time of the Conservative Annual Conference at Blackpool that year she had decided to join the band of Tory rebels led by Churchill against the new constitution. When she wrote to him promising him her support at the Conference she was a little put out to receive only 'a very brief reply'.[21] However at the second reading of the Government of India Bill in February 1935 he asked the Duchess to wind up for his group which gave the bill a stormy passage through the Commons. She based their case on the fact 'that we feel that it is entirely contrary to the spirit of the 1919 Act and its Preamble to hand over the centre until provincial self-government has proved a success',[22] and expressed fears that the antagonism between Moslem and Hindu would in any event make self-government impracticable. Throughout all the long-drawn-out stages of the bill the Duchess hardly missed a sitting, perched in a seat behind Churchill, ready to hand him any documents he might need.

Both she and Eleanor Rathbone voted against the second reading. Eleanor, Irene Ward, Lady Astor and Mary Pickford carried several amendments in committee to improve the position of women under the constitution. Eleanor voted with the Government on the third reading because, as she said : 'If you cannot get a mile, get a yard; if you cannot get a yard get a foot; if you cannot get a foot get an inch.' Defective as it was she was voting for the bill, she added, because 'it contains seeds of future growth; opportunities which, if the Indians use them properly, will enable them to secure social reforms and gain practice in the exercise of democratic rights.'[23] She would have been gratified to know that one of the seeds planted then would blossom in time to allow India a woman Prime Minister.

The Duchess of Atholl however experienced no change of heart and not only voted against the third reading, but gave up the Government Whip. Churchill tried in vain to dissuade her from this step, and for the final months of this Parliament she sat as an Independent. She addressed several large meetings in Lancashire, the heart of the cotton trade, on the implications for the industry of the constitution.

A loss to the House was the sudden death in March 1934 from pneumonia of a member of the Lothian Committee, Mary Pickford. She had not had time to realize her potential in Parliament but there is no doubt that she would have reached the front bench if she had lived. With her intellectual ability and unusual experience she was one of the ablest women to sit in the House of Commons. She had too a charming personality. She was much mourned by her friends and admirers inside and outside Parliament who put up a memorial window to her in her parish church of King Sterndale,

Derbyshire. By her death the number of women members was reduced to fourteen.

It was during this Parliament that Eleanor Rathbone found yet another cause to shoulder—Palestine. She became interested in the voting rights of Jewish women and the still persisting evils of child marriage among the Arabs in the mandated territory. She asked her first Parliamentary question about conditions in February 1933,[24] and the following year visited Palestine to see for herself.

Events nearer home, in Europe, began to exercise the minds of many at Westminster at this period. Concerned to make the League of Nations more effective, Eleanor Rathbone deplored its failure to apply sanctions when the Japanese invaded Manchuria in 1931. On Hitler's rise to power in 1933 both she and Marjorie Graves pointed to dangers for the future, Eleanor calling the Nazis' success 'a re-emergence of an evil spirit that bodes very ill for the peace and freedom of the rest of the world.'[25]

Marjorie Graves in a short but telling speech during the Committee stage on the estimates for the Foreign Office in July said :

> We know of the expansion of Germany and what it means. We know what the *Wehrsport* means. It means, for instance, that hundreds and hundreds of young men in training at eight o'clock in the morning run round a stadium to military airs. In Germany's training of her youth lies her strength. We know that Germany is capable of training to the last ounce—at present for work and in the future for world domination. . . . Whatever we may say in this Chamber, Germany at least is going to arm and she is going to arm exactly as she chooses, although for the present her arming may be secret. . . .
>
> [And later on the question of disarmament :]
> I know that every soul in this Committee hopes that we may be able to limit bombing from the air, but that Great Britain should stand out alone for the reservation [on bombing] is to my mind lacking not only in common humanity, but in common sense. . . .[26]

Not all the speeches made on this subject at that time stand up so well to scrutiny today.

Outside the House in May 1934 Mavis Tate carried out a dramatic rescue operation from a Nazi concentration camp. Herr Gerhard Seger, a Socialist member of the Reichstag, had escaped from Oranienburg camp and fled to Prague, where he made horrifying disclosures about his treatment. It then became known that his wife and child were being held in another camp at Rosslau near Dessau, the only woman and child in an all-male camp. Various

people and organizations had endeavoured to free them without
success until Mavis Tate, without a single introduction from this
country, as she was to recall later,[27] went to Berlin and spent nearly
a week interviewing various people until she got the ear of Hitler's
piano-playing friend, 'Putzi' Hanfstaengl. She persuaded him that
it would be good propaganda for Germany to release the Segers and
he took the matter up with the Führer. As a result orders were given
not only to free Frau Seger and the child but to send them and Mrs
Tate back to England at German expense in a Junkers aircraft.
Furthermore Prince von Bismarck, a member of the German
Embassy in London, met them at Croydon. It was a unique achievement even for a determined woman. In view of Mrs Tate's visit to
Belsen some ten years later, it is interesting to recall that, while she
was waiting for Frau Seger's release from Rosslau, her Nazi hosts
took her to see Oranienburg concentration camp in an attempt to
refute Herr Seger's allegations about the conditions there.

In May 1935 Marjorie Graves in a foreign affairs debate made
the then perceptive comment that Herr Hitler was 'the first of the
rulers in Europe who has discovered that the putting into uniform
of the unemployed is a cure for unemployment' and supported the
Prime Minister's appeal to Germany 'to think again before she goes
definitely into the outer darkness of isolation. . . .'[28]

Florence Horsbrugh, who was a member of the British delegation
to the League of Nations in 1934 and 1935, intervened for the first
time in a foreign affairs debate following Mussolini's invasion of
Abyssinia in October 1935. Until then her speeches had mostly concerned Scottish affairs and, in particular, the jute industry and other
industries of her constituency. She spoke, she said, 'as a woman'
in demanding adequate armaments. 'What', she asked, 'would the
feelings of the women be if this country were invaded from the air,
if we had aeroplanes of a foreign nation overhead and our aeroplanes . . . going up to fight not merely against fearful odds, but
against hopeless odds?' If warnings about the weakness of our
defences were not heeded she believed that those 'who at present
represent Great Britain will go down to posterity not with honour,
but with dishonour.'[29]

On some other matters one or two of the new M.P.s showed
knowledge unusual in their sex at that time. Mavis Tate, a pilot herself, was well informed on aviation and during the debate on the
Air Estimates in March 1934 she regretted that more had not been
done to foster inter-imperial air communications and strongly urged

training in night flying. It was no consolation, she maintained, 'to hear what we may do for this country in regard to aerial defence in two, three or four years. It is what we are prepared to do today that matters.'[30] As a keen motorist she also contributed to the debates on the Road Traffic Bill before the House in the same year, finding it unimaginative in that it failed to plan for the increased traffic of the future.[31] In 1932 Mrs Runge surprised the House by making some useful suggestions for regulating dog racing from her experience as a greyhound owner ('One of the most thrilling moments of my life', she recalled, 'was when my dog made the first dead heat that ever occurred at the White City.')[32] In 1934 Florence Horsbrugh gave the hon. members a recipe for 'red biddy' when moving the second reading of her bill to control the sale of methylated spirits. 'Instead of buying a bottle of whisky at 12s. 6d.', she advised them, 'you could buy alcohol for twopence and get . . . a drink with a kick in it.'[33] At this first attempt to carry the bill the House was counted out.

But if the women M.P.s were adding their voices to the debates of the day, Press and public comment about them collectively remained critical. So great had been the publicity surrounding their election in 1931 that, when the newness had worn off and they had settled down to work, the ensuing silence seemed to several commentators to indicate that the women M.P.s were not being as active as they might be in the Commons. In June 1932 the *News Chronicle*[34] initiated a lengthy correspondence with an article entitled 'What are Women M.P.s Doing?' Very little was heard about them—was it true to say that they were in Parliament to represent women's interests only? Megan Lloyd George was reported as saying that the 'biological interest' should not be stressed, a view supported by the Duchess of Atholl and Irene Ward, while Helen Shaw said firmly that they should speak 'only when they had something to say. Parliament is not a place to let off steam but where knowledge and experience is pooled for the good of the nation as a whole.' In 1933 *The Daily Telegraph*[35] asked itself whether women M.P.s were getting a fair share of parliamentary time or whether they were 'the victims of [the] alleged selfishness or vanity of the male members who insist on making long speeches?'; it came to the conclusion that if women were not heard frequently 'they are seen constantly and observed doing valuable work for their constituencies', or, as a subtitle had it, 'Little Talk but Much Industry'. It quoted 'an old M.P.' as saying 'The women are still a novelty in the House, but they are making their way quietly and steadily and are displaying wisdom in talking wisely and not too often.'

Was there any justification for this faint praise? While Lady Astor, the Duchess of Atholl (who complained at this time that she often prepared speeches only to fail to catch the Speaker's eye), and Eleanor Rathbone continued to speak fairly frequently, some of the new members did not intervene as often as their lively and politically experienced predecessors of the last Parliament. Florence Horsbrugh and Irene Ward spoke the most often, but Marjorie Graves, Lady Iveagh and Megan Lloyd George were seldom heard. When Marjorie Graves did speak (nearly always on foreign affairs) she had something to say; Lady Iveagh asked only two questions and made one speech during this Parliament—all on maternal mortality; Megan Lloyd George spoke once or twice on matters affecting her constituency, although as the only Liberal woman she received plenty of advance notice from her Whips to prepare a speech. Whenever she did intervene her wit and her voice were highly praised. 'It is the softest and most beautiful voice in the House of Commons', reported *The Daily Telegraph*.[36] When it came to questions Lady Astor, the Duchess of Atholl and Eleanor Rathbone were the most frequent inquirers. In the period November to Whitsun, 1933-4, for example, the *Parliamentary Gazette* recorded that Lady Astor asked 69 questions, the Duchess of Atholl 60, and Eleanor Rathbone 27.[37] In 1932 the Press reported that both Irene Ward and Thelma Cazalet had had to be silenced by the Speaker for 'flinging questions at ministers'. Miss Ward, 'a very jolly young woman', had laughed heartily at her reproof.[38] In the division list for 1933–4 the *Gazette* reported that Mrs Runge voted the most often, 224 times; followed by Mrs Shaw, 208; and eleven women in all are shown to have voted in more than a hundred divisions.[39] In committee and constituency women continued to be busy and felt that on the whole they had to work rather harder than the male M.P.s for not only were they more in demand inside and outside the House, but their mailbags continued to contain letters from women all over the country as well as from their constituents. In July 1935, for example, Mrs Tate presented a petition to the House, signed by representatives of more than a hundred women's societies throughout the Commonwealth, asking the Government to implement measures to give women equal nationality rights with men.'[40]

But the suspicion persisted that women were either not being fairly treated or were not making the best of their opportunities. The

Evening Standard, that ever faithful watchdog of women politicians' interests, in its issue of 17 July 1935 made a list of the objectives which they had so far failed to reach. They had not yet: (1) moved or seconded the Address in Reply to the King's Speech; (2) been put on the rota to deputize for the Speaker; (3) been a party Whip; (4) become chairman of a party committee; (5) become chairman of a Standing Committee. Furthermore in this Parliament no woman had been a member of the National Government nor even a Parliamentary Private Secretary.

There was still much to achieve.

4

1935-1939 'War Can be Averted'

IT WAS unfortunate from the women's point of view that the 1935 General Election, which was to be the last in the pre-war era and to usher in a long Parliament that sat until 1945, was to return so few of them. Although the sixty-seven women candidates standing on 14 November represented an increase of five over the figure of 1931, the total was less than in 1929, and of these candidates only nine, or fourteen per cent, were elected. This was especially disappointing because of the fifty-eight unsuccessful candidates thirty-two had fought before; some of them like Mrs Corbett Ashby (Liberal— Hemel Hempstead) and Mrs Ayrton Gould (Labour—Manchester, Hulme) were veterans of many campaigns.

The parties put forward the following number of women candidates:

	CONSERVATIVE	LABOUR	LIBERAL	OTHERS	TOTAL
1935	19	35	11	2	67
1931	*16*	*36*	*6*	*4*	*62*

The Labour Party had dropped their number more than the above figure indicates, for two of the thirty-five candidates belonged to the I.L.P. which by this time had split off from the Labour Party. One of the I.L.P. candidates was Miss Jennie Lee, who stood under her married name of Mrs Aneurin Bevan in her old constituency of North Lanark and was runner-up to the Conservative with over 17,000 votes to the official Labour candidate's 6,000. Earlier in the year the Labour National Agent, Mr George Shepherd, had been reported as lamenting the small number of women candidates and saying that 'women of ability were much to be preferred to a man who takes his job too easily'. The *Evening Standard*[1] reporting this added that many more women were volunteering than had been selected; the reasons advanced against them were that their voices were not strong enough for open air meetings and that they were less expert than men at answering difficult questions or dealing with interrupters.

One of the two Independent candidates in this election was

Eleanor Rathbone who was returned unopposed for the Combined English Universities, with her running mate, Sir Reginald Craddock. (This was one of only three occasions on which a woman has been returned without having to fight an election.) The other candidate was that well-known philanthropist, Mrs Violet van der Elst, whose platform at Putney was the abolition of the death penalty. About this time she was apt to send aeroplanes over London to write 'Abolish Capital Punishment' across the sky. At the election she polled 1,021 votes and lost her deposit.

Lady Iveagh did not stand again and her son-in-law took her place at Southend, but all the other twelve former members defended their seats. When the results came in from the polling stations it was found that the Labour Party had managed to regain some ground lost in the landslide of 1931 but the Conservatives and their National supporters still had a majority of 246 over all others in the House. The modest swing of the pendulum in favour of the left however had been enough to unseat five of the Conservative women M.P.s: Mrs Ida Copeland (Stoke), Miss Marjorie Graves (Hackney South), Mrs Runge (Rotherhithe), Mrs Shaw (Bothwell) and Mrs Sarah Ward (Cannock). Some other former members were also unsuccessful: Margaret Bondfield was unable to dislodge Irene Ward at Wallsend and Susan Lawrence was defeated by Captain Harold Macmillan at Stockton-on-Tees.

In this election several Conservative women fought entrenched Labour positions in East London: to increase her effectiveness Miss Dorothy Roddick used a novelty, a loudspeaker van, in her fight at Plaistow; Mrs Eleanor Tennant in Silvertown and Mrs Runge in Rotherhithe courageously visited all the public houses in their divisions. In Wales, Miss F. E. Scarborough, the Conservative candidate for Ebbw Vale, used even more unusual tactics and attempted to defeat Aneurin Bevan with song. She installed a piano in her committee room, wrote her election address in verse, and set it to music, as well as composing patriotic songs to whip up the Celtic blood. After a campaign that was reported to be 'going like an eisteddfod' she polled just over 7,000 votes. On the other hand, Labour women tackled the Tory citadels of the St George's division of Westminster, St Marylebone, Saffron Walden, New Forest, and Dorset North, and Mrs Elizabeth Pakenham (the future Lady Longford) assailed Cheltenham. Two interesting Liberals were Miss Chrystal Macmillan, a former suffragette and President of the Open Door International, who lost her deposit at Edinburgh North and Miss Nancy

Stewart Parnell, a descendant of the Irish leader, who also used a loudspeaker in Willesden East to advise the voters: 'Mind how you cross the road and how you cross the ballot paper.'

All in all, it was not a satisfactory election result from the feminist point of view and the NUSEC felt called upon to issue a statement to the Press emphasizing the women's 'rougher path to Parliament' and reminding the public, lest it draw the wrong conclusion from the results, that of the fifty-eight unsuccessful candidates two had lost to another woman and thirty-seven had stood for seats not held by their party since 1918.[2] In May of the following year at its annual general meeting the National Women Citizens Association adopted a resolution urging that: 'in view of the lack of assistance that was given to women candidates at the general election and the desirability of [having] a larger number of women in Parliament', all parties should remove discontent by giving women better opportunities and effective support. The only reaction to this resolution reported in the Press was that of Mr C. J. L. Brock, organizing secretary of the Liberal Candidates Association, who declared: 'I do not know of a single woman who approached us with a view to becoming a candidate who was unsuccessful in obtaining a constituency, but on the other hand we at this office approached a number of other well-known women Liberals to request them to become candidates but they were unwilling to do so.'[3]

The nine women returned to Westminster consisted of one Labour, one Liberal, one Independent, and six Conservative members. Of the Conservatives Lady Astor had a majority of over 6,000 at Sutton, Plymouth, and returned to the House together with her eldest son, the Hon. W. W. Astor, who was the new member for East Fulham. The Duchess of Atholl, who had reapplied for the Conservative Whip shortly before the election because, after Mussolini's invasion of Abyssinia, she felt that the Conservatives 'must close their ranks', had a majority of over 5,000 against Mrs Macdonald, the Liberal candidate. Miss Cazalet, Miss Horsbrugh and Miss Ward all managed to retain their seats with reduced majorities. Florence Horsbrugh this time topped the poll in the two-member seat of Dundee, and Irene Ward's defeat of Margaret Bondfield at Wallsend by 2,379 votes was regarded by *The Times* as one of the greatest personal triumphs of the election.[4]

Mrs Mavis Tate had accepted the invitation to stand for Frome in Somerset, a seat that had been comfortably held by Lord Weymouth. She had worked hard in Willesden West where she had set up an office which was 'a combination of labour exchange, house agency and centre for pension and accident claims'.[5] It was in fact an M.P.'s 'surgery', a commonplace today, but a novelty in the 1930s. Mrs Tate said that her move to Somerset was dictated by family reasons and the health of her husband, but there is no doubt that she was wise to go, for at this election Mr Sammy Viant recaptured Willesden West which has been held by Labour ever since. In Frome, Mrs Tate seems to have been one of the few Conservative candidates who courageously made the necessity for rearmament one of the themes of her election campaign;[6] she only just got home in a three-cornered fight by 994 votes.

Miss Megan Lloyd George was returned for Anglesey as an Independent Liberal with a majority of over 4,000.

There were no new faces among the women M.P.s who met again at Westminster, but there was one topped with auburn hair that had not been seen there for some time: Miss Ellen Wilkinson had returned fresh from her victory at Jarrow where she had converted a 3,192 Conservative majority into a Labour majority of 2,350. She had been far from idle while she was out of Parliament. She had written three books, visited India, the United States and many parts of Europe, and spoken at the last free elections in Germany before Hitler's assumption of power, making some lasting anti-Nazi contacts. She was burning to do battle for her distressed constituency of Jarrow where the unemployment figures were still extremely high compared with other parts of the country.

But if the path to Westminster had been rough, for those who managed to climb it there were certain honours and preferments in store. Early in 1936, after the death of King George V, Lady Astor was included in the deputation of members of the Commons who went to express the House's sympathy to Queen Mary. Following the abdication of Edward VIII she was asked to broadcast to America and Dr Thomas Jones, Secretary of the Pilgrim Trust and a former Assistant Secretary to the Cabinet, has left an amusing record of her preparations:

> I was due at the Fishmongers to dine . . . [he wrote] and went off . . . to dress early and then by 5.45 to St James's Square. I had promised to help her [Lady Astor] with a broadcast to America she was to do at 2 a.m. I found her full of praises of the House and of S.B.'s [Stanley Baldwin's] speech, though she felt he might have made fewer references to himself. She had a pad and was dabbing sentences on it as if she was throwing darts on a target and she kept

shouting them at me. Waldorf came in with a draft which an American had prepared for her because he knew what America would like. Then [Lord] Lothian came in full of talk and ideas of what should be said about Mrs Simpson. . . . I cleared out to Waldorf's room and wrote for an hour, with several interruptions, my notion of what she should say. . . .[7]

One suspects that as so often before Lady Astor threw all these drafts aside and used her own words.

Ellen Wilkinson contributed an article to the *Daily Herald* giving the 'women's view' of the Abdication in which she said : 'We are not going to acknowledge two sorts of women, one a wife, but a wife not good enough to be Queen.'[8] This coincided with the Labour Party's attitude.

Before then it was a woman who had for the first time moved the Address in Reply to the only Speech from the Throne that Edward VIII was to make. Miss Florence Horsbrugh was selected for this honour which *The Times*[9] found to be 'a well deserved compliment to women members of the House in general and Miss Horsbrugh in particular'. It may perhaps be asked why it did not fall to either Lady Astor or the Duchess of Atholl with their length of parliamentary service, and the answer must be that they had both in the past been guilty of independence of the party Whip. Florence Horsbrugh had followed the party line and, as *The Times* explained : 'She had always been indefatigable in her parliamentary duties and never lost an opportunity of bringing the claims of her constituents before the House of Commons.' She was told of her assignment five days before she was to move the Address. The question of dress was an immediate preoccupation, because in pre-war days the movers and seconders always wore Court dress. She consulted the Government Chief Whip and they decided on the normal Court dress then worn by a woman : a long evening dress with a train and long white gloves (but 'no tiara' stipulated the Chief Whip, which was no hardship since Florence did not possess one). A dressmaker in South Molton Street hurriedly made an elegant gown in raisin-coloured velvet, specially chosen to be a foil to the black diplomatic uniform worn by Harold Nicolson who was to second the Address. Thus attired Florence marked the occasion with a graceful speech nicely enlivened with humour.

The fact that the member selected for this honourable but onerous duty [she said] is a woman has, I believe, been appreciated as a compliment not only to women members of this House but to the vast

number of women electors throughout the country (Cheers). I will
not liken this occasion to the crumbling of some fortress wall which
has defended this citadel of male prerogative. . . . I prefer on this
occasion to regard it as an opening of a gate into a new field of
opportunity and I believe the gate is being thrown open with true
if rather tardy hospitality. . . . Whatever else may be said about me
[she added] in the future, from henceforward I am historic.

She included in her speech a strong plea for peace: 'I believe I speak
for the women of Britain when I say that if ever the time comes again
when women wait and men fight there is one form of suffering they
demand that they shall not have to undergo and that is the suffering
that comes from the knowledge that the fighting forces are not
properly equipped. . . .'[10]

Later Florence Horsbrugh made history again by being the
first Member of Parliament to appear before the television cameras
at Alexandra Palace when, wearing her velvet dress, she was interviewed by a gentleman also in evening dress and gave a summary
of her speech. Her 'historic' dress is now in the London Museum.

The women members also had the gratifying experience of being
the first to attend a Coronation ceremony in Westminster Abbey.
In the Coronation Honours Lady Astor's long service was at last
recognized and she became a Companion of Honour. Tom Jones
had suggested to Stanley Baldwin that she ought to be made a Privy
Councillor but this honour was not conferred on her.[11] In 1937 too
Reading University conferred on her the honorary degree of D.Litt.,
an honour which she had already been given by the University of
Birmingham.

But the threat of war overshadowed everything else during these
years. Mussolini's attack on Abyssinia and the terms of the Hoare-
Laval pact that came to light at the beginning of the first session
seriously disturbed the House. Eleanor Rathbone was one of those
who, by questions in Parliament and speaking and writing outside
it, agitated for stronger sanctions, including oil sanctions, against
Italy; she was again one of the members who conducted the successful campaign against the infamous pact with the result that it
was jettisoned and Sir Samuel Hoare, the Foreign Secretary,
resigned. A speech that she made at this time brought support from
an unexpected quarter. The Italian invasion of Abyssinia had forced
the Duchess of Atholl to turn her attention to the situation in Europe.
With her usual concern for detail she had got hold of a full trans-
lation of *Mein Kampf* and was so disturbed by what she read that

she decided to publicize the more revealing passages in pamphlet form. It was an attempt worth making for it is doubtful whether many of the leading politicians of the day had taken the trouble to read the book in any detail. The Duchess had come to the conclusion that, much as she distrusted Soviet Russia, Germany was now the greater danger to peace. She therefore wrote to Eleanor to congratulate her on her speech. 'She seemed more surprised than I had expected',[12] she recorded, but perhaps Eleanor can be excused because, apart from their work together for women in the colonies, they had taken opposing views on many other matters: women's suffrage and rights, proportional representation, India. Now they came together on the great question of peace.

On 5 November 1936 the Duchess made her first speech in the Commons on foreign affairs, stressing the importance of British obligations under the Covenant of the League of Nations towards the smaller nations such as Czechoslovakia, Yugoslavia, and Rumania.[13] This led to an invitation from Princess Cantacuzene, on behalf of the Rumanian National Council for Women, to visit that country. The Duchess invited Eleanor Rathbone and Lady Layton to accompany her and with the blessing of the Foreign Office they set off in February 1937 for a tour of Yugoslavia, Czechoslovakia and Rumania. They met many heads of state and influential people and their visit not only served to improve relations with these Balkan countries but they also brought away much useful information which they put to good use. As the Duchess wrote: 'The great lesson of our trip had been the danger faced by Europe as a whole. Half the continent, it seemed to our party, was trembling in the balance between dictatorship and democracy, and to a large extent the issue might depend on whether we supported the democratic forces.'[14]

The outbreak of the Spanish Civil War in the summer of 1936 had also brought the Duchess and Eleanor Rathbone into collaboration. They were instrumental in setting up an all-party Committee for Spanish Relief which met regularly in a committee room at the House of Commons during the next two years and organized among other things the evacuation of Spanish children from bombed areas. Ellen Wilkinson was also keenly interested in Spain and she, together with Eleanor Rathbone, the Duchess and Dame Rachel Crowdy set off to see the situation for themselves in April 1937, travelling overland to Toulouse and from there by air to Barcelona. They were warmly welcomed by the Spanish Republican Government and given all facilities to see what they wanted. They went by car to Valencia where they spoke to Italian prisoners, part of the Italian expeditionary force about which the British Government 'had no information'. They also met the only woman member of the Cortes known as La Passionara, with whom the Duchess was much impressed. In Madrid, the outpost of Republican resistance, they had their first experience of bombing, and a shell exploded outside an hotel where they were lunching, killing several people. The visit made a great impression on all of them and they returned fired with the desire to organize relief schemes and to press the British Government to recognize the extent to which the Franco forces were being assisted by the Axis powers. The Duchess broadcast an appeal to foreign countries for help for the children of Madrid and her committee managed to organize the reception in the United Kingdom of 4,000 Basque children. She also wrote a book on the situation called *Searchlight on Spain* which was published in the Penguin series in 1938 and sold 100,000 copies in a week, running into a second and a third edition. People began to call her 'the Red Duchess' and her interest in Republican Spain seriously affronted some of her right-wing Conservative colleagues.

In December Ellen Wilkinson paid another visit to Spain with Mr Attlee and other Labour members. It was on this visit that Mr Attlee gave the clenched fist salute that caused much criticism at home. In his autobiography *As It Happened*, Lord Attlee recalls how Ellen snubbed a British consular official in Madrid whom she suspected of pro-Franco sympathies: 'She drew herself up to her full height (which was not great) and, looking at him with blazing eyes, repeated his name twice. She then made a very deep curtsey and turned away. It was most impressive, suggesting Queen Elizabeth receiving the French Ambassador after the massacre of St Bartholomew's eve.'[15]

Ellen was already well known for her implacable opposition to the Fascist dictators. Sir Nevile Henderson, the British Ambassador in Berlin, told Hugh Dalton in 1937 that when he had suggested to Göring that he should visit England, Göring had replied: 'If I came to London all your Ellen Wilkinsons would throw carrots at me.'[16] In the same year Ellen was elected to the National Executive Committee of the Labour Party. With Sir Stafford Cripps and D. N. Pritt she was very much in favour of the formation of a Popular Front with the Communists and the I.L.P., but the rest of the executive disagreed.[17] Cripps was eventually expelled from the Labour Party for his intransigent attitude over this matter, but Ellen, although acting as his liaison officer with the rest of the party, remained within the fold.

In the meantime Germany had reoccupied the Rhineland and was arming apace. On 31 May 1937 Mr Baldwin, who had been Prime Minister since June 1935, retired and Mr Neville Chamberlain took his place. Eleanor Rathbone for one was not pleased. 'That narrow head, that narrow head', she murmured to a friend.[18] But Lady Astor welcomed Mr Chamberlain's appointment. She counted him as a friend and had entertained him and his wife at Cliveden. Soon after he became Prime Minister, Chamberlain told her that he meant to be his own Foreign Minister,[19] although Anthony Eden was now Foreign Secretary. It was about this time that the group of influential people including Lord Halifax, Lord Lothian, Geoffrey Dawson, editor of *The Times*, and J. L. Garvin, editor of *The Observer*, who were often entertained by Lord and Lady Astor became known in the Press as the 'Cliveden set'. On 4 July 1936 *Time and Tide*, a periodical that supported Winston Churchill, mentioned Lady Astor as one of a group of important people who held 'dangerous views'. In the next issue she replied in a letter : 'I have desired to restore a sense of security in Europe by treating Germany as an equal. I have worked for the reversal of the policy of goading her people and rulers into restlessness by trying to keep them in a state of inferiority.' She also supported Baldwin's policy over Abyssinia saying in the House on 4 December 1935, 'I am glad that the Government has [*sic*] stuck to their guns. No one in his senses believes that this or any other Government in the world wants war.'[20] Although her views on Germany were probably no more extreme than those of the majority of Conservative M.P.s, the idea of the all-powerful 'Cliveden set' died hard, and after Lord Halifax became Foreign Secretary the *Daily Worker* alleged that his negotiations with Hitler were backed by Lady Astor, Lord Lothian and Geoffrey Dawson. David Low in the *Evening Standard* followed this up with a series of cartoons, one of which showed Goebbels as a ballet master teaching four girls labelled Lothian, Dawson, Garvin and Nancy to dance. In June 1938 Lady Astor gave a personal explanation to the House denying a colleague's statement that the Prime Minister had by arrangement given an interview to an American journalist in her London house.[21]

In spite of this unpleasant publicity Lady Astor was still showing undiminished vitality in the House. In the United States, in spite of some adverse Press comments, she remained a popular and celebrated figure. When she visited Washington at the beginning of 1938 the Senate suspended its sitting for five minutes in order to greet her. Nevertheless it seems that she took very much to heart the accusations levelled in the Press, for Tom Jones records that on the morning of her investiture as Companion of Honour he found her weeping after dreaming about her dead sister; she told him that she was kept sane and happy by her love of reading and that Honours meant nothing to her.[22]

A minority in Parliament saw the foreign situation differently. The Duchess of Atholl added her signature to those of Winston Churchill, Clement Attlee and others in a letter to the Press on 1 January 1937 saying: 'War can even yet be averted and a stable peace permanently maintained if the nations which are members of the League will now make plain their determination to fulfil their obligations under the Covenant and take any measures required for the prevention or repression of aggression including, if necessary, military action.'

This gave Eleanor Rathbone the theme for her book *War Can Be Averted*[23] which expanded these arguments and was published the following year. In a foreign affairs debate in July the Duchess delivered another attack on the Franco régime[24] which caused *The Spectator* of 23 July to comment that there had been 'nothing in recent Parliamentary history to compare with the evolution of the Duchess'. In the debate on the King's Speech in November 1937 she said:

> I believe that the Spanish people in fighting to defend their liberties are fighting a preliminary battle to defend the liberties of other countries. I feel therefore that if we further withhold the right from that people to the means of full self-defence we shall incur a grave moral responsibility and shall greatly increase the dangers which darken our own future.[25]

But for her too the sands were running out. The resignation of Anthony Eden in February 1938 came as a shock and, growing increasingly alarmed at the continued Axis intervention in the Spanish Civil War with its threat to British communications, she wrote a long letter to the Prime Minister on 25 April explaining why she could no longer support the Government's policy on Spain. In an equally long letter (they both appeared in the Press[26]) Neville Chamberlain set forth the the Government apologia, but added that since he did not expect these arguments to alter her views the Party Whip would be withdrawn from her. It was a cold letter containing not

one word of regret for the loss of a member who had held office
and for a number of years had served the party loyally. Almost at
once the Duchess was in trouble with her constituency. The seeds
of discord had already been sown by her attitude over India, and
her espousal of Republican Spain had upset some of the Catholics
in her division. Moreover her unfortunate habit of speaking her mind
in the neighbouring constituencies held by Conservative members
of different views had also done her harm. In November the Conservatives of Perth and Kinross decided to seek another candidate.
Many of her friends felt that here she should have held her hand
and ridden out the storm, but the Duchess decided to fight a by-
election on the foreign policy issue and applied for the Stewardship of
the Chiltern Hundreds, which was granted on 20 November 1938.

In the debates on 5 and 6 October that followed the Munich
crisis Lady Astor had cried 'Nonsense' when Churchill declared,
'We have sustained a total and unmitigated defeat.'[27] Florence Horsbrugh, who by now had been replaced by Irene Ward as delegate to the League of Nations, had also claimed, 'We are starting to win for peace and the first victory has been won.'[28] Eleanor
Rathbone however applauded Churchill's speech—she had always
admired his oratorical gifts but as he was an opponent of women's
suffrage and of the Indian constitution he had not endeared himself to her in the past; as early as 1936 however she had told an
I.L.P. summer school, 'Watch that man carefully',[29] for in him she
was beginning to see a possible national leader. His later attacks on
the Government's appeasement policy had strengthened this view
and in the early days of the Munich crisis she wrote to him:

> There is a great longing for leadership and even those who are far
> apart from you in general politics realize that you are the one man
> who has combined full realization of the dangers of our military
> position with belief in collective international action against aggres-
> sion. And if we fail again, will there ever be another chance?[30]

It was against the background of the Munich Agreement that the
Duchess of Atholl fought a by-election in the cold winter of 1938.
A local laird was nominated as the official Conservative candidate,
but Sir Archibald Sinclair, who supported the Duchess's views on
foreign affairs, induced Mrs Macdonald, the Liberal candidate, to
stand down. It was therefore a straight fight between supporters of
Chamberlain and Churchill. The Duchess of Atholl had help from
many distinguished people including Captain Liddell Hart—the

military correspondent of *The Times*, Lady Violet Bonham-Carter, J. M. Keynes, Lord Cecil, Dingle Foot, Vernon Bartlett and Colonel Josiah Wedgwood; many of them came up to speak for her; Eleanor Rathbone sent her car, a spirited vehicle known as 'Jane Austen'; La Passionara sent a telegram of good wishes from Spain; and Winston Churchill rang up most evenings to hear progress reports. He sent her a message saying that the issues raised by her candidature 'went far beyond ordinary questions of parliamentary or party affairs'.

> You stand [he wrote] for the effective rearmament of our country. . . . Your victory as an Independent member adhering to the first principles of the Conservative and Unionist Party can only have an invigorating effect upon the whole impulse of Britain's policy and Britain's defence.[31]

But the euphoria induced by the 'piece of paper' which Mr Chamberlain had brought back from Munich told at the poll. On 22 December, the Duchess lost the by-election by the narrow margin of 1,313 votes. It was a bitter disappointment for she had believed that she would win.

And so there left Parliament one of the most dedicated and interesting women to sit in the Commons. As *The Spectator* said, her evolution from right-wing Conservative to a rebel on behalf of Republican Spain had been remarkable. Entering Parliament in 1923 with the desire 'to smooth things over' in the novel situation created by women in the House, she had ended by rebelling against her own Government, twice throwing off her party Whip. She has often been accused of inconsistency because of her contrasting attitudes towards India and Spain but this is perhaps to see things too much as left or right. Her opposition to greater independence for India may have been reactionary, but her support for the Republican Government in Spain was not for its policies but for its predicament. Though she distrusted Soviet Russia she recognized the German menace for what it was sooner than most people, and it was the Axis exploitation of Spain as a military training ground that caused her to take the stand she did. If the Duchess had a fault, and it was a serious one, it was that in her pursuit of causes she forgot about people; she was better at furthering an idea than in dealing with human beings. She could never, for instance, anticipate or understand the reaction of her constituents to her activities and there is no doubt that at times she treated them autocratically. Highly strung and intense, her ideas were set in rigid lines; she could never compromise and in that lay her strength and weakness.

As it turned out, events would shortly have brought her and her constituents to see eye to eye. She did in fact rejoin the Conservative Party in 1940 although she never contested a seat again. The preliminary work she had done on behalf of the canal-boat children found its fulfilment with the passing of the Education Act of 1944. The Duchess continued to be busy with various bodies that aimed to help people in beleaguered Europe during the war. Her very happy married life came to an end with the Duke's death in 1942, but she herself lived on until 1960, dying at the age of eighty-six.

Although during the period 1935–9 women seldom took part in defence discussions both Mrs Mavis Tate and Miss Megan Lloyd George became informed on some aspects of defence. Mrs Tate continued to take an active interest in aviation and many of her questions dealt with air matters. In 1936 she seconded an amendment moved by Lieutenant-Colonel Moore-Brabazon (later Lord Brabazon) to delay the passing of the Air Navigation Bill. In an able speech she criticized among the provisions of the bill the proposal to renew the Imperial Airways' charter for fifteen years, on the grounds that this monopoly would not encourage the necessary development. She touched on the failure to grant local authorities land on which to build aerodromes, criticized the aircraft in use as obsolete and the service for not extending to many parts of the world.[32] She voted against the Government in the divisions on the second and third readings of the bill. At this time she also advocated the employment of air hostesses on British passenger aircraft, but this suggestion met no favour with the authorities who regarded it as dangerously advanced.

Megan Lloyd George, more active in the Chamber during this period, took a keen interest in civil defence about which she became an enthusiast. In June 1938 she pleaded for better air raid precautions and asked the Government to appoint someone to have overall responsibility for these in London.[33] In April 1939 she spoke ably during the second reading of the Civil Defence Bill.[34]

Although the drift towards war overshadowed everything else at this time it was nevertheless a period when much useful work was done by women M.P.s on the domestic front; no fewer than four private bills reached the Statute Book as a result of their efforts. Early in this Parliament many of them combined to defeat the Government by 156 votes to 148 in support of an amendment,

moved by Ellen Wilkinson during a Civil Estimates debate dealing
with Civil Service pay, that 'in the opinion of this House the time
has come when the Government should give effect to the Resolution
adopted by the House on 19 May 1920, and forthwith place women
employed in the common classes of the Civil Services on the same
scales of pay as apply to men in those classes.'[35] The Duchess of
Atholl, true to her anti-feminist convictions, was the only woman to
vote with the Government. In a second division Florence Horsbrugh
was among those who abstained from voting and the amendment
was defeated; but it had been a near thing and the Government
later decided to divide the House on a vote of confidence. Thelma
Cazalet expressed the opinion of many Conservatives when she said :
'No matter what my views are on equal pay, I think it is of vital
importance that the National Government is in power during this
serious period of our history.'[36] The Government gained a handsome
majority.

Another bill that invited the joint attention of women members
was the Widows, Orphans and Old Age Contributory Pensions Bill
and several of them combined to fight the clause whereby the upper
income limit for women contributors under the scheme was fixed at
£250, as opposed to £400 for men.[37]

When Ellen Wilkinson got back to the House in 1935 she lost no
time in bringing the distressed conditions of the seaport of Jarrow
to its attention. In 1936 she walked for much of the way at the head
of the march of unemployed men from Jarrow to Westminster and
after the refusal of the Government to allow the men to present
their petition at the bar of the House she recalled :

> As I marched down that road with those men, all of whom I know
> well, whom I had worked with in my own constituency, as I marched
> with them hour after hour just talking . . . I began to understand
> something of what it meant day after day, to get up and not know
> what you were going to do and never have a copper in your pocket
> for anything. . . . Is the House quite sure it can dispense with that
> kind of direct experience?[38]

She herself presented the petition reminding the House that in the
steelworks alone where formerly 8,000 people were employed now
only 100 worked on a temporary scheme.[39] She continually bombarded the President of the Board of Trade with questions concerning the re-establishment of industry in Jarrow and it was regarded
as her personal triumph when, in 1937, Mr Oliver Stanley announced plans for a new steel plant there; she was cheered as she

rose to thank him. Later she wrote an indictment of past Government policy concerning Jarrow in a book called *The Town that was Murdered*.

Ellen was cheered again when her private bill to give greater protection to hire-purchase customers passed its third reading in May 1938. After considerable amendment it had been supported by all parties and all sections of the trade and was the first legislation on this method of payment.[40]

In her own party circles however she became very unpopular in 1939 for writing articles in the Press suggesting that Herbert Morrison would make a better leader of the Labour Party than Clement Attlee (who was away ill at the time). At a party meeting she just escaped a vote of censure.[41]

In spite of her concern with foreign affairs Eleanor Rathbone found opportunity to press on with her campaign for righting the wrongs of family inheritors. She tried to introduce another bill in 1936 without success but, as a result of pressure which she and other members exerted on the Government, in 1938 it facilitated the introduction of a private Family Inheritance Bill which became law.[42] Eleanor was not altogether pleased with the terms of this bill; nevertheless it was another campaign successfully concluded and this one must have saved many unfortunate spouses and families from being entirely cut out of their relations' wills without redress. One other cause for satisfaction this year was that her own University, Oxford, honoured her with the degree of D.C.L.

On the Government side of the House the women had some notable successes. In December 1937 Irene Ward successfully introduced the Poor Law (Amendment) Bill under the ten-minute rule to give pocket money, not 'exceeding 2s.', to old people in Poor Law Institutions.[43] She was applauded by both sides of the House and the bill had a smooth passage before becoming law the following year; it was notable as the first measure of social welfare ever introduced for the elderly.

Mavis Tate, a dynamic and rather emotional speaker who was always much concerned with medical and health questions such as maternal mortality, the midwifery service, mental health, abortion and suicides, supported a private bill that attempted unsuccessfully to ease divorce procedure.[44] There was an element of tragedy in this for her own marriage broke up about this time (it was dissolved during the war) and she was involved in financial difficulties. Early in 1939 she told the Frome Conservatives that she could not afford to contest the seat again. (Later, at a Conservative Party gathering held during the war, she disclosed that she had contributed £1,000 towards her election expenses, £400 annually for three years to the local Conservative Association, and £5,000 over ten years to the Conservative Party.[45]) The Frome executive committee disagreed about accepting her resignation. Although the majority wanted to keep her Mrs Tate persisted in her determination to stand down. This caused a tremendous upheaval; the executive committee resigned and a new one was elected which declared that never again would it lose a good member because of financial considerations. The outbreak of war shelved the whole question for the time being.

In June 1938 Miss Thelma Cazalet's work on educational matters was recognized by her appointment as Parliamentary Private Secretary to the Parliamentary Secretary at the Board of Education, Mr Kenneth Lindsay, and sat on the second Treasury bench. After Susan Lawrence, Ellen Wilkinson, and Mary Agnes Hamilton (see Appendix A) she was the fourth woman to be appointed a P.P.S. and the first Conservative to hold the position. Already it was being asked in the Press, and has continued to be asked intermittently until the present time, why comparatively few women are appointed to this unpaid, honorary position which is regarded as the first step up the ladder to ministerial promotion. One of the reasons sometimes advanced by political commentators is that part of a P.P.S.'s job is to keep his minister informed of news and comment from every quarter and that since women seldom if ever go into the Smoking Room of the House of Commons, where most of this information is picked up, they are at a disadvantage in this job. The argument continues that the Lady Members' Room is in no way a substitute, for their numbers being so small the women M.P.s find it better to keep off political discussions and nowadays, to quote Dame Irene Ward, 'simply zip each other up'. Even so, these points do not seem valid. Thelma Cazalet served successfully in the post until 1940, but before that she had set up another record by being the first woman M.P. to marry. In June 1939 her wedding to Mr David Keir, Chairman of the Press Gallery, was a splendidly all-party affair with Megan Lloyd George in attendance, Malcolm MacDonald as best man and both Neville Chamberlain and Lloyd George there as guests.

Florence Horsbrugh was the first woman to have two private bills to her credit. At her second attempt in 1937 she successfully piloted through the House the Methylated Spirits (Scotland) Bill,[46] to regulate the sale of this intoxicant, and in 1938 introduced the Adoption of Children (Regulation) Bill[47] which was the outcome of the work of a departmental committee, set up by the Chancellor of the Exchequer, of which she was chairman. After much amendment in Committee by lawyer members it received the Royal Assent in 1939, the year that Florence was awarded the C.B.E. But better was to come. In July of that year she was working one day in the Library of the House of Commons when Lord Dunglass (now Sir Alec Douglas-Home), the Prime Minister's young Parliamentary Private Secretary, told her that Neville Chamberlain wanted to see her. Florence immediately imagined it was because she had written some amendments to the Government's proposals for a pension fund for members which she did not think adequate. 'Oh, Alec, say you can't find me', she said. But Lord Dunglass remonstrated : 'You must come, Florence. It isn't about your amendments, I promise you.' He escorted her still protesting to the Prime Minister's door. As she went in she was still murmuring : 'You know, the Prime Minister did say the pension debate could be left to a free vote.' 'What *are* you taking about?' said Chamberlain in mild surprise, 'I asked you here to offer you the post of Parliamentary Secretary to the Ministry of Health.' It was a post she was to hold until the end of the Coalition Government in 1945, serving under four different ministers. For the first time for eight years a woman sat on the Treasury bench in the post once held by Susan Lawrence. Florence was immediately plunged into the grim preparations for evacuation of mothers and children in the event of war. She found Neville Chamberlain a fair-minded Prime Minister to work with.

By this time there were twelve women in the House, for though the Duchess of Atholl had lost her seat four new members had arrived as the result of by-elections. In June 1937 Lady Davidson o.b.e., wife of Sir John Davidson, former Conservative Chancellor of the Duchy of Lancaster, inherited her husband's seat of Hemel Hempstead on his elevation to the peerage. She came of a family with strong political traditions; her father, Lord Dickinson, had been one of the few M.P.s of his day to campaign for women's suffrage ('When will Asquith see these women mean business?' he exclaimed after Emily Wilding-Davison flung herself in front of the King's horse at the 1913 Derby.) Lady Davidson retained the seat with a comfortable, if reduced, majority. The runner-up in the three-cornered fight was the Liberal candidate, none other than the redoubtable Mrs Corbett Ashby, here fighting her sixth election.

Joan Davidson, a very attractive woman, became a loyal member on the Government benches although she did not speak often in the Chamber; she and her husband were close friends of Stanley Baldwin and at party headquarters Lady Davidson wielded great influence. She made her maiden speech in a debate on the Population Statistics Bill.[48]

The three other women joined Ellen Wilkinson on the Labour benches. In August Mrs Agnes Hardie, the widow of Mr George Hardie, Labour M.P. for Springburn, Glasgow, and sister-in-law of the late Keir Hardie, took over the Labour candidature in the by-election following her husband's death, and won comfortably. She had had considerable trade union experience having been the first woman organizer of the National Union of Shop Assistants and from 1918 to 1923 Women's Organizer of the Labour Party, a post she relinquished when her husband became an M.P. In spite of her professional qualifications her arrival was heralded in left-wing circles as that of a much needed representative for the 'working class housewife', a role which she played up to in her maiden speech during the second reading of the Annual Holiday Bill when she castigated the Government party as being like 'the housewife who polishes up the parlour and leaves the kitchen alone'.[49]

In April 1938, as the result of a by-election in West Fulham, Dr Edith Summerskill entered the House. She had won a resounding victory for the Labour Party by converting a Conservative majority of over 3,000 to one of 1,421 in her favour. She had fought twice before: at a by-election in Putney and at Bury in Lancashire in the General Election of 1935. During this West Fulham by-election she made criticism of the Government's foreign policy and the weakening authority of the League of Nations the main issues of her campaign. Dr Summerskill was one of the women destined to make her mark in Parliament in a long career that still continues. She came of a family of doctors and it was medicine that brought her into politics when she was co-opted on to a maternity and child welfare committee of an urban district council; subsequently she became a member of the Middlesex County Council. Although she was happily married to another doctor, Dr Jeffrey Samuel, and had a son and daughter, she used her professional name for politics, for Dr Edith, a tall, attractive young woman given to wearing severe hats, was a firm advocate of women's rights. A good platform speaker, she was apt to deflate hecklers by finding clinical explanations for their obstructive behaviour. (It was a method she was also to apply to her

(a) Miss Ellen Wilkinson speaking at a 'Save Peace' demonstration in Trafalgar Square during the Munich crisis, September 1938.

(b) The Rt Hon Edith Summerskill, Minister of National Insurance, 1950.

(a) The Rt Hon. Florence Horsbrugh, Minister of Education 1951-54, arrives at 10 Downing Street for a Cabinet meeting.

(b) Baroness Swanborough (Stella, Marchioness of Reading) on her introduction into the House of Lords as the first woman peer, 21st October 1958.

opponents in the House.) Her maiden speech on the Budget proposals deplored the effect that the economic depression had had on the social services, protested against the rise in the tax on tea and its effect on modest budgets ('in hundreds of homes the Chancellor of the Exchequer is a woman') and touched on the weakened position of the League of Nations.[50] She lost no time in asking the Minister of Health the first of many questions about the use of analgesia in childbirth,[51] for the campaign for painless childbirth was one of her great interests. Later in 1938 she went to Spain at the invitation of the Spanish Government to investigate the conditions of women and children there.

The third woman to reach the Opposition benches also won a by-election victory at Dartford at the end of 1938, with a majority of 4,238. She was Mrs Jennie Adamson, wife of the Labour Member for Cannock, who had already contested Dartford in 1935. She too fought her campaign on foreign policy, resisting conscription (which was the official Labour Party policy) and she also demanded an improved standard of living. She was welcomed by her Labour colleagues as another 'working class housewife', a role she supported by saying that she would 'still cook the Sunday joint'. She and her husband were the fourth married couple to sit together in the House. Her maiden speech in the debate on the King's Speech concerned unemployment.[52]

By the end of 1938 therefore the twelve women members consisted of six Conservatives, four Labour, one Liberal, and one Independent.

By 1939, after the rape of Czechoslovakia, hopes of saving the peace were fading. During the Adjournment Debate on foreign affairs on 22 August 1939 Winston Churchill in a powerful speech remarked that it was 'an odd moment for the House to declare that it will go for a two months' holiday'. Eleanor Rathbone was the only woman to intervene. She appealed for a more generous policy towards refugees and reminded the House 'that while we are enjoying ourselves by sea or mountain there are hundreds of thousands of men and women who are wandering about in the utmost destitution, many of them hiding by day, many of them already in the hands of the Gestapo and being beaten up daily in concentration camps and prisons.'[53]

On the recall of Parliament three weeks later, after the signing of the German-Russian pact, she spoke once more: to ask for a National Government to lead the country.[54]

F

1939-1945 Woman-power

SURVEYING THE war-time parliamentary scene after an interval of two decades it is clear that it was at this period, as at no other, that the women members of Parliament came nearest to acting as a women's party, speaking with one voice on behalf of their sex, whatever their political backgrounds. Although women had often before crossed party lines in support of each other, on only one isolated occasion had they acted as an organized group—in 1928, when they supported Margaret Bondfield's measure to provide shoes for poor children. Now, several months before the formation of an all-party Coalition Government under Mr Churchill, the women members had begun to act as a pressure group and they continued to do so throughout the war. It was ironic that while the First World War created a climate of gratitude for women's war effort that made their enfranchisement and entry into Parliament possible, the Second or 'total' World War soon disclosed a marked reluctance on the part of officialdom to use woman-power to the best advantage and this attitude created a women's 'front' in the House of Commons, committed to putting this right.

In the early days—the period of the 'phony' war—some thoughts still strayed towards the possibility of peace. During a debate on the war situation in October, Eleanor Rathbone wondered 'has everything been done; could it have been stopped?' and asked, 'if at this late hour Hitler were given some kind of ladder to climb down, [whether] we should not in the long run achieve an honourable and secure peace without war?'[1] The following speaker, Mrs Mavis Tate, disagreed. Speaking from her knowledge of Germans and reminding the House that she claimed to be the only person in the country who had ever been able to get anyone out of a concentration camp, she said she felt sure that the Germans would take any gesture of conciliation as a sign of weakness.[2]

In the spring of 1940 when the German offensive in Western Europe had started, those looking with critical eyes at Mr Chamberlain's leadership included Eleanor Rathbone, Mavis Tate and Lady

Astor who in peace had so firmly supported him. She now thought that Lloyd George would make a better Premier.[3] Before the Norway debate on 8 May, which led to Neville Chamberlain's resignation and the formation of a Coalition Government under Winston Churchill, both Mavis Tate and Lady Astor decided that if the Opposition divided the House they would vote against the Government. They told Ellen Wilkinson this and, according to an article which Lady Astor wrote in *The Observer* after Ellen's death in 1947, this knowledge passed on by Ellen caused Herbert Morrison to change his speech and divide the House which he had not intended to do. Thus Lady Astor claimed that she, Mavis Tate and Ellen Wilkinson played a key role in changing the Government at this critical juncture.[4] Both she and Mavis Tate were among the thirty-three Government supporters who voted in defiance of a three-line Whip; 'it was not an easy thing to do', as Mavis was to recall later in the war.[5]

When Churchill formed his all-party Coalition Government he kept Florence Horsbrugh in her post as junior Health Minister and appointed Ellen Wilkinson to the post of Parliamentary Secretary to the Ministry of Pensions. He sent for Florence at the end of several other interviews with newly appointed ministers. He was by then tired and keyed up to a high pitch at the magnitude of his task, and for Florence's benefit outlined a challenging prospect in which, fighting to the last, they and their colleagues rolled in the gutter and died or alternatively set up Government in Canada. 'Can you bear it? Can you stand up to it?' he demanded. When she left him she assumed, correctly, that she had been reappointed to her post, although in three-quarters of an hour the Ministry of Health had not been mentioned.

As for the interview between a former right-wing Tory opponent of women's suffrage and Ellen Wilkinson, an ex-Communist suffragette, it must have been an interesting experience for both of them. Afterwards the Prime Minister told his friends with pride : 'I have formed the most broad-based Government that Britain has ever known. It extends from Lord Lloyd of Dolobran to Miss Ellen Wilkinson.'[6] She, for her part, told a *Daily Herald*[7] reporter : 'After I had been interviewed by Mr Churchill I felt that I had been in the presence of a very great man and a very great leader.' Certainly his trust in her was not misplaced for, as often happens, office had a sobering effect on the fiery backbencher and she became a loyal and hard-working member of the Government. Ellen Wilkinson was at the Ministry of Pensions for a few months and then in October

1940, after the London blitz had started, she was transferred at Herbert Morrison's request to his Ministry of Home Security as an extra Parliamentary Secretary with special responsibility for the provision of air raid shelters. She worked there in great harmony with her chief until the end of the war.

Both women ministers were therefore key figures in the organization of civil defence. At the Ministry of Health Florence Horsbrugh was responsible for the casualty service, evacuation, billeting, the creation of day nurseries, rest centres for the bombed out, and health in air raid shelters as well as for the normal affairs of her department. In the House she had to satisfy many questioners on these subjects. The manifold problems of evacuation and billeting were matters that particularly exercised her at the beginning of the war and again in 1944 when the flying bomb attacks began. She covered many hundreds of miles visiting all parts of the British Isles and on one occasion was reported to be in Coventry after a raid before the flames had died down. She was twice bombed out of her flat and injured her leg in an air raid in 1944.

One of her most difficult assignments was to house and cater for some 12,000 evacuees from Gibraltar who raised many problems. Often she had to go and listen to their grievances, when 'they either kissed me or spat at me' as she remembers. Lord Leathers, Minister of Transport, provided a liner to take some of the evacuees to Northern Ireland. Their Ulster hosts behaved well, arranging transport, porters to carry their luggage and so on. It was therefore unfortunate that one grateful guest should exclaim on landing : 'How nice it is to come to a Catholic country !'

In the worst London raids Ellen Wilkinson was constantly inspecting the air raid shelters amid dust and rubble before the smoke cleared away, driving herself about in a small car so as not to put a driver at risk. In the early days there was much to be done to improve conditions both in the shelters and in the London underground stations where throughout the war thousands of people slept on the platforms. 'Safety, Sanitation and Sleep', Ellen announced as her watchwords in making arrangements for the people in the shelters. She also approved all attempts to keep up morale. 'I do think', she said on one occasion, 'that life should consist of something more than work and shelter.'[8] She was also responsible for organizing the voluntary army of firewatchers who, after their day's work, took their turn in guarding city buildings against incendiary bombs. Ellen was never afraid to upbraid young men who were suspected in certain places of shirking these duties and when women factory workers complained that they had no time for shopping she told their husbands roundly in her speeches that they should do more in the home—advice that was not always well received. In the middle of 1942 her colleague at the Ministry of Home Security, Mr Mabane, was transferred to another post and Ellen Wilkinson became responsible for the duties of both junior ministers. In addition, on more than one occasion she successfully mediated in shipyard strikes on Tyneside and in other ports. Never of strong physique, there is no doubt that she sacrificed her health to overwork and she also had bad luck, for she fractured her skull in a motor accident in 1942 and the following year hurt her leg in a glider accident. She still kept going with her leg in an iron, refusing to be considered an invalid, but towards the end of the war her health began to give way. At the end of 1944 she was in hospital ill with pneumonia and bronchitis. That was the year she was elected Chairman of the Labour Party.

In October 1940 Mrs Jennie Adamson, the Labour member for Dartford, was appointed Parliamentary Private Secretary to the Minister of Pensions, Sir Walter Womersley. Her special responsibilities were the pension claims affecting women and children, particularly war orphans.

For the backbenchers too the war imposed its strains. Eleanor Rathbone was bombed out of her house in Romney Street, Westminster, and Lord and Lady Astor suffered air raid damage to their house on the Hoe at Plymouth; they were there a good deal during the war, because for five years they were Lord and Lady Mayoress of the much bombed city. It was Lady Astor who, after the first blitz on Plymouth, agitated for a National Fire Service, which Herbert Morrison, as Minister of Home Security, inaugurated in 1941. She also helped to revive the morale of the people of Plymouth by organizing band music and dancing on the Hoe.

Just after the House of Commons was bombed in May 1941 Irene Ward and Thelma Cazalet-Keir went to examine the ruins. As they made to pass round the remains of the Speaker's chair a policeman barred their way. 'You must wait a minute,' he said, 'His Majesty is inspecting the ruins.' It seemed to them a strange quirk of fate that it needed a Hitler bomb to make it possible for the Monarch to re-enter the Commons.

During the war the Labour and Conservative Parties agreed on an electoral truce whereby vacant seats were filled by the party in possession uncontested by the other. In this way Mrs Beatrice Rathbone entered Parliament unopposed in 1941. Her husband, Flying Officer J. B. Rathbone, Conservative member for Bodmin, Cornwall, and a great-nephew of Eleanor Rathbone, had been shot down in a bombing raid over Germany and his wife was nominated in his place. She was American by birth and had been active in organizing from her house in Dean's Yard, Westminster, the distribution of the 'Bundles for Britain' sent over from the United States. She made her maiden speech during the debate following the fall of Crete, calling on the Government for 'action, vigorous action' in the conduct of the war and reminding it that 'it is not the eleventh hour, it is half past the eleventh hour'.[9] Sir Percy Harris, the Liberal member for Bethnal Green, with more chivalry than geographical accuracy, said her speech 'was like a breath of fresh air from America across the moors of Devonshire'. For a short time there were two women with the same name in Parliament, but Mrs Rathbone ended this confusing situation by marrying an Army officer in 1942 and becoming Mrs Wright. The mother of two young children by her first marriage, she served on a Ministry of Health Committee on maternity and child welfare. She gave birth to a daughter in 1943 and was thus the first woman to have a baby while a member of the House.

In 1943 another war widow entered the House in place of her husband, bringing the number of women M.P.s up to fourteen. Lord Apsley, the Conservative member for Bristol Central, was killed on active service in the Middle East, and his widow, Viola, fought a spirited by-election campaign against three Independent candidates (including Jennie Lee). She did this from a wheelchair for she had been badly injured in a hunting accident some years previously. She made a great impression when, in deep mourning, she appeared before the Bar of the House in her wheelchair and nimbly negotiated it to take the oath and sign the roll. She had been keenly interested in politics for some time and had also been active in work for the British Legion, the Red Cross and, since the early days of the war, the Auxiliary Training Corps (forerunner of the WAAC). She again roused the attention of the House when, seated in her chair at the the end of the Chamber, she spoke for the first time and from personal experience in a debate on the rehabilitation of the disabled, in which she quoted Shakespeare's lines :

> Yield not thy neck
> To fortune's yoke but let thy dauntless mind
> Still ride in triumph over all mischance.[10]

In the first months of the war various women's organizations began making representations to the women M.P.s about the unsatisfactory attitude of the authorities towards the employment on war work of well qualified women; a mere handful of all the thousands who had been placed on the Central Register of women available had even been interviewed, let alone offered posts. It was soon clear, as Dr Summerskill was to remark in a later debate, that the Government 'was in some respects too gallant to women and in others not chivalrous enough.'[11] In February 1940 all the women backbenchers went in a body to the Financial Secretary of the Treasury to demand that women should be given a more responsible role in the war effort. They submitted a memorandum which gave details of the poor response from public and private enterprises to applications for war work by well qualified women. No immediate improvement was forthcoming, and Lady Astor, at the suggestion of Dame Caroline Haslett, got together at her home a committee composed of all the women backbenchers and certain other prominent women including Lady Violet Bonham-Carter (now Baroness Asquith), under the chairmanship of Miss Irene Ward. For the duration of the war it met at fortnightly intervals while the House was in session. The committee issued regular reports on the use of womanpower, investigated complaints and where necessary forwarded them to the appropriate departments. The Hon. Secretary was Mrs Ethel M. Wood c.b.e., aunt of Mr Quintin Hogg M.P., who on her own responsibility later published a booklet *Mainly for Men* which outlined some of the inequalities in the employment of women with which the committee had to deal.

In September 1941, at the request of the National Council of Women, the committee organized a deputation led by Thelma Cazalet-Keir to the Foreign Secretary, Anthony Eden, to ask that the ban on women entering the Diplomatic and Consular Services should be lifted. After agreeing to give favourable consideration to this at the end of the war, he called Thelma back to inquire: 'But what are you going to do with all the husbands?' Another deputation went to see Sir John Anderson, the Chancellor of the Exchequer, to ask that the marriage bar to women in the Civil Service should be lifted and this too was done at the end of the war. The wider and more purposeful use of women police was another matter that concerned the committee, as it had earlier women M.P.s, and frequent representations were made about it.

In the spring of 1941 the women M.P.s managed to persuade the

Government to allow time for a debate on the whole subject of woman-power. It took place on 20 March and was the first comprehensive discussion on the employment of women ever held.[12] Mr Ralph Assheton, the Parliamentary Secretary to the Ministry of Labour, opening the debate, immediately showed that misplaced chivalry of which the committee complained when he said: 'No man with whom I have discussed the matter views with equanimity the possibility of having to use compulsory powers in regard to women.' He was followed by Irene Ward who said:

> This debate creates another milestone in British parliamentary history. Today, for the first time when we are officially discussing matters relating to women, we have got the women members of Parliament of all parties united in a common policy. . . . We want to reaffirm . . . our determination to support the Government in whatever action they may think necessary in connection with the organization of woman-power in their effort to achieve victory at the earliest possible moment. . . .

After outlining some of the matters at issue: wages and conditions for women workers, training facilities, the desire to share in the planning of policy, differentials in compensation rates for war injuries, pay and conditions for nurses and servicewomen, she announced that to avoid overlapping and waste of time each of the other women M.P.s would deal with a different aspect of the subject. One after another, interspersed with observations of the other sex, the women members spoke like a well rehearsed team. Only Agnes Hardie, who made no secret of her pacifist views, struck a slightly discordant note by opposing the conscription of women. Florence Horsbrugh, as Parliamentary Secretary to the Ministry of Health, dealt with the shortage of day nurseries for working mothers and other points raised, and Sir John Anderson, the Lord President of the Council, wound up the debate, saying he felt sure that the House would agree that it had served a useful purpose. But perhaps Thelma Cazalet-Keir summed up the situation best when she remarked in the course of her speech:

> If we had 40 or 50 women members of Parliament instead of the present small number, I doubt whether this debate would have been necessary, because many of the things we are discussing today would either never have occurred or would have been automatically rectified at a much earlier date. . . . I am sure that one of the tests of the civilization of a country—and by civilization I mean democratic way of life—is the position and status given to women.

But if the debate cleared the air temporarily, the same grievances had to be brought up again on several other occasions during the war. When, in December 1941, during a three-day debate on the war effort,[13] it was announced that single women between the ages of twenty and thirty would be called up, all the women members, except Mrs Hardie who declared 'war is not a woman's job', supported the measure, but at the same time they reminded the House of the lack of training facilities for women, the misuse of ability, the low wages, unfair compensation, lack of welfare facilities and so on. There was also renewed criticism of the Government's appeal to women to join the Services. Eleanor Rathbone wanted less stress on smart uniforms and more appeal to public spirit, while Lady Astor did not feel that posters of A.T.S. girls sitting at a bar with drinks before them would help recruiting. Warming to her theme she asked what the Government expected when they could not even deal fairly with women in political life. She cited the cases of Margaret Bondfield and the Duchess of Atholl who never regained their positions of influence in their parties while 'men fail time after time and back they come to the front bench'. 'I say', she declared, determined not to miss this opportunity, 'that no Government and certainly not this Government has ever understood, trusted or even tried to use, women.'

During this debate Mavis Tate revealed that, disguised as a worker's mate, she had got into an aircraft factory. She described an alarming wastage of manpower, with men sleeping away the day between wheeling aircraft out in the morning and back into the hangars at night, and coach drivers earning good wages, idle for several hours between driving workers to and from the factory.[14] Her revelations made a great impression on the House.

During another debate on woman-power in March 1942[15] Dr Edith Summerskill said she was tired of serving on committees on which men had been appointed to deal with questions affecting women. 'I am beginning to feel', she said, 'that the war is being prosecuted by both sexes and directed by one.' A particularly remarkable instance of this had occurred the month before when the Government proposed to set up a committee composed entirely of men (the Parliamentary Secretaries of the three Service departments) to inquire into the welfare of the women's Services. The inquiry had been made necessary by rumours and allegations of 'immorality', particularly in the A.T.S. It was Thelma Cazalet-Keir's question whether 'it would be a good thing to set up an all-woman committee to inquire into conditions in the male Services?'[16] that brought home the absurdity of the situation, with the result that the Government later announced the appointment of a new committee with Miss Violet Markham as chairman and composed of five women (including Thelma Cazalet-Keir and Edith Summerskill) and three men. As Eleanor Rathbone remarked: 'The Government are sometimes willing to listen to reasonable criticism.'[17]

During the woman-power debate in 1942 Mavis Tate tried to move an amendment to the effect that civilians should receive equal compensation for war injuries. This question, originally raised by Jennie Adamson in 1939[18] and regularly aired at every discussion on woman-power in the House, was one that agitated many members of both sexes for three years. Under the existing legislation single women received compensation at a rate of some seven shillings less than single men. This was strongly resented in the civil defence services: in April 1942 Edith Summerskill presented a petition from 8,100 women in London and the Home Counties asking for the compensation scheme to be amended.[19] But it was the lively and energetic Mrs Tate who, at the request of the Woman-power Committee, led this campaign to a successful conclusion. Mavis Tate was never afraid to go against the Government in defence of her principles. In this she resembled her great friend, Lady Astor. After raising the matter several times in debates and at Question Time, on 25 November 1942 she finally forced the matter to a division during the debate on the King's Speech.

'I would impress upon the House', she said, 'that this is not a fight for women. It is a fight for human justice and nothing else.' With deadly logic she demolished successive arguments advanced against equal compensation and wound up an arresting speech by saying: 'I beg hon. members, no matter what they came prepared to do, to look into their own hearts and consciences, to forget party, to forget whether it is to their advantage or to their disadvantage, to join me in the lobby against the Government for the sake of justice.'[20] Edith Summerskill seconded her appeal and ninety-five members, including all the women backbenchers, followed her into the division lobby. It was one of the very rare occasions on which a speech from the back benches has influenced the opinion of the House and brought about a change of policy, for so large an adverse vote moved the Government to set up a Select Committee on which Thelma Cazalet-Keir, Megan Lloyd George, Agnes Hardie, Edith Summerskill and Mavis Tate served. It reported in favour of equal

compensation and on 7 April 1943, in reply to a question from Mrs
Tate, Sir Walter Womersley, Minister of Pensions, announced that
the Government had accepted the committee's recommendations
and that in future civilians of both sexes would be compensated at
the same rate.[21] It had been a long battle and when Mavis Tate
rose to thank the Minister she was cheered on both sides of the
House.

Few opportunities were lost by this very active group of women
to uphold the rights and dignity of their sex. Lady Astor was concerned that no women had been awarded the Victoria Cross[22] and
Edith Summerskill objected strongly to what she considered to
be the offensive implications of a security poster proclaiming:
'Be like Dad, Keep Mum'.[23] She also fought for and in 1943
secured the right for women to serve as auxiliaries in the Home
Guard[24] and she herself served in the Home Guard of the House of
Commons.

If the Government had, as Lady Astor told it, a blind eye for the
usefulness of women to the war effort, it certainly availed itself of
the services of the women M.P.s. For security reasons details of
public expenditure on the fighting Services could not be revealed in
open debate, but a Select Committee on which both Lady Davidson
and Irene Ward served was set up to keep an eye on this and issue
reports from time to time. In 1941 the Minister of Labour appointed
Irene Ward and Megan Lloyd George to serve on the Women's
Consultative Committee to advise him. Agnes Hardie and Beatrice
Wright served on a consultative committee set up by the Minister
of Health and Edith Summerskill gained valuable experience as a
member of a consultative council appointed by the Minister of
Food, Lord Woolton. All the women in the House served on a parliamentary advisory committee on salvage set up by the Minister of
Supply who appointed Megan Lloyd George as chairman. Her success in this job led later to her appointment to the Ministry's Salvage
and Recovery Board.

The women M.P.s' watchfulness over the interests of their sex was
continued in the debates held towards the end of the war on the
major measures to improve the post-war world. The only occasion
on which the Coalition Government under Mr Churchill was
defeated on a vote of the House was during the committee stage of
the Education Bill, introduced by Mr R. A. Butler in 1944, when
Thelma Cazalet-Keir courageously moved an amendment to give
equal pay to women teachers.[25] In the division that followed the

Government was defeated by 117 to 116 votes, recalling a similar occasion in 1936 (see page 123-4). Churchill, who was not present was very annoyed and the next day told the House that a vote to delete the amended claused would be treated as a vote of confidence. At that critical juncture of the war, he said, 'there must be no doubt or question of the support which the Government enjoys in the House of Commons'. Before the vote was taken the perpetrator of the defeat said : 'In this great democracy of ours, convention, for once, seems to have overruled common sense. I believe in the clause as it stands but I shall vote against it to show my measureless confidence in the Prime Minister now in view of the stupendous days that lie ahead.'[26] The Government got its vote of confidence by an overwhelming majority and the equal pay question was again shelved. Soon afterwards Thelma met the Prime Minister in a corridor; he had quite regained his good humour and remonstrated genially : 'Thelma, Thelma, you are trying to put an elephant into a perambulator !'

In the country Thelma Cazalet-Keir's stand was not favourably received by everybody. Angry correspondents in the columns of *The Daily Telegraph*[27] under the headline 'Women M.P.s' Obsession. Are They Abusing Their Power?' accused women M.P.s of putting their sex before their country and concentrating too much on women's issues. The correspondents included Mr Remer who wrote : 'My only criticism of my woman colleagues in 20 years in Parliament is that they concentrated entirely on domestic politics.'

In the last weeks of the war in Europe a bill to grant family allowances, one of the outcomes of the Beveridge Report, came before the House. It was however as speaker after speaker was to affirm at its final reading in June, really the result of the efforts of a single woman, Eleanor Rathbone who, starting in the early twenties, inside and outside Parliament, prepared the ground for family endowment. In 1940 she had re-stated the argument for it in a Penguin book *The Case for Family Allowances* and throughout the war she had pressed the Government on many occasions to declare its intentions. The falling birth rate had aided her cause, and opinion in Parliament and the country was now ripe for the measure. In recognition of her work, for, as she said, she was 'generally regarded as the grandmother of the proposal', Eleanor was given the honour of initiating the debate on the second reading.[28] The bill, she reminded the House, set up a new principle of public responsibility in that it proposed that the State should make a money contribution not merely to bringing children into the world and to their education, but to maintaining them as well. Some of the proposals did not accord with her ideas : she would have liked the first child to be eligible for an allowance and for the allowance (then five shillings) to be higher. On one point she and other women members fought their last great feminist battle of the war : the proposal that the allowances should be paid to the father. Here Eleanor and her supporters were adamant; outside opinion came to their aid and a campaign on familiar lines was waged, with the result that the Government accepted an amendment that the allowances should be paid to the mother.

Following the passing into law of the Family Allowance Act, Eleanor Rathbone received many congratulations and tributes. To-day in the changed circumstances of the 1960s, in an affluent society with a relatively high birth-rate, some may think the family allowance policy needs revision, but for the period in which it was conceived no one can deny Eleanor Rathbone's achievement. Another —the greatest—of her campaigns had ended triumphantly as a result of her 'brick by brick' technique, but there were plenty of other causes to take its place. Her concern for refugees had increased rather than diminished. At the time of the internment of enemy aliens in 1940 she was one of the first two M.P.s to visit Huyton camp near Liverpool where anti-Nazis had been hurriedly impounded with Nazi Germans and conditions left much to be desired.[29] Eleanor campaigned for improvements and for the release and employment of a number of well-disposed aliens, which eventually came to pass. When news was received of the mass extermination of Jews in enemy-occupied Europe she and Mr Richard Grenfell, a parliamentary colleague, set up an organization called the National Committee for Rescue from Nazi Terror of which she became vice-chairman. In the House she pressed the Government to take more positive action by allowing increased Jewish immigration to Palestine. In the last speech which Victor Cazalet made in the House of Commons in May 1943 before his death on active service he paid a remarkable tribute to Eleanor's work for refugees, calling her 'an honourable and noble lady' in the true rather than the parliamentary sense of the words.[30]

Eleanor did not always see eye to eye with Churchill over certain aspects of his conduct of the war but she continued to uphold and feel grateful for his overall leadership, and in March 1943 electrified the House by leaping to his defence after one of Aneurin Bevan's

more virulent attacks on him. Barely controlling her white-hot anger
she said :

> The Prime Minister needs no defence from me. History will judge
> and will be able to say what we owe to him. But there is just one
> thing. I do not think we ought to part on an occasion like this with-
> out someone saying it and perhaps I may say it because I am so
> completely outside this issue and not a member of the Prime
> Minister's party, and that is with what disgust and almost loathing
> we watch this kind of temperament, these cattish displays of feline
> malice.[31]

These were almost the last words spoken in the debate and made
a lasting impression on all who heard them. As the Press recalled
after Eleanor's death : 'It was a piece of vehement denunciation
packed into a couple of minutes such as no woman has ever achieved
in the House of Commons.'[32]

Apart from their work in Parliament and in committee and constituency several women members travelled abroad under difficult
conditions during the war. One of them, Edith Summerskill, was
the first woman to be included in a Commonwealth parliamentary
delegation, and visited Australia and New Zealand in June 1944.
The woman who travelled farthest and longest was Irene Ward
who in 1943 set out to visit China on behalf of the Ministry of
Information : a journey that covered 30,000 miles and lasted seven
months, and during which she travelled in wartime unpressurised
aircraft. When she was asked on her departure whether there was
anything she wanted she requested only 'some oxygen for when I
go over the hump'.

In the New Year Honours of 1945, when victory was in sight,
the two junior ministers, Florence Horsbrugh and Ellen Wilkinson,
were made Privy Councillors, the first women to receive this honour
since Margaret Bondfield's appointment sixteen years before. In
March they were both included in the delegation which the Foreign
Secretary, Anthony Eden, led to San Francisco to discuss the formation of the United Nations Organization. On her return from San
Francisco Ellen Wilkinson presided over the Labour Party Conference at Blackpool. According to Hugh Dalton she made an admirable chairman who was always prepared to give younger delegates
a chance to speak from the floor. Behind the scenes she was taking
an active part in the discussions with Mr Churchill about the timing
of a general election. She and Professor Harold Laski had reopened

their campaign to try to persuade Clement Attlee to step aside in favour of Herbert Morrison as leader of the party, but they collected little support.[33] Ellen's devotion and loyalty to Herbert Morrison were remarkable, and in view of their many years of close collaboration in Government and party it is strange and perhaps less than generous that when Lord Morrison of Lambeth came to write his autobiography he made no mention of her at all.

Just after the German surrender Mavis Tate undertook the task for which she is perhaps best remembered today : to visit Belsen concentration camp as the only woman of an all-party delegation dispatched in haste by the Speaker at General Eisenhower's urgent request. Newsreels shot at the time show Mrs Tate at Belsen standing transfixed with horror at the sight of the sub-human shadows wandering around her. It was on this visit that she contracted a virus infection that undermined her health with tragic consequences later.

Only fifteen days after the European war ended on 23 May 1945 the Coalition Government ceased to exist and Mr Churchill appointed a National caretaker Government that lasted for three weeks before the dissolution. In San Francisco Florence Horsbrugh heard that she had at last left the Ministry of Health and had been appointed Parliamentary Secretary to the Ministry of Food; with characteristic urgency Churchill wanted her to come home at once but Anthony Eden and Lord Halifax held up her departure for a few days. In London Thelma Cazalet-Keir was awakened in the early hours by the telephone ringing. A familiar voice, struggling with loosely fitting dentures, inquired whether she would accept the post of Parliamentary Secretary to the Ministry of Education. 'But mind, Thelma', it added with a chuckle, 'none of this equal pay nonsense.' Now ensued a few hectic weeks in which she not only had to get to know her department but to act at the dispatch box for her Minister, Mr Richard Law, who was away ill.

On 15 June the thirty-seventh Parliament of the United Kingdom and the fourth longest ever to sit was dissolved in anticipation of a general election on 5 July. But some six months before this another memorable record had been set up. On 1 December 1944 Lady Astor, the first woman to sit in the House, had celebrated the completion of twenty-five years as a member of Parliament. Her silver jubilee was marked with many gatherings inside and outside Parliament including a luncheon at the House attended by twenty-eight women members, past and present, and a meeting arranged by fifty-one women's organizations at Grosvenor House at which Lady

Astor summed up the contribution of women M.P.s thus : 'I do not
say we have been brilliant or glamorous, but we have been useful.'[34]
These celebrations were tinged with regret because at the same time
she did 'the hardest thing of my life' and announced her retirement
at the next election, giving Lord Astor's health as the reason. She
made little secret of her reluctance to go for she felt it was the wrong
time to be getting out of public life. 'We are going to have the same
shams after this war as after the last if we are not careful', she said.
'The Left will have its wild people and the Right will have its dead-
who-won't-lie-down kind of people.'[35] She felt she ought to be there
to deal with both of them.

Many were sorry to see her go for, although of late her interventions had become less reasoned and more obstructive, she was, like
Eleanor Rathbone 'a great institution' and life in the House would
certainly be duller without her. But she herself had no illusions. On
her last day in Parliament, still dressed in the same type of neat black
and white ensemble that she had worn with little variation since
1919, she told a reporter : 'The House won't miss me. It never misses
anybody. I've seen them all go, Lloyd George, Asquith, Baldwin,
Snowden, MacDonald and the rest and not one of them was missed.
The House is like the sea and the M.P.s like little ships that sail
across it and disappear over the horizon. Some of them carry a light
and some don't. That's the only difference.'[36]

What was her true worth in the House? It is certainly a fact that
she was as popular with many in the Labour Party as she was with
some of her own party, or conversely as disliked. 'Your place is over
here', Labour members had cried on more than one occasion and
Lord Attlee has written that at heart Nancy Astor was a Socialist.[37]
This seems too sweeping a statement for she adhered to most of her
party's principles and could be scathing about the policies and
performances of a Labour Government. She was always on the left
of the Conservative Party on domestic matters, and on the issues that
really interested her, whether it was drink, nursery schools, gambling,
clean milk, or the all-important question of women's status and
rights, she never saw things on party lines : she was truly independent.

As to the women who sat in Parliament with her, their opinion
has always been divided, and not on party lines. Some feel that her
constant waging of the sex-war, her irritating interruptions, and her
habit of speaking extempore without doing any preparatory home-
work on the matter in hand did the women's cause no good. Others

say that her courage and spirit, her kindness and generosity to her colleagues, as well as her way of illuminating basic truths by unforgettable turns of phrase made her a fitting 'First Lady'.

From a detached point of view it is easy to dismiss Nancy Astor as a lightweight figure whose fame in Parliament rested on her nuisance value. She was more than that. From her earliest days as an M.P. she had progressive social ideas well ahead of her time, ideas which shocked her party then but which are part of its policies today. Her difficulty was that while she possessed all the necessary courage, vision and energy to pursue her aims, by temperament and limited training she lacked the mental discipline and application required; she had to substitute provocative extempore tactics for documented argument and planned strategy so that she became an agitator rather than a reformer. As regards international affairs she shares in retrospect the odium of the 'Cliveden set', but her support of a pre-war policy of appeasement was endorsed by the majority of her Conservative colleagues; of these she was one of the few who had the courage to vote against the Chamberlain Government in the Norway debate of 1940. To use her own analogy, Nancy Astor was a ship which carried a light, even if it was a spasmodic, flashing one.

The end of the Second World War and Lady's Astor's departure bring to an end another clearly defined era in the history of women members of Parliament. During the sixteen years since 1929 thirty-two women had sat in the House of Commons, although never more than fifteen at a time. Even so it was an increase over their very small numbers between 1919 and 1929. They were still coming very largely from the middle classes and reaching Parliament around the age of forty. More of them were being elected in their own right and not through inheriting seats from relatives, but the majority of women candidates were still fighting difficult constituencies. Of the two main parties, although at most elections the Labour Party had fielded nearly double the number of women sponsored by the Conservative Party, the political climate had favoured them less, with the result that since 1919 the number of women of the two parties to have sat in Parliament was remarkably even : seventeen Conservative, sixteen Labour. With the addition of the four Liberals and one Independent the total of those who had sat in Parliament since 1919 was thus thirty-eight.

It cannot be denied that as might be expected, with their dual responsibilities to their constituencies and to women electors, the majority of women members did concentrate on domestic matters and they had for the period of the war acted together as a feminist pressure group, but as has been frequently shown in this book some of them had also interested themselves very much in external affairs.

This period had had its triumphs, but it had also had its disappointments. The first woman had attained Cabinet rank, but only for a short time and in difficult circumstances; for much of the period no woman had occupied a seat on the Government front bench. Individually and collectively women had made some notable achievements but their numbers were still pitifully small. Now in 1945 a new spirit of equality engendered by the war, and the general acceptance of the need for women to play their part in shaping the post-war world seemed to offer greater prospects of success for those seeking to enter Parliament. Another organization had appeared, committed to helping women parliamentary candidates and known as Women for Westminster. According to a brochure, 'Names of women with suitable qualifications will be recommended by the Women for Westminster committee of the party concerned for inclusion in the party panel of candidates.' A series of lectures and speakers' classes were arranged to help women prepare themselves. The brochure included this call :

> Reconstruction after the last war gave a world which had been shaped by men alone. Are women content that this should happen again? Unless women prepare now and become prospective parliamentary candidates in large numbers, we cannot hope to see after the next election a much higher proportion of women members. . . .

PART THREE
1945-1966
Slow Progress

1945-1950 The Era of the Housewife *(I)*

THE 1945 General Election campaign was conducted, as might be expected, in unorthodox and makeshift conditions. No parliamentary register had been compiled since 1939 and the election had to be fought on a wartime emergency one based on civilian identity cards. There were many omissions including that of the name of Mr Churchill who was therefore deprived of his vote. Party organization was makeshift, full-time agents being a peacetime luxury, and no constituency party could be sure of the extent of its support. In addition there was the unknown quantity of the Service votes which had to be cast and flown home from different parts of the world. Naturally constituency parties were only too pleased if they could put up a candidate returning from some battlefield with a chest full of medal ribbons and, as in 1919, these were not the most favourable circumstances for women to find seats. Nevertheless of the 1,683 candidates nominated on 25 June, eighty-seven were women, the greatest number at any one time to have sought election. They were made up as follows :

	CONSERVATIVE	LABOUR	LIBERAL	OTHERS	TOTAL
1945	14	41	20	12	87
1935	19	35	11	2	67

The increase in the Independents was accounted for by four who belonged to the left-wing Commonwealth Party that had come into being during the war, two Communists, and the first woman Welsh Nationalist candidate. Mrs van der Elst, in spite of a bad attack of laryngitis, was putting up at Hornchurch and Mrs Mary Stocks, the principal of Westfield College, another Independent, was contesting the London University seat.

Thirty-five of the eighty-seven candidates had fought elections before; among them were eleven members of the last Parliament. Two women besides Lady Astor—Mrs Agnes Hardie (Springburn, Glasgow) and Mrs Beatrice Wright (Bodmin)—had decided not to put up again. It had been rumoured that Eleanor Rathbone, now over seventy, would stand down but she decided to carry on in order to see through her work for various causes: this time her candidature for the English Universities was opposed and she had to campaign. Among the new candidates Miss N. A. Cooper (Ulster Unionist—Fermanagh and Tyrone) was the first woman to fight an Irish seat since 1918 and Lady Violet Bonham-Carter, the daughter of the Earl of Oxford and Asquith, the former Prime Minister, had resigned as a Governor of the B.B.C. in order to fight her first contest in the Liberal cause at Wells.

In spite of the increase of women candidates by nearly 25 per cent not everyone was satisfied. Bernard Shaw in a letter of support to the Labour candidate for Flint, Miss Eirene Lloyd Jones, daughter of Dr Tom Jones, the former deputy secretary of the Cabinet and secretary of the Pilgrim Trust, wrote: 'I know what I am talking about when I say that men cannot be trusted to behave themselves properly in the absence of women when the interests of their better halves are concerned.' In order to get more women into Parliament he was in favour of what he called 'the coupled vote' by which each elector would vote for a man *and* a woman, all votes cast for a single candidate of either sex being declared invalid.[1] Less radically, a letter written to *The Times*[2] by 'Elector' suggested that it should be an unwritten rule that a woman should be included in every short list of candidates interviewed by selection committees. Other Press comment stressed the difficulty of attracting well-qualified women to a political career because of the wartime lack of domestic help.

After a campaign in which the war leaders seemed a little out of character talking about milk for babies and other social measures, polling took place on 5 July, but the declaration of the results was delayed until 26 July to allow the Service votes to be flown home and counted. Before this however one of the women candidates was sure of her result. Mrs Bessie Braddock, the Labour candidate in the Exchange division of Liverpool, previously held by a Conservative, called in a mathematical genius from the local dog track and on the basis of his calculations toured the division in her loudspeaker van telling everyone she had won. When the poll was counted her expert had under-estimated her majority by only 45 votes.[3]

The landslide to Labour that was revealed on 26 July gave it an overall majority of 152 and carried the record number of twenty-four women into the House of Commons. As in 1923 and 1929 a swing to the left had increased the number of women M.P.s.

Twenty-one of them were Labour, one Conservative, one Liberal and one Independent.

Lady Davidson (Hemel Hempstead) was the only Conservative returned, with a 5,000 majority over another woman, Miss Doris Mobbs, the Labour candidate. All the others lost their seats by decisive majorities. For Florence Horsbrugh and Irene Ward this meant only a temporary absence from Parliament, but Lady Viola Apsley (Bristol Central), Mrs Thelma Cazalet-Keir (Islington East), and Mrs Mavis Tate (Frome) were not to return. Lady Apsley contested Bristol North East unsuccessfully in 1950, but neither Thelma Cazalet-Keir nor Mavis Tate was to fight another election. Thelma Cazalet-Keir who, like Mary Agnes Hamilton in 1931, had suffered the irony of a brief taste of front bench office before losing her seat, was a loss to Parliament but went on to do other useful public work. About her time as an M.P. she says, looking back, that while it could be intensely interesting and exciting, the greater part of it consisted of hard, unrewarding work. Her services were recognized in 1952 by the award of the C.B.E.; she became a Governor of the B.B.C. and she is, among her other interests, chairman of the Fawcett Society, the descendant of Dame Millicent Fawcett's suffrage organization, whose premises house what is probably the most comprehensive library of books on women's activities in the world.

A tragic fate overtook Mavis Tate who was found dead in a gas-filled room of her house in Pimlico in 1947. It was revealed at the inquest that she had suffered from depression due to financial and other troubles, and aggravated by the illness which she had contracted at Belsen. She had been readopted for Frome, and although this division was redistributed before the next election it is very probable that if she had lived she would have returned to Parliament. She was a woman of considerable ability, and although emotional and highly strung her independence, enterprise, and vigour made her a valuable member. As mentioned earlier, she was one of the very few members of either sex who could claim to have made a speech (on civilian compensation for wartime injuries) from the back benches that influenced the thinking of the House.

When Parliament met on 1 August to re-elect Colonel Clifton-Brown as Speaker, the Lady Members' Room on the terrace may have been overcrowded but the atmosphere was that of a happy reunion for most of the members had known each other through working in the Labour movement for many years. It was remarked in the Press that many of them were in their forties or fifties and married and that a surprising number of them had been teachers, while the *Manchester Guardian*[4] remarked that several, although well qualified in other directions, described themselves as 'house-wives'.

Lady Noel-Buxton, Miss Jennie Lee and Mrs Leah Manning had returned to Parliament for the first time since 1931. Lady Noel-Buxton had topped the poll in the two-member seat of Norwich formerly represented by Miss Dorothy Jewson; Jennie Lee had left the Independent Labour Party in 1942 because of its attitude to the war and rejoined the Labour Party in 1944. She had been adopted for Cannock—a seat formerly represented by Mrs Adamson's husband who had retired—and held it with a 19,000 majority. She was now the wife of Aneurin Bevan. (Their wedding in 1934 created quite a stir in the Press because they decided to dispense with wedding rings.) Since she was last in the Commons Jennie had, as she put it, 'hoboed round the world' writing and lecturing. Her political sympathies still veered much to the left. Mrs Manning was back to the House after winning Epping by the narrow majority of 987.

Eleven of the twelve new Labour members had won Conservative-held seats, some with as spectacular a turn-round of figures as any in the country. Like the Conservative victors of 1931, several of those elected in 1945 were probably surprised to find themselves in Parliament.

The three youngest members were still in their thirties and had got into Parliament at their first attempt. They were all destined for long and successful parliamentary careers. Two of them, Miss Alice Bacon (Leeds North East) and Miss Margaret Herbison (Lanark) had very similar backgrounds : both were the daughters of miners, both were schoolteachers, and both had come into the Labour movement when they were quite young. Alice went to elementary and secondary schools in the Yorkshire village of Normanton, where her father was for many years secretary of the Miners' Federation, before she trained as a teacher. She joined the Labour Party at sixteen and when she was elected to the National Executive Committee in 1941 she was its youngest member. She had been an official of the National Union of Teachers and chairman of the Standing Joint Committee of Working Women's Organizations which represented two million women in the trade union, Labour Party and Co-operative movements. Margaret, petite and with an attractive low-pitched Scots voice, was born in Shotts, a large mining village in her constituency, and was educated there. After taking her M.A. degree at Glasgow University, she taught history and English at a school in Glasgow and, although active in the Labour movement, had no thought of a parliamentary career; she loved teaching and had no desire to leave it. Towards the end of the war however a burly miner called at her parents' cottage in Shotts with an invitation from the local Miners' Federation to become the prospective Labour candidate for the Lanark division, Jennie Lee's old seat. 'Go away', she said, 'and find a man.' A week later three burly miners were on the doorstep with the request that she should reconsider her decision; they could think of no better candidate. So Margaret became 'the miners' little sister' representing them and her other Lanarkshire constituents at Westminster. Her story is a refreshing contrast to some of the other grim struggles.

Mrs Barbara Castle, at thirty-four the youngest woman member, and quite the most glamorous with her auburn hair and colourful clothes, had captured Mary Agnes Hamilton's former seat at Blackburn. She came from the middle classes; her father, Frank Betts, had combined a career as a tax inspector in Bradfield with editing a socialist paper, the *Bradfield Pioneer*. Barbara therefore grew up in political atmosphere and at the age of six wrote her first election address: 'Vote for me and I will build you houses.' From Bradford Grammar School she won a scholarship to St Hugh's College, Oxford. While she was up at Oxford she was treasurer of the University Labour Club. On coming down she became a journalist. She was elected in 1937 to the St Pancras Borough Council as one of the youngest members and eventually became deputy leader of the Labour Group. During the war she was a temporary civil servant in the Ministry of Food and then joined the *Daily Mirror* as its housing correspondent and also wrote a weekly column for the Forces, dealing with demobilization and other problems. In 1944 she married Ted Castle, another journalist on the *Mirror*. Apart from housing, she was particularly interested in economic and overseas affairs.

The other new members were all middle-aged or elderly and had long histories of endeavour in public service and party circles with the result that their backgrounds and careers were in many cases remarkably similar; they were worthy women but perhaps not so interesting as a group as some of their predecessors or successors. They were all married except for Miss Grace Colman (Tynemouth) who was an intellectual and came from a Conservative family; she was the daughter of a canon of Worcester Cathedral and by way of contrast cousin of Ronald Colman, the film actor. A former rowing blue, Grace became a Socialist when she was up at Newnham College, Cambridge. She had been a tutor at Ruskin College, Oxford and at London University and during the war served as a temporary civil servant in the Board of Trade. Aged fifty-three she had had long apprenticeship in the party, having contested Hythe in 1929 and 1931 and Hallam, Sheffield, in 1935. She had rather an abrupt manner and made no concession to fashion.

Mrs Barbara Ayrton Gould (Hendon North) was perhaps the most prominent of the group. She had fought every general election and one by-election since 1922 and in 1929 at Northwich lost the seat by only four votes. She was Jewish, the daughter of two distinguished scientists and widow of Gerald Gould, the poet and associate editor of the *Daily Herald*. Their son is Michael Ayrton the artist. Barbara was one of the few active suffragettes to reach Parliament; she had gone to prison for militant activities and once rode at the head of a procession as Joan of Arc. She was a graduate of London University and worked for a time as publicity manager of the *Daily Herald* before becoming organising secretary of the National Society for Lunacy Reform; and in 1929 she was a member of the Royal Commission on the Civil Service. She had been on the National Executive Committee of the Labour Party since 1930 and for the year 1939–40 its Chairman. One of her chief interests was the care of neglected children.

Many of the other new members came from the ranks of local government: Mrs Freda Corbet (Camberwell North West), a barrister known in her party as 'a great little propagandist', had been a member of the L.C.C.; Mrs Muriel Nichol (Bradford North), daughter of a former Labour M.P. for Merthyr Tydfil, sat on the Welwyn U.D.C.; Mrs Clarice McNab Shaw (Kilmarnock; not to be confused with Mrs Helen Shaw, former Conservative member for Bothwell), was one of the oldest at sixty-three, and a member of the Ayr County Council; Mrs Edith Wills (Duddeston) had sat on the Birmingham City Council for many years. Representing the Co-operative movement were the oldest of the group at sixty-six, Mrs Caroline Ganley (Battersea South), who was also a local councillor, and Mrs Mabel Ridealgh (Ilford North), a former National President of the Women's Co-operative Guild. Mrs Lucy Middleton (Plymouth, Sutton), a teacher and wife of a former Secretary of the Labour Party, had a background of political organization, first with the Peace Movement and later as adviser to the Hindu minorities at the Round Table Conference on India in the 1920s. Mrs Florence Paton (Rushcliffe), a magistrate, joined her husband, one of the two members for Norwich, in the House of Commons.

There were in addition two who, although similar in background and experience to the others, stand out by virtue of their striking personalities and were to become well known at Westminster. They were Mrs Bessie Braddock (Liverpool, Exchange) and Mrs Jean Mann (Coatbridge and Airdrie). 'Watch Mrs Braddock' the *Daily Herald* advised its readers on 27 July. 'A big woman who is capable of playing merry hell at any moment when she is roused by injustice'. Bessie had been reared in politics for her mother, Mary Bamber, had been a trade union organizer and one of Liverpool's first women magistrates. Bessie married Jack Braddock in 1922 and they were both for a time key members of the Communist Party from which they were expelled in 1924 for refusing to reveal to party head-quarters the identities of the agents whom they had recruited. As members of the Liverpool City Council in the 'thirties they had cam-paigned hard with Sydney Silverman, now Bessie's colleague in the House of Commons, for an improvement in the health and housing services and there had been noisy scenes in the City council chamber to which the police had twice been called in order to escort Bessie from it; as the *Daily Herald* now explained, 'she does not under-stand what mincing words means'. She was strongly partisan and professed it difficult to see a redeeming feature in any member of the Tory party.

Mrs Jean Mann was an equally lively if less violent politician who had fought two previous elections and had been a propagandist for her party since the early twenties; a witty and popular speaker she could always draw a crowd. She was the daughter of an iron moulder, the mother of five children and was a grandmother as well. Since her husband had been unemployed for some time between the wars there was little about domestic difficulties Jean did not understand or could not expound on; of all the 'housewives' in this Parliament she was to be the most vocal. She also knew a good deal about local affairs, particularly housing, for she had for many years been a member of the Glasgow City Council and was for some time vice-president of the Scottish Housing and Planning Council, honorary secretary of the Town and Country Planning Association of Scot-land and member of Scotland's Advisory Council. She was also, with another newly elected M.P., a member of the first Rents Tribunal in Scotland and this delayed her arrival at Westminster, because, although the remuneration was negligible and did not cover the expenses involved, it was held to be an office of profit under the Crown. She had to wait to take her seat until a special Act of Parliament had been passed to exempt her and her colleague from the £500 fine which they might otherwise have had to pay under an Act of 1707.

By the time Parliament met however the congestion in the Lady Members' Room on the terrace had been relieved to some extent by the appointment to office of all three of the senior women members who now had rooms of their own. Mr Attlee made Ellen Wilkinson Minister of Education with a seat in the Cabinet. He had originally thought of Mr Chuter Ede for this post, but he was needed at the Home Office and Ellen with her interest in education became the second choice.[5] She was now the first woman after Margaret Bondfield (see Appendix A) to achieve a Cabinet post and in the photograph of the new Cabinet taken in the garden of 10 Downing Street she, like Margaret, looked a brave but slight figure among the regiment of men. Dr Edith Summerskill was appointed Parliamentary Secretary to the Ministry of Food under Sir Ben Smith, the post held by Florence Horsbrugh in the caretaker Government and one for which Dr Edith was well qualified. Mrs Jennie Adamson, with her wartime experience, was an excellent choice as Parliamentary Secretary to the Ministry of Pensions. She did not however hold the position long, for in May 1946 she was made Deputy Chairman of the Assistance Board in place of Miss Violet Markham and had to leave Parliament.

Some interesting appointments were made among the backbenchers. Sir Stafford Cripps, the President of the Board of Trade, chose Barbara Castle as one of his two Parliamentary Private Secretaries, with special responsibility concerning clothes rationing. In November she made a notable maiden speech on demobilization in which she quoted letters from skilled men in the Services who complained of delay in their release and expressed the suspicion that 'some wangling was going on' in the demobilization arrangements.[6] Jennie Lee was appointed to the Central Advisory Committee on Housing set up by the Ministry of Health of which her husband was Minister. Both she and Barbara Castle were chosen by the Parliamentary Labour Party to inquire into conditions of old age pensioners.

Alice Bacon, who first spoke during the second reading of the National Insurance (Industrial Industries) Bill,[7] was appointed a member of the Women's Consultative Committee of the Ministry of Labour which was now turning its attention to the resettlement of women in civilian life, and in December she also became a member of a Home Office committee to consider shop hours and general working conditions of young people. Lucy Middleton went to the Estimates Committee of the House of Commons. She was chairman of a party committee on the blitzed areas, a post for which as member for devastated Plymouth she was particularly well qualified. She also sat on a party committee on agriculture and food. Muriel Nichol joined the committee set up by the Home Office under the chairmanship of Miss Myra Curtis (the Curtis Committee) that was to make far-reaching recommendations for the care of children.

The male members of the House of Commons now had to get used not only to seeing a larger number of women about but also to rather more eye-catching clothes. The new members did not all subscribe to Lady Astor's idea of sober parliamentary wear and the honourable members were sometimes loud in their appreciation. Ellen Wilkinson, endeavouring to answer questions in a smart little hat with a green feather perched on her head, was held up for several minutes by Opposition cheers.[8] Barbara Castle did not often cover her auburn hair but when she did it was with a creation of so dashing a style that her arrival became for the parliamentary correspondent of the *Manchester Guardian* 'the sartorial moment of every parliamentary day'.[9] Leah Manning, who like Bessie Braddock was of generous proportions, drew applause when she entered the House dressed for a Buckingham Palace Garden Party, while Jean Mann never again wore a brown velvet ensemble after some members hissed 'dressed like a bride' when she rose to ask a question.[10] If women members had to come back to the Chamber after an evening function they invariably changed out of evening dress first, otherwise the reaction of male members, who frequently attended in dinner jackets, might have been embarrassing. On the other hand one woman, Grace Colman, went to the other extreme and was reported as staying away from the first post-war Buckingham Palace Garden Party because she refused to wear a hat, saying that it was 'preposterous that nowadays we should be ruled by out-of-date etiquette like that'.[11]

Bessie Braddock was one of the many new members waiting to catch the Speaker's eye to make her maiden speech at the beginning of the new session. She was not disappointed for long, nor disappointing, for—fixing the Opposition with her eye—she dealt with their responsibility for the housing situation: 'Right throughout this country and particularly in industrial areas', she said, 'people are living in flea-ridden, bug-ridden, lousy hell-holes which have been allowed to develop throughout the industrial areas of this country.'[12] The honourable members had never heard anything quite like this from a female voice before.

It was not long after her maiden speech that Bessie was heard again, this time making an unusual announcement on 2 November during a dock strike. Her statement, she told the House, was the agreed order for the strikers to resume work on the following Monday morning pending negotiations for a permanent settlement; she was, she said, speaking for all the dockers in the country. In congratulating her Mr Tom Driberg, the Labour member for Maldon, said that it was an historic speech in that it was an operative order and added: 'I would like . . . to say with the greatest possible friendliness that I would always much rather be on her side than against her in any dispute or negotiation.'[13] It was certainly the first time that a woman M.P. played a key role in settling a dispute of this kind, although Ellen Wilkinson had acted as mediator in shipyard disputes during the war.

One sad event occurred before the post-war Parliament was very old. Eleanor Rathbone, who had again topped the poll for the English Universities, died suddenly without any previous illness at the beginning of January 1946 at the age of seventy-three. In the last few months her friends had noticed a change in her. She seemed strained and almost haunted, they thought, by the plight of the distressed people in Europe and elsewhere whom she was seeking to help; but she had never relaxed her efforts nor her liaison work with her university constituents, travelling all over the country to speak at meetings and sending out regular newsletters. 'What a rebuke she was', commented the *Manchester Guardian*[14] recalling that she was fifty-seven when first elected, 'to those—so vocal in recent days—who would make youth the sole criterion of the capacity to serve in Parliament and who would, if they could, fix a maximum age for Parliamentary candidates at, say, 40.' It must also be claimed that Eleanor did much to justify the university vote which was to be abolished by an act passed during this Parliament. She was truly independent, finding cause for praise and blame in all parties: she condemned the Chamberlain policy of appeasement as strongly as she criticized the Labour Party's pre-war pacifism. She filled a use-

ful role in being able to say and do things that few party politicians
could afford, but she, like all Independent members, had to pay the
price for her freedom in her lack of the support from party colleagues
and the research facilities of party organizations. Years before, she
had told members of her Oxford college, Somerville, that if women
wanted to carry through any reform to its final stage they must
combine the qualities 'of the giant Sisyphus, King Bruce's spider, the
Ancient Mariner and the Importunate Widow'[15] and she obeyed
her own advice. But in spite of her determination she always had
a sense of the possible; she knew the moment to hold back and never
overdid her propaganda so that it rebounded on itself. As a result,
in nearly all the campaigns she mounted over the years, whether it
was for votes for women, the enfranchisement of Indian women, the
status and welfare of women in the Colonies, the treatment of aliens
in this country and refugees abroad, the Zionist cause in Palestine,
or family allowances, she was able to look back on solid achievement;
the 'brick by brick' technique had paid off.

She will perhaps be best remembered for her work for family
allowances. At her death it was forecast that these might become
known as 'the Rathbone', rather as old age pensions were once known
as 'the Lloyd George'. Instead they have become part and parcel
of the Welfare State and have recently been under criticism in the
changed social conditions of the sixties; but for the pre-war circumstances of the greater part of the population, with its declining birth-
rate, they were a notable reform. In Parliament Eleanor was admired
and respected but never popular. She often irritated the House by
her persistence and importunity, but on occasion, as in her dramatic
rebuke of Aneurin Bevan in 1943, she could astound it.

It has been said that Eleanor, like her fellow campaigner the
Duchess of Atholl, cared more about causes than people. In her
case this is not true, for she knew and cared about the unhappiness
of disconsolate people more than many reformers did. 'Spinster
though I am,' she once asserted, 'I claim to be a real expert upon
the unhappily married woman'; she knew all the 'possible permuta-
tions or combinations of domestic discord'.[16] Eleanor's real difficulty
was that with few exceptions she never found it easy to get on intimate terms with others; and she lacked the art of casual com-
munication. But, aloof blue-stocking as she seemed, many people
in different parts of the world had reason to mourn her as the great
number of posthumous tributes to her showed.

Many eminent people, including Winston Churchill, sponsored

a memorial fund which was able to endow an Eleanor Rathbone Lecture on a social or political theme which is given annually at one of the universities that she represented; in Liverpool University there is now the Eleanor Rathbone Chair of Social Science. Israel has its own memorial to her work for the Jews in Rathbone House, a building for cultural activities attached to a children's agricultural school near Tel Aviv. So Eleanor's good works go on and not least because, after certain bequests, she left the residue of her considerable fortune to be used for the charities in which she was interested. The sum of £7,000 was set aside for the benefit of refugees, particularly those from Czechoslovakia and Spain.

The members on the Government side of the House began their work with the uplifting sense that a golden era of social reform was now beginning, undeterred by the fact that in order to get through all the legislation outlined in the King's Speech they would have to put in long hours with all-night sittings and no time for private bills. The message from the Government Whips' Office to the ladies was, according to Jean Mann, 'Keep mum and let the bills go through.'[17] But if the Government now had the power to put through its programme it had not got all the material resources, for the post-war economic situation gave increasing cause for concern and necessitated tight economy in the spending of foreign currency, particularly dollars, and the continuance of restrictions on the home front. The 'housewives' of Westminster found themselves in the difficult position of having to interpret the Government's austere policies to the housewives in their constituencies, who after six years of war were tired of rationing, queueing, mending and making do.

Edith Summerskill at the Ministry of Food suffered to the full the difficulties and frustrations of this period, for it was often her job to justify not only the continuance of rationing but also to explain the necessary reductions and its extension to cover foods never previously rationed (such as bread and potatoes) because of poor harvests and the shortage of dollars to import more wheat. The Government's policy was to continue to subsidize the cost of basic food to the consumer; therefore any increase in the amount allowed meant heavier bills for the Exchequer to pay. Edith set about her job well aware of the difficulties but determined to make her Ministry 'a very human Ministry, always in contact with the people'.[18] Soon after her appointment she was reported as going on a tour of food shops to study the queues. She received deputations of housewives who came

Women M.P.s on the terrace of the House of Commons, 1959. Standing, left to right: Mrs Harriet Slater, Mrs Lena Jeger, Mrs Patricia McLaughlin, Mrs Alice Cullen, Miss Joan Vickers, Miss Alice Bacon, Lady Megan Lloyd George, Lady Gammans, Mrs Bessie Braddock, Miss Elaine Burton, Hon. Mrs Evelyn Emmet, Mrs Barbara Castle, Mrs Mary McAlister, Mrs Jean Mann, Mrs Joyce Butler, Dame Irene Ward. Seated: Lady Davidson, Rt Hon. Edith Summerskill, Miss Edith Pitt, Miss Mabel Howard (New Zealand Minister for Women and Children), Miss Pat Hornsby-Smith, Rt Hon. Florence Horsbrugh, Miss Margaret Herbison.

(a) The Rt Hon. Barbara Castle, Minister of Transport.

(b) The Rt Hon. Jennie Lee, Minister of State, Department of Education and Science.

(c) The Rt Hon. Margaret Herbison, Minister of Social Security.

(d) The Rt Hon. Alice Bacon C.B.E., Minister of State, Home Office.

from Birmingham to complain that they could get 'cod, nothing but cod' at the fishmongers, while those from Plymouth complained of nothing but plaice.[19] Many found her sympathetic. But the House-wife's League became something of a thorn in the Government's side with its constant complaints which were suspected of being politically inspired—'Woolton's Whimpering Winnies', Alice Bacon called them.[20]

In Parliament Edith Summerskill was called upon to answer a constant battery of questions; the index of Hansard under her name might be mistaken for that of Mrs Beeton's cookery book, embracing what seems to be the whole range of edible—and even potable— commodities. The women members were among her most frequent questioners and a debate on the food situation in 1947[21] found many of them raising complaints: Barbara Ayrton Gould appealed for more sugar and bacon, Barbara Castle was worried about the loss of vitamin C as the result of potato rationing, Alice Bacon attacked the rationing of bread and the reduction in the bacon ration to one ounce per person per week, Leah Manning wanted meals made avail-able to every child at school. In another debate a few days later, Jean Mann, a most persistent questioner, while approving the Government's policy of holding down prices and 'fair shares for all', echoed the grumbles of Scots housewives when she said that putting oatmeal on ration points was almost the last straw. What were they to give their families for breakfast? 'We cannot fry a bit of bacon . . . that is out of the question. We cannot give stewed fruit or prunes be-cause they are on points. We cannot give fried potatoes because we have not the fat and potatoes are rationed.'[22] Dr Edith stood up well to this bombardment and to the taunts about groundnuts, eggs from Gambia, and bulk buying, patiently explaining the Govern-ment's economic difficulties in the importation of food. Not unnatur-ally she sometimes got irritated by incessant complaints. During a debate initiated by a member who wanted the control order on cheese lifted she resented the fact that some imported cheese was referred to as 'mouse trap' and reminded the House that it all had the same nutritional value. 'The function of the Ministry of Food is not to pander to an acquired taste', she said firmly, 'but to ensure that the people who have never had time to acquire these tastes are suitably fed.'[23] She attributed a longing for big juicy steaks to snob-bery[24] and at a speech to the Oxford University Club in 1949[25] defied anyone to tell the difference between butter and margarine, a remark that was not easily forgotten and has to this day been a boon to the

G

organizers of advertising campaigns for at least one brand of margarine.

Then there was the rather unfortunate business of snoek. Seeking for some addition to the British diet that did not cost hard currency, the Ministry of Food imported this tinned fish from South Africa in 1948. Jean Mann for one did not think much of it and in a supplementary question to one asked by the member for Ayr snapped : 'Is the hon. lady aware that as far as snoek is concerned the rest of Scotland could not care less?'[26] Another member suggested that it should be called by a more appetizing name. But snoek remained snoek, and a good deal of it remained on the grocers' shelves, while it provided much sport for the cartoonists and music hall comedians.

Edith Summerskill was however able to fulfil one lifelong ambition in 1949 by piloting the Milk (Special Designations) Bill[27] through the House that made it compulsory for milk to be tuberculin tested or pasteurized. This end to a long campaign for clean milk she called 'her finest hour' for both she and Dr Somerville Hastings, another Labour member, had been pressing for it for a long time; it was a measure for which several other women, including Lady Astor and Mrs Wintringham, had fought since the 1920s.

In 1946 Edith Summerskill led the British Delegation to the United Nations Food and Agriculture Organization's Conference in Washington and the following year she spoke at the F.A.O. meeting in Geneva on Britain's contribution to the solution of the world's food problem. In 1949 she was made a Privy Councillor.

Housewives' difficulties were not of course confined to food. There were shortages and restrictions in every department of domestic life. Clothes rationing was one that raised a great deal of ill feeling. When fashion designers daringly introduced a 'new look' into women's clothes in 1947 by making skirts appreciably longer, there was an anxious demand from Mabel Ridealgh that Mr Harold Wilson, who had succeeded Sir Stafford Cripps at the Board of Trade, should take a lead against it in view of the extra material it would use (a request that cannot have been very popular generally).[28] Bessie Braddock took up the cause of the fuller figure, demanding extra coupons and a better supply of garments. She and Leah Manning established their point without words on one occasion when they made a stately progress arm-in-arm into the Chamber and bowed low to the Speaker while Sir William Darling, a clothing manufacturer, was holding forth on sizes in women's clothing. The House took it in a gale of laughter.[29] Outside the House Bessie acted as a model for outsize garments once or twice and did a good deal to encourage a greater variety and enterprise in the design of these clothes which were uniformly dreary and tentlike. It was the first time the sturdy sizes had had representatives of their own in Parliament to take up the cudgels for them.

In a debate on consumer goods in June 1947 Lady Davidson voiced the plight of housewives all over the country when she said, 'today I have not a sheet which is not end to middle or middle to end with patches all over it', and asked for more generous treatment from Sir Stafford Cripps who, she said, she knew was 'a very austere man.'[30] Mrs Wills agreed with her that 'men do not know what it is to manage a home without all the things and comforts which women like to have.'[31] There was indeed a feeling that the housewife was not being sufficiently considered. 'I have said it before,' declared Mabel Ridealgh in a debate a few months later, 'and I say again, the splendid job of the housewife is not being fully recognized.'[32]

When Princess Elizabeth became engaged to Prince Philip twelve women were among the Labour members who voted against the proposed allowances for the Royal couple on the grounds that they were excessive in a time of austerity for the general public.

The troubles on the home front came to a peak in the hard winter of 1946–7 when there was a severe fuel crisis; coal supplies failed, factories came to a standstill, transport suffered, and unemployment figures rose, while restrictions had to be put on the domestic use of power and fuel. Margaret Herbison and Jennie Lee had been particularly active during the stages of the Coal Nationalization Bill and after the fuel crisis Jennie criticized the treatment of the miners by the newly formed state-run Coal Board which she claimed to be callous and unimaginative and to have 'opened old wounds' afresh.[33]

It was in this hard and bitter winter that Ellen Wilkinson died. Since becoming Minister of Education she had had the frustrating task of trying to implement the Education Act of 1944 and raise the school leaving age to fifteen at a time when many school buildings had been bombed and were quite inadequate and teachers in very short supply. In spite of rapidly deteriorating health she went into the job with all her customary drive and enthusiasm, determined, as she said when receiving the honorary degree of Doctor of Laws at Manchester University in 1946, to see that 'secondary education shall be secondary and not elementary with frills on'.[34] She realized the high priority of scientific and technological education in a nuclear age, saying 'it's a race between education and extinction',[35] but she also believed in the importance of the arts and the humanities. In spite of the difficulties she kept to the provisions of the 1944 Act, piloting only a small amending measure through Parliament that raised no great point of principle,[36] and one of her last public actions was to confirm that the raising of the school leaving age would come into force as planned on 1 April 1947.

Early in the new Parliament she had got into trouble by forecasting in a speech in her constituency only a month before the measure was taken that bread might have to be rationed. With her usual frankness she apologized for the lapse in a statement in the House.[37] She had travelled abroad, visiting schools in the British Zone of Germany in 1945 and 1946, and she took the chair at the Preparatory Conference of UNESCO. But all the time asthma and bronchitis continued to trouble her and she was becoming more dependent on relieving drugs. She had always overworked and friends like Margaret Bondfield now noted with concern how completely exhausted she seemed at times when she was caught off guard. She spent part of the summer recess in Switzerland trying to regain her health, but strongly denied reports that she had been advised to take things more easily. Her last public appearance was a fortnight before she died when she opened the Old Vic School and made a speech saying that she hoped England would become a Third Programme nation, an idea that was not altogether well received by the public at large. A few days later she was found in her flat in a coma following a bad attack of asthma. She was taken to St Mary's Hospital, Paddington, where she never fully regained consciousness and died ten days later on 6 February. At the inquest the coroner, after hearing evidence from her doctor, found that she had accidentally taken an overdose of sleeping pills in addition to her other drugs.

It was a sad ending for a gallant spirit. Like Eleanor Rathbone, Ellen Wilkinson had done much for many people, in her constituency of Jarrow, in the trade union movement, in Germany and Spain and many other parts of the world; her courage had broken down several barriers for women in the House of Commons. Possessed of great fire and drive, she never, unlike Eleanor, carried out a sustained policy in advancing her particular causes from the back benches. Her speeches were often passionate emotional outbursts; she could have tears in her eyes pleading for Republican Spain and choke with anger over the injustices suffered by Jarrow. Yet in office she steadied and was a most efficient administrator. To her friends she was always loyal: she made herself unpopular campaigning for Herbert Morrison and it was Ellen who, alone on the Government benches, raised a cheer when after the election of 1945, Churchill entered the Chamber for the first time as Leader of the Opposition. 'Don't ask me about Churchill', she would say to critics, 'I am biased in his favour.' Although she had her ups and downs inside her own party she inspired affection on both sides of the House. She was very friendly with Irene Ward—they had great respect for each other—and also with that most Tory of Tories, Lord Winterton, and his wife. She wrote better than she spoke but she was responsible for many witticisms that are often wrongly attributed. It was Ellen, for instance, who said of the House of Commons, 'This place is full of ex-future Prime Ministers',[38] and compared the Houses of Parliament to 'a highly decorated cake outside and a Victorian railway station inside, with the House of Lords as the first-class waiting room and the House of Commons as a second-class one.'[39]

In the House of Commons tributes were paid by all the party leaders and at the memorial service to this small woman, who in fifty-five years had risen from the back streets of Manchester to sit in the Cabinet, were representatives of the King and the Duke of Gloucester, and the Prime Minister and his ministers in person.

Ellen's death reduced the number of women M.P.s to twenty, because besides Eleanor Rathbone's death and Jennie Adamson's retirement, Mrs Clarice McNab Shaw, the elderly member for Kilmarnock, had had to apply for the Stewardship of the Chiltern Hundreds in October 1946 because of ill health. She had never been really fit while in the House and after her years of struggle to get there had been unable to take an active part. She died only a month later. In December however another woman representing a Scottish constituency took her seat, bringing the number of women up to twenty-one. She was Lady Priscilla Grant of Monymusk who won a by-election at Aberdeen South for the Conservative Party with a majority of 3,839. She had the typical British good looks of fair hair and blue eyes and the added appeal of being a war widow with two small daughters; her husband, an officer in the Grenadier Guards, had been killed at Arnhem. During the war she had been a welfare supervisor in an Aberdeen factory and at the general election in 1945 had contested Aberdeen North. Now at the age of thirty-one she was the youngest woman in the House and, according to Jean Mann, the glowing Press accounts of a 'Glamour Girl for Parliament' had rather prejudiced the inmates of the room on the terrace against her. When they met her however they succumbed to her quiet charm. As she was being introduced into the House some members permitted themselves a low wolf whistle amid Conservative cheers, and one Labour member shouted 'Grace Darling to the rescue!'[40] She herself remarked, 'It's rather like entering a school at half-term and a boy's school at that.'[41] She became an assiduous member. In her maiden speech in March 1947 she accused the Government of squandering both time and victory and told it bluntly that it would never attract large numbers of women into industry while the difficulties of housekeeping were so great.[42] In the summer recess of 1948 she married Lord Tweedsmuir, the son of John Buchan, the author and former Governor General of Canada, who was the youngest peer to sit on the front benches of the House of Lords.

In the same month that Priscilla Grant entered Parliament, Florence Paton made history by being the first woman to be appointed to the Speaker's Panel of Chairmen of Committees. She first presided over a committee in May 1948 when she sat at the Clerks' Table (committee chairmen do not occupy the Speaker's chair) during a debate on Scottish aviation estimates and was cheered and congratulated by members on both sides of the House.[43]

In 1947 Margaret Herbison was the first woman since the war to be chosen for the honour of seconding the Address in Reply to the King's Speech. It was no longer necessary to wear Court dress and so in ordinary day clothes Margaret, mindful of the difficult times, warned the Government in the course of her speech that although it had the right to ask much of the people 'they have a right to ask much from us in return.'[44] In December that year it was announced that Lady Davidson had been elected to the executive of the 1922 Committee, the influential Conservative backbenchers' committee. It was the first time a woman had been so honoured; Lady Davidson however had always wielded considerable influence in Conservative Party circles inside and outside the House. Although she was never a very effective speaker in Parliament, at party gatherings, such as the Conservative Women's Annual Conference, she could make just the right appeal.

The number of women M.P.s was increased to twenty-two when in October 1948 Mrs Alice Cullen, a widow of fifty-six with three daughters, won a by-election for the Labour seat of Glasgow, Gorbals —the first Roman Catholic woman to be elected. She had been a member of the Glasgow Corporation for ten years. In her maiden speech in December she gave the House a graphic description of the congested housing conditions in her overcrowded constituency.[45]

Although the women of Parliament were of necessity much preoccupied with the rationing problems of the home front during the whole of this period, this did not prevent many of them from making valuable contributions on other questions. Many, like Alice Cullen, Bessie Braddock, Barbara Castle and Jean Mann, were well qualified from local government experience to speak on housing. Lucy Middleton, the member for Sutton in much-bombed Plymouth, took a leading part in all deliberations on war damage claims and was instrumental in getting the War Damage Commission to consider claims for compensation from those who through ignorance or other reasons had not submitted their claims before the closing date. This included many small householders who had not been aware that they could claim.

Women were active too in the great debates on the National Health Service and drew attention to some of the initial problems. Bessie Braddock campaigned against the provision of pay-beds in hospitals;[46] Alice Bacon, on the motion for the Adjournment in July 1948, startled the House by alleging that general practitioners were refusing to accept chronically ill or 'bad risk' patients on to their panels, and later revealed that she had received some hundred letters on the subject.[47] Many women contributed also to the various debates concerning the care of children and adoption, following the report of the Curtis Committee. In the very last days of this Parliament Barbara Ayrton Gould persuaded the Government to allow time for a debate on cruelty to children, which she introduced.[48]

In the post-war period women travelled abroad frequently on parliamentary and party delegations. In 1949 Barbara Castle was an alternate delegate to the General Assembly of the United Nations in Geneva where she specialized in social and humanitarian questions; in May that year she visited Canada on a trade mission. Margaret Herbison was one of only two women at the first meeting of the Consultative Assembly of the Council of Europe. In 1946 she, Barbara Castle, Bessie Braddock and Jennie Lee added their names to a critical amendment to the King's Speech, concerning the Government's foreign policy, demanding 'socialist planning as a constructive alternative to conflict between American capitalism and Soviet communism'.[49] Barbara Castle's signature was unusual because as a P.P.S. she was expected to refrain from open criticism of Government policies. Perhaps one of the most powerful inter-

ventions on the question of peace was made by Leah Manning in
a civil defence debate in March 1948 when she stunned the House
with a sudden burst of revulsion against the renewed threat of war.

> The Iron Curtain, [she said] which we are told exists between
> East and West, has today given place to a kind of sheet in a shadow
> play across which both sides see a phantasmagoria of distorted,
> horrible, grotesque people passing. Someone has to tear down the
> sheet and show people on both sides that we are all ordinary human
> beings hating war and longing for peace. Unless the Government can
> do that, the Government have failed in all that they set out to do.[50]

In spite of the growing distrust of Russia many Government members were unhappy at the continuation of national service. Margaret
Herbison, Muriel Nichol, Mabel Ridealgh and Florence Paton were
among those who in 1946 tabled an amendment to the King's Speech,
regretting the Government's intention of embarking on a policy of
peacetime conscription,[51] and in 1948 Alice Cullen, Leah Manning,
Muriel Nichol, Florence Paton, Mabel Ridealgh and Lady Megan
Lloyd George[52] were among the fifty-one members who voted against
the bill to increase the period of national service from twelve to
eighteen months.[53]

Outside Parliament some of the livelier spirits met trouble one
way or another which sometimes ended in a court of law. Barbara
Castle was sued by the *Daily Express* for saying in a B.B.C. discussion
that the results of a 'hustings ballot' which it was running on the
necessity for a change of Government were rigged. The matter was
finally settled out of court with Barbara paying costs and donating
twenty-five guineas to the Newspaper Press Fund as a token of the
sincerity of her apology. A rather more protracted affair was the
libel case which Bessie Braddock brought against the *Bolton Evening
News* in the autumn of 1948 for carrying a story (which was copied
by other newspapers,) headed 'Revelry by Night' which reported
that on 1 May 1947 Bessie 'had danced a jig on the floor of the
House ending up on the seat vacated by Mr Churchill, our greatest
House of Commons man'. It appeared that after Opposition members had left the Chamber in protest at the guillotining of the Transport Bill, some Labour members, including Bessie, had crossed the
floor to occupy the vacated seats and give their front bench an
audience; it was then that she was said to have trod a measure. A
special Act had to be passed in Parliament to allow witnesses from
the floor of the House and the Press Gallery to give evidence for both

sides as to how Bessie had crossed the floor of the House that night. (Did she walk or did she 'mince' or did she 'jig'?) Bessie's turbulent past in the Liverpool City Council chamber was revived by the defence which recalled how she once called someone 'a blasted rat' and imported a megaphone into the council chamber, but Bessie in the witness-box was straightforward and, as the presiding judge, Lord Goddard, said, 'as good a witness as ever I want to see'.[54] The jury found against her and after her appeal failed Bessie apologized in the Commons for inconveniencing members and assured the Speaker that she had meant no disrespect to the House.[55]

Jean Mann upset the Tommy Handley fans by referring to 'a little twerp Itma' in a debate on broadcasting.[56] Handley retaliated by slightly altering his slogan to 'It's that MANN again.'

At the beginning of 1949 Megan Lloyd George became deputy leader of the Parliamentary Liberal Party. It was said that her appointment would please the more radical element in the party that then numbered twelve, for Megan was showing left-wing tendencies. In June she celebrated the completion of twenty years in Parliament with a tea-party for all the women members.

When Parliament rose for the Christmas recess in December 1949 it was not to meet again. In the middle of January the Prime Minister announced the dissolution for 3 February with polling in a general election on 23 February. So in the middle of winter the parties prepared themselves for the fray.

1950-1951 *The Era of the Housewife (II)*

IT WAS obvious from the start that the 1951 General Election was going to be very largely a housewives' election with domestic discontents well to the fore. In spite of Dr Summerskill's assurance, in a discussion on nutrition introduced by Mrs Ganley at the end of the previous Parliament, that 'the hard-pressed housewives of the country can feel satisfied that the dark days of 1947, so far as food supplies are concerned, have gone and that they can look forward with confidence to the future',[1] Conservative campaigners made great play with the continued existence of queues, ration books, austerity and spivs five years after the end of the war. Leading ministers, including Edith Summerskill in Fulham, were heckled vigorously and many of their more unpopular statements were used in evidence against them. Perhaps the most unfortunate and the one that had the most damaging effect from the Labour's point of view, second only to Bevan's 'vermin' taunt at a later date, was Douglas Jay's statement in a Socialist pamphlet that 'Housewives as a whole cannot be trusted to buy all the right things where nutrition and health are concerned . . . For in the case of nutrition and health, just as in the case of education, the gentleman in Whitehall really does know better what is good for the people than the people know themselves.'[2] Probably no other statement has ever annoyed the women of this country more and the Conservatives made the most of it. Indeed if the women's vote can ever be said to have decided the result of an election it came nearest to doing so in 1950 and 1951. The war had long been over but housewives were still struggling with wartime conditions and they were sick of it.

In this election women were pushed onto the platform or the soapbox to 'give the women's view' as never before. Party managers suddenly discovered that they were invaluable because men, it was thought, sounded foolish talking about the size of the bacon ration or the price of tea. All three parties put up women for their party political broadcasts. Margaret Herbison, in her Scots voice—'low enough for a torch singer', as one Press report said—answered Mr

Churchill's and Lord Woolton's charges about bulk buying. Florence
Horsbrugh, now a candidate for Midlothian and Peebles, and Megan
Lloyd George spoke for the Conservative and Liberal Parties respec-
tively.

It was probably the importance of the housewife in this election
that led to the record number of 126 women candidates which has
not so far been exceeded or even approached. For some time before,
the adoption of more women had been the subject of party concern.
The question was discussed at the Conservative Women's Conference
in 1947 and correspondents in *The Daily Telegraph*[3] had then suggested that women candidates should be encouraged by some kind
of financial help. When nomination day came it was revealed that
all three parties, especially Conservative and Liberals, had increased
their number of women candidates :

	CONSERVATIVE	LABOUR	LIBERAL	OTHERS	TOTAL
1950	28	42	45	11	126
1945	*14*	*41*	*20*	*12*	*87*

The comparatively large number of forty-five Liberals reflected
the much increased total of candidates of that party fighting this
election. The number of Conservative candidates—and consequently
of women members—might have been increased by one if Dr Pearl
Hulbert, wife of Commander (later Sir Norman) Hulbert, the member for Stockport, had not resigned as prospective Conservative
candidate for Colchester in 1948. She had originally been adopted in
preference to a male applicant by a majority of two to one, but later
her platform manner was criticized by the Young Conservatives and
a certain section of the Association favoured putting up Mr Cuthbert
Alport in her stead. Seventy outraged Conservatives called a meeting
to support Dr Pearl but she resigned saying, 'Men in the local Conservative Association are woman haters,' and that she was not prepared to stand while the present executive committee held office.[4]
Mr (later Lord) Alport was then adopted in her place and embarked
on a successful parliamentary career by carrying the seat with 931
votes. This case is interesting in that it is one of very few, if not the
only one, in which a woman candidate once adopted has met trouble
of this kind.

Lady Noel-Buxton (Norwich) and Mrs Edith Wills (Duddeston)
did not defend their seats but all the other former members including seventy-year-old Mrs Caroline Ganley (Battersea South) stood
for re-election. Irene Ward was fighting again, this time in opposition

to Grace Colman at Tynemouth. Florence Horsbrugh however had not really wanted to return to Parliament. When pressed by Lord Woolton, the Chairman of the Conservative Party, she agreed to stand provided it was for a seat where she was unlikely to be returned; accordingly she was adopted for Midlothian and Peebles, a Labour-held seat.

Only forty of the 126 candidates, including the former members, had fought elections before. Many of the new candidates were university women and about a dozen were under thirty.

To set the seal on this housewife's election Bernard Shaw wrote a letter in support of the Labour candidate for Croydon East, Miss Marion Billson, saying: 'Many of the male parliamentary candidates in all parties are mere yes-men and superannuated gossips. Women who all have to manage homes and rear and bring up children are practical, know where the shoe pinches and will vote for anything sensible and necessary, party or no party.'[5]

Although the election was quiet the results were looked forward to with excitement tinged with uncertainty for, while the tide seemed to be changing in favour of the Conservatives, there had been boundary changes in all but eighty constituencies of the 625 that might lead to unpredictable results. Nor did the verdict of the polls fail to live up to expectations for it was one of the closest contests for a hundred years, ending with an overall majority for Labour of six seats. One of the last eagerly awaited results to come in at the photo finish was that of Coatbridge which revealed that Jean Mann had held it for Labour with over 6,000 votes.

Of the 625 newly elected members only 21 were women, a disappointing result from the greatly increased number of candidates, but the swing to the right had unseated seven of the former Labour members and brought in only three new ones and four more Conservatives, making the total: 14 Labour, 6 Conservatives and 1 Liberal. Irene Ward, upholding her reputation as a trouncer of women, had defeated Grace Colman at Tynemouth by a 5,637 majority, and Barbara Ayrton Gould (Hendon North), Leah Manning (Epping), Muriel Nichol (Bradford North), Mabel Ridealgh (Ilford North) and Florence Paton (Carlton, a newly drawn disvision), all lost their seats, Florence Paton by only 395 votes. Of those that survived, Freda Corbet (Peckham) and Jennie Lee (Cannock) had two of the largest majorities, of over 19,000 and 17,000 respectively, and Lucy Middleton held Sutton, Plymouth by a narrow 924. Only nine Liberals were returned and Lady Megan Lloyd George did well against strong opposition to hold Anglesey by 1,929 votes.

The election brought five new women M.P.s into the House of Commons. For the Labour Party there was Miss Elaine Burton who held Coventry South. She was cast in a different mould from many of the women elected in 1945 for she was an athletic woman of forty-six, daughter of an Olympic hurdler, who had herself been a champion sprinter at the age of sixteen and had played cricket and hockey for Yorkshire. (She now gave up cricket as a concession to her parliamentary duties and took up skating instead which some wits thought appropriate.) She had taught for several years and had also worked for the South Wales Council of Social Service. During the war she fought a by-election at the Hartlepools as a Common Wealth candidate and in 1945 had contested Hendon South for the Labour Party which she joined that year. She had a taste for exotic millinery which brightened up the Commons.

The other new recruits were both elected for Welsh seats. Mrs Eirene White (née Lloyd-Jones), fighting the seat for the second time, won East Flint with a majority of 97 votes. A graduate of Somerville College, she had done a variety of jobs. She had been readers' adviser to the New York Public Library and had studied housing in various parts of Europe. During the war she was a temporary civil servant at the Ministry of Labour and then became lobby correspondent for the *Manchester Guardian*, a job rarely held by a woman. She was therefore no stranger to Westminster. She married another journalist in 1948 but had no children. A Fabian, she was a member of the National Executive Committee of the Labour Party. Her particular interests were overseas and industrial affairs, education and child welfare.

Mrs Dorothy Rees had won Barry by the narrow majority of 1,025 votes. She belonged to the older tradition of Labour women candidates for she was a former schoolmistress aged fifty-one, the daughter of a docker and widow of a Channel pilot. She had been active in the Labour Party for thirty years and was an alderman of the Glamorganshire County Council as well as a member of various bodies including the National Advisory Committee for National Insurance.

Mrs Eveline Hill (Manchester, Wythenshaw) and Miss Pat Hornsby-Smith (Chislehurst) were two more post-war Conservative women M.P.s to be elected and were of a different type from the 'O.B.E. women' of pre-war days. Mrs Hill, who was fifty-two, had lived in Manchester all her life and had been a member of the City Council for fourteen years. Together with a brother she ran a family catering business and therefore had some practical knowledge of the business world. Pat Hornsby-Smith's fame had preceded her into Parliament. She was a dynamic, auburn-haired woman of thirty-five who had come into prominence in her party in 1946 after a challenging speech at a party conference. Soon after that she was adopted for Chislehurst out of twenty applicants, nineteen of whom were men. The daughter of a small shopkeeper in a London suburb, she was educated in local elementary and secondary schools and after her father's death supported her mother on a salary of three pounds a week. Eventually she became Private Secretary to the Earl of Selborne while he was wartime Minister for Economic Warfare. She joined the Conservative Junior Imperial League (forerunner of the Young Conservatives) when she was sixteen and had been a member of Barnes Council. At Chislehurst she fought an enthusiastic campaign as 'our Pat' and captured the seat with the small majority of 167. With her mixture of charm and aggressiveness Pat was hailed by the Press as 'a second Lady Astor' and rapid promotion was predicted for her. She made her maiden speech on Anglo-Canadian trade when she asked for another Ottawa Conference.[6]

The last of the twenty-one women to reach the House was Florence Horsbrugh. Her calculations had gone astray : she had been decisively defeated at Midlothian and Peebles according to plan, but when on the day before the poll Squadron-Leader Fleming k.c., the candidate and former member for Moss Side, Manchester, died suddenly, party headquarters put great pressure on Florence to stand in his place, a sign that the Conservative Party was anxious to have her back in Parliament. Her polling day was on 9 March when she was returned with the respectable majority of 8,578.

In his new administration Mr Attlee appointed Edith Summerskill Minister of National Insurance. She was therefore the third woman after Margaret Bondfield and Ellen Wilkinson to hold full ministerial office. She was delighted by the appointment, for family welfare had always been one of her main concerns, and declared : 'I want to be a Minister of Human Relations.' But lack of financial resources made this a frustrating job, especially when she had to resist pressure for increasing pensions which the rise in the cost of living had reduced in value. She appointed the newly elected Dorothy Rees to be her Parliamentary Private Secretary, a post for which, with her experience on the National Advisory Committee, she was well qualified. Margaret Herbison was appointed to be one of the two Joint Under-Secretaries for Scotland.

Alice Bacon seconded the Address in Reply to the King's Speech on 6 March.[7] It heralded a short, uneasy Parliament in which the first serious cracks in the Government ranks began to appear with the resignation of Aneurin Bevan, the Minister for Health, Harold Wilson and John Freeman over the proposed Health Service charges. Barbara Castle, who had been P.P.S. to Harold Wilson after he succeeded Sir Stafford Cripps at the Board of Trade, was one of those responsible for the *Keep Left* pamphlet issued by the *New Statesman* in 1950, which set forth the Bevanite principles of extended nationalization and unilateral disarmament. On the other wing of the party Jean Mann, for long a supporter of the Government's food policy, created a sensation when in February 1951 she wrote an article in a Lanarkshire paper[8] suggesting a two-tier system of rationing whereby extra food could be bought at a higher price. She maintained that it was no good pretending that there were fair shares for all for 'the big purse' won every time, and complained 'I've been short of tea, short of sugar, short of butter, short of eggs, short of butcher-meat and, I am sure, so has everybody else.'

During this period of eighteen months, three women introduced interesting private bills. Eirene White and Eveline Hill attempted to do something for the victims of broken marriages : Eirene, although (as she stressed) a happily married woman herself, introduced a Matrimonial Causes Bill to amend the law so that divorce could be allowed after the parties had been separated for not less than seven years. Although feminine opinion was divided on this issue the bill passed its second reading and the Government agreed to set up a Royal Commission to consider the whole question of divorce.[9] It is interesting that sixteen years later this particular matter was still under consideration by Church and State.

Eveline Hill tried to legislate for deserted wives in her Deserted Wives Bill so that a woman could not be turned out of her home after her husband's desertion, but could have the tenancy transferred to her. However, as Irene Ward remarked during the second reading, it was something of a lawyer's day and, although supported by Freda Corbet, Eirene White, Irene Ward, Joan Davidson and Edith Summerskill, the bill failed on the closure motion by 44 votes to 51.[10]

Barbara Castle's measure, the Criminal Law Amendment Bill,[11] introduced under the ten minute rule, to amend an Act of 1885 in order to give protection to prostitutes (hitherto outside the law) against misuse and abduction, fared better and it passed swiftly through all its stages to become law. Barbara was inundated with messages of approval while the bill was going through and when it passed its third reading the Association of Moral and Social Hygiene told her, 'you have done what we have attempted to do for 50 years' and gave a luncheon in her honour.

One of Irene Ward's main preoccupations on re-entering the Commons was the question of equal pay. She reminded the Government in a debate on the King's Speech in November 1950[12] that the Royal Commission set up by the Coalition Government had reported in its favour, and she left it in no doubt that she would carry the matter further for 'women are very tired of promises without performance', she said. She also asked the Prime Minister 'whether in view of the publicity given to vital secret operations during the war he has appointed an authority to ensure that no vital information is disclosed and no breach of the Official Secrets Act committed'.[13] Irene, who had close connections with the First Aid Nursing Yeomanry (FANY) during the war and had recorded its achievements in a book, *F.A.N.Y. Invicta*, was already worried by some of the war-time exploits that were being revealed in books and B.B.C. broadcasts.

Megan Lloyd George's position was becoming more difficult. With two other Liberal members she had often voted with the Government when the other Liberals voted with the Opposition. At a meeting of her Anglesey constituents in November 1950 she defended her actions successfully but already the *Manchester Guardian*[14] was expressing the suspicion that 'if the ship of Liberalism increased what she called "its list to starboard" she might be tempted to take a dive overboard to port.'

By this time women M.P.s were no longer, in spite of their battles for the housewife, viewed quite so much as representatives for women generally. Unless they had broadcast or made a speech that was widely reported they did not now receive the great volume of letters from women outside their constituencies that their predecessors had in pre-war days. Their modest increase in numbers and the fact that all M.P.s of both sexes were now expected to do a great deal of constituency work, holding regular 'surgeries' to which electors could bring their problems, had spread the load in this respect. To this limited extent only had the novelty of women in Parliament begun to wear off, for they still attracted a good deal of comment, some of it critical. In 1949 on the occasion of the thirtieth anniversary of Lady Astor's introduction into the House of Commons, A. J. Cummings of the *News Chronicle*[15] found that women in Parlia- ment had not had a noteworthy record and that 'with one or two exceptions, they have not yet got rid of a suppressed sense of sex in- feriority.' They were treated by their male colleagues with a faintly patronizing air 'which a facade of courtesy cannot completely con- ceal', but if there were a hundred women members he thought they would be a power to be reckoned with and 'the gentle air of male patronage would disappear like the mists of the morning.'

Some harsh things were said by Mrs Helena Normanton K.C. at a Suffragette Fellowship meeting at the beginning of 1950. Women M.P.s did not concentrate on the main issues such as peace, she said; there had by now been about a hundred and twenty of them (this was a slight exaggeration; see Appendix A) and she doubted whether anyone would remember the names of ten of them; none of them had ever resigned on a matter of principle; 'It's disgusting. None of the women have the guts to do it.' (She must have forgotten the Duchess of Atholl.) She firmly advocated a separate Women's Party. Lady Astor, another speaker, was also disapproving: what she thought of the Labour women in the House was not fit for her audience to hear. 'They have done things that we fought against for years' and they had not insisted on equal pay. It was most dis- appointing to see women putting party loyalty before their prin- ciples.[16]

And so it was on a note of general dissatisfaction that this difficult Parliamentary period came to an end.

1951-1955 In the Shadow of the Bomb

DURING THE summer recess of 1951 Mr Attlee brought his administration to an end and was the first Prime Minister to announce the
date of a General Election, 25 October, on television. The election
healed the divisions in the Labour Party temporarily, although not
long before the campaign opened the Bevanites published another
pamphlet, *One Way Only*, in advance of the Party Conference at
Scarborough at which Bevan and Barbara Castle secured the first
two places in the election of the National Executive Committee. For
Barbara her election was the result of a shrewd move : realizing that,
as a Bevanite, she would not win many trade union votes in the
women's section, she went forward this year for the section elected
by the more left-wing constituency parties. This manoeuvre she had
discussed with that clever tactician, Hugh Dalton, during a walk he
had organized at Whitsun for budding young politicians.[1] Barbara's
victory displaced the veteran Emmanuel Shinwell from the Executive.

There were 1,376 candidates in the 1951 election, nearly 500 less
than in 1950; the Liberals crippled by the cost of the previous election sponsored many fewer candidates this time, while the Communists only mustered 10 as opposed to 100 in 1950. These changes
were reflected in the number of women standing which had also
fallen considerably.

	CONSERVATIVE	LABOUR	LIBERAL	OTHERS	TOTAL
1951	25	41	11	—	77
1950	*28*	*42*	*45*	*11*	*126*

Of the seventy-seven women candidates no fewer than fifty-four, or
two-thirds, had fought before, including the former M.P.s who were
all defending their seats. One of the candidates was Lady Violet
Bonham-Carter who was again representing the Liberals, this time
in the Colne Valley, with the support of the local Conservatives who
did not contest the seat. Her old friend, Winston Churchill, came to

speak for her during the campaign and it was confidently expected that she would win.

Another organization to promote women candidates, the Women's Electoral Committee, emerged at this election. It seems to have been a small affair run by a lady in Herne Hill who circulated to women's organizations lists of the women candidates. This was resented by some of them who felt it suggested that they were only concerned with their own sex. The Women for Westminster group had faded away soon after 1948; like earlier organizations of its kind it had found overwhelming the difficulties of operating on a non-party basis.

During the campaign in which the parties exchanged plenty of scares and accusations concerning the rise in the cost of living under Labour, 'the sixpenny eggs' likely under Conservatives, the Bevan split, and the dangers of a Tory finger on the trigger, television was used for party political broadcasts for the first time, but the main broadcasting medium was still sound radio on which both Margaret Herbison and Pat Hornsby-Smith spoke for their parties. Polling took place in fine weather with a record number casting their votes. Again there was a closely-run finish but the swing away from the Labour Party continued and the Conservatives were returned with a small overall majority of 17 to form a Government under Mr Churchill. The result as far as the women candidates were concerned was that only seventeen of the former twenty-one members were returned and no new members; the Labour benches lost Mrs Caroline Ganley (Battersea South), Mrs Lucy Middleton at Sutton, Plymouth (where the Hon. J. J. Astor regained the seat for his family), and Mrs Dorothy Rees (Barry), all of them defeated by narrow majorities. The Liberals too did badly, returning only six members to the House and both daughters of the twin Liberal dynasties were defeated. Lady Megan Lloyd George, after twenty-two years as M.P. for Anglesey, lost to the Labour candidate Mr Cledwyn Hughes but, said the *Manchester Guardian*, 'one thing is certain we have not heard the last of Lady Megan.' In the Colne Valley Lady Violet Bonham-Carter failed to unseat Mr Glenvil Hall by 2,189 votes.

The Conservative women were nearly all returned with increased majorities; Pat Hornsby-Smith did particularly well to increase her tiny majority of 167 to 980. But even with the national swing against Labour the Labour women M.P.s still outnumbered the Conservatives by nearly two to one (Labour eleven, Conservative six), and two, Bessie Braddock (Exchange, Liverpool) and Alice Cullen (Gorbals, Glasgow), had even managed to increase their majorities. The Conservatives were becoming worried about their poor showing of women in the House and early in 1952 a correspondence was initiated in *The Times*[2] with a letter signed by Lady Davidson, Mrs Eveline Hill, Lady Tweedsmuir and Miss Irene Ward asking Conservative and Unionist Associations to give more consideration to women in selecting candidates. 'Far too often', they wrote, 'women fight the hopeless seats over and over again. . . . Women candidates ask no favours, only to be considered on their merits.' Mrs Elsie Olsen, the prospective Conservative parliamentary candidate for Edmonton, wrote bitterly of her experience after reducing the Labour majority at Ealing North in 1950 :

'Far too often the only chance for a woman candidate after she has proved her merit in tough constituencies is either to withdraw from the candidates' list altogether or to resign herself to being a "perpetual candidate". Having had to make way in one constituency after reducing a majority by nearly 14,000 votes, I hope I may be forgiven for being a bit sensitive on the topic.'[3]

In drawing up his list of ministerial appointments Mr Churchill, with the example of the Labour Government before him, appointed two women. Florence Horsbrugh remembers that it was a pouring wet day when she and several Conservative colleagues were sitting in the Smoking Room of the House of Commons (she did on occasion brave this sanctum) where every so often one or other received a telephone summons to Downing Street, to be greeted by the cheers or jeers of their companions. Eventually to cries of 'Well played, Florence' she too received a call and drove away to Downing Street to be offered the post of Minister of Education. She thus became the fourth woman and first Conservative woman to be made a senior minister; but, unlike Ellen Wilkinson, she was not at first given a seat in the Cabinet. This caused a good deal of comment in the Press since no Minister of Education had been left out of the Cabinet since the National Government formed under Ramsay MacDonald in 1931. The reason was that Churchill wanted to have a small Cabinet, but to many it seemed to be because he jibbed at the idea of having a woman seated at the Cabinet table at Number 10. Pat Hornsby-Smith was appointed to Florence's former post of Parliamentary Secretary to the Ministry of Health and at thirty-seven was the youngest woman so far to become a minister.

On the Opposition front bench Dr Edith Summerskill was a mem-

ber of the Shadow Cabinet dealing with health, and Miss Herbison
was a spokesman on Scottish affairs.

As the new Government settled down to the job of trying to deal
with the economic situation and the manifold problems overseas,
controversy between the parties still ran high, as a remarkable incident concerning Bessie Braddock showed before the session was
very old. During a debate on the National Health Service, in which
the Opposition was hotly contesting the Government's plans to implement the health charges, Bessie appealed to the Speaker on a point
of order. She had, she said, been punched by a Conservative member on her way from the division lobby—was this in order?[4] The
Speaker said it most certainly was not; the House had not been so
astounded since Nancy Astor had tugged at Sir Frederick Banbury's
coat-tails, for, as one lobby correspondent had it, 'One might nearly
as soon expect to find an M.P. accused of jostling Cleopatra's Needle
or the Clock Tower of Westminster itself.'[5] The wicked Tory turned
out to be Mr Arthur Colegate who denied the charge, and a somewhat confused story unfolded itself, during which Bessie maintained
that had such a thing happened outside the House the hon. gentleman would not have been on his feet for two seconds, a statement
that few were disposed to doubt. In the end all parties took the
Speaker's advice to forgive and forget and Bessie accepted Mr Colegate's apology. This incident got Lord Mancroft into trouble a few
months later when he lightheartedly told a meeting of the Primrose
League that unlike members of Parliament he was not 'paid a thous-
and a year for larking about in the division lobbies at night with
Bessie Braddock and the rest of the girls'. Barbara Castle raised this
witticism as a matter of privilege[6] and the Speaker ruled that there
was a *prima facie* breach, but after Lord Mancroft had written a
letter of apology Barbara withdrew her motion.

It seems always to have been the fate of women senior ministers,
from Margaret Bondfield onwards, to have to meet heavy demands
with inadequate resources and Florence Horsbrugh was no exception. The Ministry of Education did not escape the axe wielded by
a Government committed to pruning public expenditure severely in
order to meet its obligations at home and abroad and to redress the
economic situation. This placed the Minister of Education in a great
deal of difficulty because her tenure of office coincided with the
post-war bulge of pupils entering the primary schools when buildings and teachers were still insufficient; and she was debarred from
voicing the claims of her department in the Cabinet unless specially

invited to attend. Early in 1952 she had to send out a circular to local authorities asking them to try to achieve a five per cent cut in educational expenditure while at the same time maintaining the essential fabric of the educational service unimpaired. This involved her in a good deal of criticism and attacks from the Opposition, many of which were led by Alice Bacon. Florence Horsbrugh insisted both in and outside Parliament that she aimed, in spite of administrative economies, at increasing the available school places by a million by 1956 and at recruiting as many as 14,000 new teachers a year, for the large size of the classes was, she maintained, 'the greatest blot on education today'.[7] In the meantime the building of new schools had to be halted temporarily in order to complete those that were already in hand. Later she had to disappoint the teachers over their superannuation claim, which did not increase her popularity.

In September 1953 she was at last admitted to the Cabinet, the first and only Conservative woman so far to attain this rank. This was not a very happy experience because the Prime Minister did not take kindly to her presence. He could be extremely offensive, as when she dared to express any opinion on foreign affairs in which, after having frequently represented her country abroad—she had gone as a delegate to the United Nations Assembly in 1951—she had some experience. 'Fancy the Minister of *Education* taking an interest in foreign affairs', he would say sarcastically, but the Foreign Secretary, Anthony Eden, and Lord Salisbury took her side, Eden often saying kindly that he valued her opinion more than most. The Prime Minister would sometimes use strong language, to which Florence had no objection, but then, realizing her presence, he would become embarrassed and make her and everybody else embarrassed too. He had comparatively little interest in her department and often threw out impracticable suggestions for economies. She soon learnt how to deal with these by saying firmly, 'Yes, Prime Minister, but that will need legislation', which always ended the matter. This ordeal did not last long because just after a year in the Cabinet she resigned her office, having been asked to make way for Sir David Eccles whom the Prime Minister wanted to reward for having, as Minister of Works, organized the Coronation so efficiently. In spite of the unpopular measures which Florence had had to carry out there were many expressions of regret among the teaching profession and tributes to her work and her courage appeared throughout the Press.[8] Her reward was the G.B.E. and she retired to the back benches as Dame Florence Horsbrugh. She had been an efficient administrator but often gave the erroneous impression that she lacked humanity. While her predecessor in office, Ellen Wilkinson, had sometimes tended to let her heart rule her head, Florence kept her head very much in control and to many people she seemed cold and remote.

Pat Hornsby-Smith at the Ministry of Health assisted in all the vexed stages of the implementation of the health charges, including the shilling prescription charge for which the preparatory work had been done under the previous Government.[9] She had to answer from the dispatch box questions on such diverse matters as hearing aids, the arsenic content of cigarettes, the closing of day nurseries, food hygiene, hypnotism, security at Broadmoor, elastic stockings, and false teeth. In the early autumn of 1953 she visited the United States at the invitation of their Government to study health and welfare services throughout the country.

In the Coronation Honours two backbenchers were rewarded: Lady Davidson received the D.B.E. and Alice Bacon the C.B.E. They and their woman colleagues covered an even wider range of subjects during this Parliament. Naturally housing, health, welfare, education and the cost of living were matters that continued to occupy them a great deal. Labour members such as Bessie Braddock, Jean Mann and Alice Cullen continued to keep close watch on the activities of the Ministry of Housing and Local Government, where Harold Macmillan and Ernest Marples were seeking to implement their pledge of 300,000 new houses a year and later introduced a bill to allow increases of rent in cases where certain repairs were carried out by the landlord, which was strongly contested by Labour members.[10] Bessie Braddock was appointed by Mr Churchill to the Royal Commission on Mental Health. She had never spoken to the Prime Minister until one day, as she was standing at the bar of the House, he tapped her on the shoulder to tell her that he was going to announce her name that day as a member of the commission. She felt his tone was a trifle patronizing so she said: 'Oh! Will you? Well, you ought to be very honoured indeed that I'm prepared to allow you to mention my name as one of *your* Royal Commission.' This highly amused the Prime Minister.[11]

Irene Ward was by now much concerned at the rise in the cost of living and had become the champion of all those living on small fixed incomes. She did not hesitate to harass her own ministers in the same way as she had their Labour predecessors. 'Will my right hon. friend please answer my question . . . ?' 'When will my right hon. friend be able to tell me . . . ?' 'Is my right hon. friend aware that I

wrote to him some months ago on this matter . . . ?' were often the
rather querulous preliminaries to her questions. On an adjournment
motion in June 1952 she raised the whole subject of the effect of the
cost of living on pensioners and others, quoting from letters written
by her constituents,[12] and strongly opposed any increase in members'
pay before the claims of pensioners had been considered, although
on this question she got the reply from Mr Churchill that 'I think
it would be an inconvenient rule if nothing could be done until
everything can be done.'[13]

There were still some outstanding feminist grievances to be righted.
In 1952 Mr Charles Pannell, a Labour member, initiated a debate
on equal pay in the public services, reminding the Government that
it was thirty-two years since Major Hill's motion on the subject was
passed by the House of Commons and demanding a date for its
implementation. Irene Ward, Alice Bacon, Lady Davidson, Elaine
Burton and Jennie Lee were among those who took part in the
debate.[14] The Chancellor of the Exchequer, Mr R. A. Butler, who
was in sympathy with the principle of equal pay, promised to consult
the Whitley Council and other civil service staff organizations, but
time dragged on and the women M.P.s organized deputations and
presented petitions; and on one occasion Irene Ward and Edith
Summerskill drove in an open horse-drawn carriage from the Fawcett
Society headquarters in Tufton Street to the Houses of Parliament
in order to draw attention to the out-of-date attitude to the payment
of women. Irene devised intricate questions to prod the Chancellor
into fulfilling the pledge made in the 1950 Conservative manifesto.[15]
He for his part blamed staff organizations for the delay. At last, in
May 1954, he was able to announce in reply to her question that
agreement had been reached and that equal pay in the civil and
local government services would be gradually implemented over a
period of time. He added, 'in regard to the hon. lady herself I am
sure the whole House will recognize that she has been extremely
pertinacious and sincere in pressing this subject.'[16] The end of
another long-drawn-out campaign that had been fought over the
years by Lady Astor, Mrs Wintringham, Ellen Wilkinson and several
others was celebrated by the Milestone Dinner organized by Mrs
Cazalet-Keir in 1955, at which Mr Butler was guest of honour.

Twice during this Parliament Edith Summerskill attempted to get
a Women's Disabilities Bill on to the Statute Book, which would
make it possible for deserted wives to obtain arrears of maintenance
through deductions made from their husband's earnings; for savings

from housekeeping funds to be divided between the partners as the court saw fit, instead of being claimed by the husband, in broken marriages; for a wife's rights to certain goods and furniture to be safeguarded; and for the transfer of a tenancy of a dwelling to her to be allowed. In 1952 and 1953 the bill met with considerable opposition from lawyer members and was talked out.[17] But four private bills sponsored by women in this session did receive the Royal Assent. Elaine Burton introduced the Disposal of Uncollected Goods Bill early in 1952 to authorize shopkeepers to dispose of unclaimed goods left with them for cleaning or repair, giving some remarkable statistics of the thousands of pairs of unclaimed shoes worth many thousands of pounds piling up in cobblers' shops, some of which were deliberately not collected by mothers because their children had outgrown them.[18] Lady Davidson and Lady Tweedsmuir who secured places in the ballot for private bills in 1953–4 both successfully introduced measures which were welcomed by animal- and bird-lovers: Lady Davidson's Protection of Animals (Anaesthetics) Bill[19] and Lady Tweedsmuir's Protection of Birds Bill[20] which was piloted through the House of Lords by her husband, a keen ornithologist. Irene Ward's Rights of Entry (Gas and Electricity Boards) Bill[21] was a useful little measure to protect the rights of householders, which she introduced with the blessing of the National Gas Consultative Council and which was passed through unopposed in all its stages. Irene now had two private bills to her credit (her earlier one in 1937 had provided for pocket money for old people in institutions; see Appendix C). Although Margaret Herbison's Foundry Workers (Health and Safety) Bill[22] did not reach the Statute Book it achieved its object for it forced the Minister of Labour, Sir Walter Monckton, to put into practice existing legislation dealing with industrial injuries. When he agreed to do this she withdrew the bill.

Elaine Burton had by now achieved the distinction of being the first woman chairman of a sub-committee of the Select Committee on Estimates and was campaigning for more informative labelling of textiles. Although Mr Nabarro, a Tory Member, called her 'a meddlesome Matty' she did a great deal to prepare the way for the Merchandise Marks Act and other measures of consumer protection that were brought in by the next Parliament.[23] Bessie Braddock as the Member for the [Cotton] Exchange division of Liverpool was also interested in textiles and was highly incensed when, after an all-night debate on the industry in March 1952, she had not caught the

Speaker's eye by nine o'clock in the morning. She stood up and protested and refused to give way and sit down, so that the Speaker had to name her and a motion was carried suspending her from the House. She then withdrew from the Chamber in order to save the elderly and rather frail Serjeant at Arms the formidable task of removing her by force.[24]

Another matter on which the uninitiated might well have been surprised to find women sparring with each other across party lines was boxing, but Edith Summerskill, freed from the strait-jacket of ministerial office, was now revealing herself as an ardent campaigner against boxing and prize fighting—'the ignoble art' as she called it—which she felt to be both dangerous to health and degrading to the spirit. Her opponent in the ring, when she spoke against reducing the entertainment tax on the sport during a Budget debate in 1954, was none other than battling Bessie Braddock who, as vice-president of the Professional Boxing Association, got in some shrewd blows in the first of many fierce but good-humoured bouts between the two ladies which diverted the House.[25]

Several women spoke in the debate on the bill to set up commercial television; Alice Bacon was one of the Labour members who was critical of its proposals, fearing the effects on children.[26] Women M.P.s were themselves beginning to appear on television. In reply to a question at the beginning of 1954 the Assistant Postmaster General disclosed that since May 1952 Mrs Castle and Lady Tweedsmuir had appeared twice in discussion programmes and Miss Herbison and Miss Ward on one occasion each.[27]

During 1953 the number of women members had again risen to twenty-one by the addition of two Conservative and two Labour women returned at by-elections. At Stoke-on-Trent North Mrs Harriet Slater was returned with a 15,000 majority in March 1953 following the death of the previous Labour member. She was a former schoolteacher who had been National Organizer for the Co-operative Party and was an alderman of Stoke-on-Trent City Council. The following month the first woman representing an Irish constituency took her seat in Parliament; she was also the first to be elected after Constance Markievicz (1918) but she came from north of the border where she was returned unopposed for Down North. She was Mrs Patricia Ford, the daughter of the former member, Sir Walter Smiles, who had been drowned in the sinking of the ferry steamer *Princess Victoria* in the Irish Sea. Patricia was thirty-one and had two young children; she had appeared on her father's platforms frequently but she was inexperienced politically. Almost at once she got into trouble by putting her name to an article in the *Sunday Express* describing her impressions of the House of Commons which reported among other things : 'There is even a room upstairs with a couple of beds and the old stagers seem to get there first. One night I found both Mrs Bessie Braddock and Dr Edith Summerskill stretched out on them and both snoring.'

Bessie raised this passage as a matter of privilege and Mrs Ford at once apologized saying : 'I can only add that it is sometimes very difficult to see in the dark.'[28] The Committee of Privileges ruled that she should be treated with indulgence as a new member.

In July 1953 Conservative cheers welcomed Miss Edith Pitt into the House as the new member for Edgbaston. They were warmer than usual for she was a type of member of which the Government was proud and her election for this safe seat was a break with tradition : she was one of six children of a Birmingham working man and had left school at fourteen. Now forty-seven she had worked her way up to become an industrial welfare officer. Originally the Conservative executive committee in Edgbaston had selected Colonel Douglas Glover (now Sir Douglas Glover, M.P. for Ormskirk) to fight the by-election, but the association reversed this decision in favour of Edith Pitt who was well-known as a member of the City Council for ten years, and as the doughty candidate at Stechford in 1950 and 1951 and at the Smallheath by-election in 1952. Colonel Glover stood down with good grace. A spokesman in the Conservative Central Office in London was reported as saying that Edith's adoption marked a change of heart of constituency Tories towards women candidates.[29] The Government showed its pleasure by selecting her to second the Address in Reply to the Gracious Speech in the autumn of 1953. This was also her maiden speech.[30]

The fourth woman to win a by-election (a very exciting one) was Mrs Lena Jeger at Holborn and St Pancras. She was the widow of Dr Santo Jeger, the former Labour member who had held the seat by a majority of under 2,000. The by-election was hotly contested by the Conservative candidate, but Lena Jeger was a first-class candidate who fought the campaign mainly on the subject of the Government's bill to permit 'repairs' increases in rents, which was unpopular in this highly overcrowded constituency. Her victory by 1,976 votes was considered a jolt for the Government. Mrs Jeger, a graduate of London University, had been a member of the St Pancras Borough Council and the L.C.C. She speaks Russian and has worked in the

Ministry of Information and the Foreign Office and was at one time
assistant editor of *British Ally*, a newspaper which the British
Government published in Moscow. She is on the left of her party.
In her maiden speech on the Berlin Conference she made a powerful
plea for peace.[31]

During this period the situation in the Far and Middle East and
in Africa engaged much of Parliament's attention. It was on foreign
affairs and defence that the Bevanite group, including Barbara
Castle and Jennie Lee, took their independent line. Jennie Lee was
actively engaged in running her husband's newspaper, *Tribune*,
which was one of the mouthpieces for their views. Early in 1952
she and Barbara were among the 55 Labour members who voted, in
defiance of the Opposition Whip, in a defence debate.[32]

At the Party Conference in 1952 Barbara retained her place on
the National Executive with an increased number of votes, while
veteran leaders Herbert Morrison and Hugh Dalton lost theirs. Towards the end of this Parliament the Bevanites opposed German
rearmament and split the Labour Party on this issue. Barbara Castle
was so incensed by a passage in a speech at Woodford by Mr Churchill, in which he recalled his instructions to Field Marshal Mont-
gomery at the end of the war to arm Germans to resist a further
Russian advance, that she cancelled her contribution to the House
of Commons' presentation on his eightieth birthday.[33] (Bessie Braddock also refused to sign the book presented to Churchill because,
remembering Tonypandy, she could not endorse the gratitude expressed in the Bunyan quotation which read, 'You have been so faithful and so loving to us, you have fought so stoutly for us, you have
been so hearty in counselling us that we shall never forget your
favour towards us. . . .[34]')

The activities of the Bevanites seriously upset at least two of the
Labour women M.P.s : Eirene White withdrew from the contest for
the National Executive in 1953 saying : "Neither the bludgeons of
the right wing nor the poisoned arrows of the left are in my opinion
proper weapons to be used against one's comrades in the Labour
movement',[35] and Alice Bacon threatened to resign from the organizing sub-committee of the executive after being accused in *Tribune*
at the end of 1954 of witch-hunting for 'Trotsky-ites' in the party.[36]

During this Parliament Alice Bacon and Priscilla Tweedsmuir
were delegates to the Consultative Assembly of the Council of
Europe. Barbara Castle visited the Middle East in an all-party group
and was already showing an interest in Africa, particularly in Kenya

where the Mau Mau troubles were causing concern. Eirene White
was also informing herself on African affairs through her visits to
various parts of the continent in party and parliamentary groups.

Over the final years of this Parliament hung the shadow of the
nuclear weapons now being developed. In March 1955 some women
members had their own debate on this great issue. Dr Summerskill
moved the motion supported by eight Labour women :

> that this House urges upon the Government the need to give further
> consideration to the long-term and remote effects of the continuing
> nuclear explosions by the Government of the United States and the
> U.S.S.R. and the United Kingdom and expresses its fears as to the
> dangers facing humanity as a result of continuing radioactive con-
> tamination of the world's atmosphere, particularly to future genera-
> tions; and asks that the suggestion of the Leader of the Opposition
> [Mr Attlee] be carried out and a conference of scientists from the
> United States, the U.S.S.R. and the United Kingdom and France
> be held to advise on the dangers facing mankind.[37]

In a sincere and non-partisan speech she spoke of the possible
effects of radioactvity on the human reproductive organs and quoted
the findings of well-known authorities. Iain Macleod, the Minister
of Health, in moving the Government's amendment to the motion
went to some length to try to allay the fears of the House, pointing
to the expanding research facilities available in collaboration with
other countries, and upset some of the sponsors of the motion by
saying that at present it seemed unlikely that there was anything more
than 'an interesting scientific problem' that would have to be
watched. Barbara Castle accused the Government of adopting a 'do-
nothing policy' and Irene Ward leapt to its defence with such critical
comments that the Speaker said mildly, 'I do not think the hon.
ladies should call each other names.' Winding up for the supporters
of the motion Elaine Burton accused the Government of an inhuman
approach, but the Government's amendment was carried by 290
votes to 250.

1955-1959 Travellers' Tales

IN APRIL 1955 after Sir Winston Churchill resigned the Premiership his successor, Sir Anthony Eden, announced a General Election for 28 May. All the women M.P.s prepared to defend their seats except Mrs Ford (Ulster Unionist—Down North) who decided not to stand again. (She later became Mrs Nigel Fisher, wife of the Conservative M.P. for Surbiton.) One or two had to face difficulties as a result of boundary changes. Dr Summerskill had to find a new constituency since the two Fulham seats had shrunk to one for which Michael Stewart, the other sitting member, had been adopted. Dr Edith was not particularly popular with some sections of her party at this time because she was associated with memories of food rationing and because of her outspoken views on boxing; but shortly before the election she was adopted for the safe Labour seat of Warrington. Boundary changes had also altered Barbara Castle's constituency; Blackburn East resolved into the entirely newly-drawn division of Blackburn and was not expected to be so favourable to her. Pat Hornsby-Smith's very marginal seat of Chislehurst had also been altered considerably with unpredictable results and this time, to add to her difficulties, a Liberal was standing.

Bessie Braddock had had troubles of a different and more unpleasant kind. An extreme left-wing faction in her constituency party in the Exchange Division of Liverpool had tried very hard to prevent her from being readopted as the Labour candidate, making the rearmament of Germany, on which Bessie endorsed the official Labour policy, one of the points at issue. An inquiry carried out by the National Executive Committee of the party had found in Bessie's favour in 1954, but shortly before the election her constituency party again decided, by 40 to 39 votes, not to support her. After another inquiry by the National Executive it was made clear to the rebels that if they voted against Bessie they would face expulsion from the party. This resulted in a 31 to 7 vote in Bessie's favour and in the removal of her critics from their positions in the constituency party.

A leaflet sent out from the Conservative Central Office to

divisional parties some time before the election stressed the need for more women and trade union candidates, although 'the final choice must rest on merit alone.'[1] Whether this had the desired effect is uncertain but it is a fact that at this election the Conservatives managed to put thirty-two women candidates into the field, more than ever before or since. Indeed in ten years the women had more than doubled their number, which in 1945 had been fourteen. Among the thirty-two there was even one, Mrs Evelyn Emmet, who had been selected for the safe Conservative seat of East Grinstead— and without having fought before. The parties were represented as follows:

	CONSERVATIVE	LABOUR	LIBERAL	OTHERS	TOTAL
1955	32	43	14	2	91
1951	*25*	*41*	*11*	—	*77*

There was a higher proportion of new candidates than in 1951, although fifty, over half of them, had fought before. There were two all-female contests: at Aberdeen South where Mrs Judith Hart was the Labour candidate challenging Lady Tweedsmuir, and at Coventry South where Mrs M. E. Williamson was standing for the Conservatives against Elaine Burton. Mrs Anne Papworth had been adopted as the Conservative candidate to fight Bessie Braddock in a three-cornered contest in Exchange, Liverpool, and the Conservative Mrs Mabel de la Motte, who had attached herself to various boxing clubs in Fulham in order to knock out Dr Summerskill, found herself in the ring with Michael Stewart. Many constituency parties were inclined to look more kindly on a woman candidate if the sitting member was a woman, on the grounds that 'it takes a woman to defeat a woman'.

At the beginning of the campaign the Labour Party was encouraged by the announcement that it had acquired an important convert: Lady Megan Lloyd George. In a letter to Mr Attlee she said she was convinced that 'in the changed situation of today it is only in the Labour Party that I can be true to the Radical tradition.'[2] Although not a candidate in this election she toured Wales and other parts of the country speaking from Labour platforms and took part in the Labour Party's final television broadcast. Dr Edith Summerskill also appeared on television when she talked about food prices. It was a quiet election. The Conservatives made great play with the suggestion that if the Labour Party were returned it would mean rationing again and this was backed up by the circulation of mock ration books printed by an unofficial Tory source in Luton. When

the results begin to come in it was evident that there had been a
further swing to the right, but it was not uniform throughout the
country and there were several interesting results. All the former
women members were returned and with them four new members
to bring their strength up to the 1945 figure of twenty-four. Pat
Hornsby-Smith beat off the Labour and Liberal challenge at Chislehurst and increased her majority to 3,870; Lena Jeger did extremely
well to hold Holborn and St. Pancras for Labour with a majority of
931 votes; Barbara Castle held Blackburn by 489; a new Conservative woman, Miss Joan Vickers, on the other hand, scored a notable
victory by 100 votes at Devonport over Barbara's Bevanite colleague,
Michael Foot, which caused great rejoicing among Conservatives;
in Belfast West, by what *The Times* called 'a freak of local politics',
Mrs Patricia McLaughlin converted an Irish Labour majority of
25 into an Ulster Unionist one of 18,141, as spectacular a turn-round
of votes as can ever have occurred.

With four new members the party strength of the women in the
House of Commons was now fourteen Labour and ten Conserva-
tives. The new Labour member was Mrs Joyce Butler, who, like Mrs
Emmet, had been adopted for her safe seat at Wood Green without
previously having fought an election. She was aged forty-four and
described herself as a 'housewife'. But she had lectured in the United
States on foreign policy and local government and was leader of the
Labour group on the Wood Green Borough Council. She was par-
ticularly interested in education. The Hon. Mrs Evelyn Emmet
(Conservative, East Grinstead) was aged fifty-six, a widow with
four children and the daughter of a former ambassador to Italy,
Lord Rennell of Rodd. She was a graduate of Lady Margaret Hall,
Oxford, had been a member of the L.C.C. and was now an alderman of the West Sussex County Council. She was connected with
influential Conservative circles and that year was chairman of the
National Union of Conservative and Unionist Associations. In 1952
and 1953 she had been appointed a full member of the British delegation to the United Nations Assembly with ministerial rank, an unusual honour for a woman outside Parliament. Mrs Emmet is a
quiet woman with a shrewd and penetrating grasp of affairs but,
although she was influential behind the scenes and active in committee, she was never a very effective speaker and did not often
intervene in debates in the House.

Mrs Patricia McLaughlin (U.U., Belfast West) was quite a
different type. She was the lively daughter of an Ulster clergyman

and had been educated at Trinity College, Dublin. She was forty-three and married to a civil engineer and had three children; for some time she had been a leading member of the Ulster Unionist Women's Council. She was determined to promote the interests of the Ulster textile industry at Westminster and was reported to be preparing a large and varied wardrobe all 'Ulster made' to wear in Parliament.

Miss Joan Vickers (Conservative, Devonport), the only new member who had fought before, had contested Poplar South in 1945. She had also served on the L.C.C. and done Red Cross welfare work in the Far East; for her work among prisoners-of-war there she had been awarded the M.B.E. A tall and distinguished-looking woman with blue-tinted hair, wearing dog collars of pearls and often dressed in black with hats to rival Elaine Burton's creations, she was particularly interested in welfare subjects on several of which, such as divorce and the death penalty, she held liberal views.

By this time the Lady Members' Room on the terrace was rather crowded but there was now another small room for their use upstairs near Mr Speaker's chair; there Dr Summerskill established herself.

When Sir Anthony Eden reformed his Government there was only one woman among the ministerial appointments, Pat Hornsby-Smith who remained Parliamentary Secretary at the Ministry of Health with Iain Macleod as Minister; but in December of the same year Edith Pitt replaced Mr Ernest Marples as one of the Parliamentary Secretaries at the Ministry of Pensions and National Insurance. Her promotion had come rapidly but this was a post that matched well with her previous welfare experience and her work on the Birmingham City Council. Moreover she represented a section of the public with which the Conservatives were anxious to ally themselves; during one of her speeches from the dispatch box she told the House of her own old-age-pensioner father who lived contentedly on his pension of two pounds a week.

Among the backbenchers Mrs Eveline Hill was elected chairman of the Conservative Health and Social Services Committee and Lady Davidson was re-elected to the 1922 Committee. On the Opposition front bench Dr Edith Summerskill remained the spokesman on health and Miss Herbison one of two on Scottish affairs.

The first measure of this Parliament that attracted much attention from the women members was Mr R. A. Butler's 'pots and pans' Budget in the autumn of 1955 which aroused criticism on both sides of the House by raising purchase tax to 30 per cent on such basic

H

household necessities as washboards, washtubs, and clothes-pegs, as part of the measures to curb inflation. On the Opposition benches the women moved several amendments to exclude certain items. Jean Mann, in asking the Chancellor to exempt baths, washtubs and washboards, among other things said that the song of men in their baths or women at the washtubs was now likely to be :

> All of me,
> Why not take all of me?[3]

Eirene White acidly inquired whether the Chancellor had consulted the gipsies before raising the tax on clothes-pegs and had arranged for the altered schedules to be translated into Romany,[4] while Freda Corbet wanted pot scourers, pastry boards, rolling pins and coal sieves to be exempted.[5] But the Chancellor did not give way and his 'pots and pans' Budget was something that remained in the public memory for a very long time. In April 1956 Irene Ward found the Budget 'barren and abominable' for it did little for 'those gallant and thrifty people' who lived on fixed incomes, and she gave the Government fair warning that she would seek every opportunity to embarrass it and make herself unpleasant to ministers on these matters.[6]

The major event of this Parliament was the Suez intervention. In September 1956 Parliament had to be recalled from the summer recess to deal with the situation created by Egypt's seizure of the Canal. British negotiations with Egypt failed and after Israel attacked Egypt the Anglo-French action followed. The Suez Canal not only flowed through Lady Eden's drawing room at 10 Downing Street, as she described it later, it also swept in torrents through the House. Although Mr Anthony Nutting, the Minister of State for Foreign Affairs, and Sir Edward Boyle, Economic Secretary to the Treasury, resigned from the Government in disagreement with its policy and about fifteen Conservative backbenchers abstained on a motion approving its actions, the Conservative women members all supported the Prime Minister. Lady Tweedsmuir spoke strongly in support of the Government's action during a foreign affairs debate.[7]

On the other side of the House all the woman backed Mr Hugh Gaitskell, then Leader of the Opposition, in denunciation—particularly Barbara Castle and Jennie Lee. After the British and French cease-fire Edith Summerskill went out to Egypt on her own responsibility in the New Year to visit the hospitals in Port Said and see the extent of Egyptian casualties. She found the Egyptian charge that the British had neglected civilian casualties caused by the bombardment substantiated and said that British conduct had been 'inhuman, callous, horrible'.[8] The news that she was entertained as a guest of the Egyptian Government and had an interview lasting an hour and three-quarters with Colonel Nasser in Cairo did not make very popular reading at home, for on the whole the public were behind the Government in its intervention and deplored the ceasefire. Moreover Sir Edwin Herbert, the President of the Law Society, who had already carried out an official inquiry for the Government into casualty figures in the Canal Zone, disputed her findings. Finally Dr Summerskill's disclosure in an article in an evening paper[9] on her return that she had described herself as a Norwegian in Egypt 'because she was ashamed to be British and remembered her Nordic ancestors of 400 years ago' called down widespread condemnation on her head. A police guard had to be placed on her house in Highgate following threatening telephone calls, and in Warrington the Conservatives met to debate the question : 'Should this Doctor be in the House?' 'We come to bury Edith, not to praise her', declaimed a Young Conservative. There was a noisy scene in the House of Commons when the member for Southend East, Mr Stephen McAdden, asked the Speaker whether it was in order for those 'who have renounced their British nationality and adopted Norwegian to ask questions?'[10] Later that year Dr Summerskill lost her place in the election for the parliamentary Shadow Cabinet of which she had been a member since 1951. She regained it the following year but she then lost her place on the Labour National Executive Committee. She refused to retract her remarks and took all these ups and downs with an equanimity and good grace which even her critics had to admire.

The resignation of Anthony Nutting, Minister of State for Foreign Affairs, over the Suez intervention led to the return of another woman to the House of Commons in a critical by-election in his former division of Melton in December 1956. Out of 101 applicants and a short list of 9, Miss Mervyn Pike, aged thirty-eight, the managing director of a firm of pottery manufacturers, was chosen. She had contested Pontefract in 1951 and Leek in 1955 where she was narrowly defeated. A businesswoman was a rarity (Mrs Eveline Hill was the only other in the House) and the fact that Miss Pike had been adopted for an agricultural seat was also exceptional, for selection committees in rural areas are usually not well disposed to women candidates. Her adoption did not go entirely smoothly : a splinter group of Conservatives campaigned against her, saying that they thought it unwise to put up a woman 'in these times to deal with Nasser, Dulles and those sort of people [*sic*]'.[11] Mervyn overcame this opposition and during the hotly contested campaign her photographs even appeared on beer mats in one public house. Anthony Nutting's majority had been over 10,000 and when she won the by-election by only 2,362, some commentators tried to blame it on her sex but, since the proportion of Government votes dropped by 5 per cent at another by-election at Chester about this time, it seems that the result in Melton simply confirmed the feelings of bewilderment and disapproval among Conservative voters at the failure of the Government to carry through the Suez operation successfully. Mervyn made her maiden speech during a debate on shop and non-industrial establishments arising out of the Gowers Report; she dealt with conditions of employment and vocational training for women.[12]

In February 1956 Lady Megan Lloyd George returned to the House as Labour Member for Carmarthen. In a by-election she had managed to wrest the seat from her former party which had held it with a 3,333 majority. This was a considerable victory, for the election was an extremely difficult and bitter struggle between conflicting loyalties; her former supporters attended some of her meetings with their coats turned inside out and both Liberal and Labour parties displayed her father's photograph and interpreted his utterances about socialism in ways to suit themselves. But the magic of the Lloyd George name and the swing towards Labour told : Lady Megan won the seat by a 3,069 majority and to the pleasure of her friends returned to Parliament at the age of fifty-seven, taking her place on the Opposition back benches below the gangway. She shared the small room behind the Speaker's Chair with Edith Summerskill and devoted herself as before to Welsh and constituency affairs, but seems never to have regained the wit and fire of earlier years.

In May 1957 the number of women was raised to the record level of twenty-seven by the arrival of another Conservative member, Lady Gammans, representing Hornsey, whose husband, Sir David Gammans, the former Assistant Postmaster General, had held the seat since 1941 until his death in February. Muriel Gammans was fifty-nine and well liked in her constituency. Having lived in the Far East and Canada, she was particularly interested in Commonwealth and foreign affairs. But she is a quiet, retiring person and did not speak often in the House.

There were now fifteen Labour and twelve Conservative women in Parliament.

Cyprus was another trouble spot during this Parliament, for the Greek Cypriots' campaign for *enosis* or union with Greece had given rise to the guerrilla warfare of the Eoka terrorists against the British occupation. In 1958 Barbara Castle, by then vice-chairman of the Labour Party (she became chairman later in 1958), visited the island on a fact-finding mission. She saw Archbishop Makarios, the leader of the Greek Cypriots, and was able to make some valuable suggestions towards reaching an agreement for a new constitution, but at the same time she was reported as saying that British soldiers had been 'encouraged' to be 'unnecessarily' tough in their handling of Eoka Cypriots.[13] Since there had been a fair number of British casualties her remark caused a great deal of resentment in Britain which her subsequent allegations that she had been misreported failed to lessen. The Labour Party was again embarrassed by the outspoken comments of one of its women M.P.s; a trade union member of the National Executive, Mr J. Matthews, wanted Barbara excluded from the chairmanship of the party and the Conservatives seized upon her reported statements as useful propaganda for the 1959 election.

Barbara also visited Kenya in 1955 to look into the case of a Kikuyu chief who had been found dead in suspicious circumstances after his arrest for complicity in the Mau Mau troubles. Her criticism of the Government's handling of this affair brought her into conflict with the Colonial Secretary, Alan Lennox Boyd (now Viscount Boyd of Merton) in December 1955. In answering a question on this affair in the House he quoted some of her conversations with colonial civil servants to support his allegation that she had gone to Kenya looking for trouble.[14] These disclosures incensed Barbara who a few days later raised on the adjournment the whole question of the administration of justice in Kenya. The Colonial Secretary apologized for quoting her private conversations but maintained that the object of her visit had been 'to support conclusions at which she had already arrived.'[15] Throughout this Parliament Barbara continued to question the Colonial Secretary on Kenya and towards the end of it she made one of her greatest speeches as a backbencher, and one of the very few that from time to time make a lasting impression on members on both sides of the House. It was in a debate of 27 July 1959 on the deaths of eleven Mau Mau detainees who, it was disclosed, had been beaten to death in Hola detention camp. In a

speech remarkable for its powerful indictment of the Government
and its passionate sincerity Barbara laid the responsibility for these
deaths squarely on the shoulders of the Minister, and her case as
she presented it was a formidable one.[16] The Colonial Secretary
denied ministerial responsibility but conceded the gravity of the
affair by announcing that a special commissioner would be appointed
in Kenya to oversee these camps in future. The Hola speech really
established Barbara's reputation as a politician. Unpopular as she
was with the other side of the House and the right-wing elements
of her own party her ability was now unquestioned and she began
to be talked about as of ministerial calibre. 'Barbara Castle', *The
Observer* had remarked some months earlier, 'has the ability and
energy to follow in the steps of Ellen Wilkinson and to reach high
Cabinet rank, if she should learn to use them properly.'[17]

The future of Germany, the complex problems of disarmament,
and the testing of nuclear weapons continued to concern the House
and divide the Labour Party. Jennie Lee was reported as criticizing
the party at a meeting in 1956 organized by the Victory for Socialism group, a newly formed left-wing ginger group which was pressing for unilateral disarmament.[18] In 1959 Lena Jeger paid a visit
to East Germany which was said to be embarrassing to Mr Gaitskell
who was at the same time paying an official visit to West Germany.[19]

At the beginning of 1957, in the Government formed by Mr
Harold Macmillan following Sir Anthony Eden's resignation, Pat
Hornsby-Smith after five years at the Ministry of Health was
appointed as one of the Under-Secretaries of State at the Home
Office under Mr Butler, and Edith Pitt was reappointed as junior
Minister to the Ministry of Pensions and National Insurance. Pat
was the first woman to have a post in the Home Office since Ellen
Wilkinson's tenure of office during the war. These appointments
caused the Press to draw the conclusion that 'Education, Health and
Pensions are the Ministries thought most suitable for women Under-
Secretaries'.[20] At the Home Office Pat made a special study of the
refugee problem and visited Vienna in February 1957 to investigate
the refugee situation there following the Hungarian uprising. She
was appointed a United Kingdom delegate to the General Assembly
of the United Nations the following year and was one of the delegates to sponsor the resolution to hold a World Refugee Year.

In Parliament she assisted in passing through the final stages of
the controversial Homicide Act which confined the death penalty
to certain types of murder. To some extent women's opinion had

always been divided across party lines on the subject of the death penalty; broadly speaking the Labour women wanted it abolished (Jean Mann had earlier opposed abolition but later altered her views) and most of the Conservatives wanted it retained; but Evelyn Emmet and Joan Vickers were among those who in 1956 had voted for Sydney Silverman's bill to abolish the death penalty.[21] Another bill with which Pat Hornsby-Smith had much to do was the Children's Bill (which had originated in the House of Lords) to improve the law on the adoption and fostering of children. Many of the women members took part in the debates on this bill and, winding up the second reading in June 1958, Pat was able to pay tribute to a 'heartening, constructive and helpful debate . . . wholly non-party and on a subject on which members from both sides of the House have sincerely expressed their views'.[22] In November Mervyn Pike also became connected with the Home Office as Parliamentary Private Secretary to the Joint Under-Secretaries of State (she eventually became P.P.S. to Pat alone). She successfully piloted through the House in 1958 a Government measure on drainage rates.[23]

Towards the end of the same year Mr Butler introduced the Street Offences Bill to implement those recommendations of the Wolfenden Report which dealt with female prostitutes; this bill made it an offence for a 'common prostitute' to loiter or solicit in public and increased the penalties. In the debates on this controversial subject, which were of very high quality, many women took part; most of them approved the measure but among the ninety or so members, led by Mr Anthony Greenwood, who voted against the bill were Bessie Braddock, Elaine Burton, Megan Lloyd George, Harriet Slater, Edith Summerskill, Lena Jeger, Jennie Lee and Eirene White. They complained that the bill merely 'swept the crumbs under the carpet' and did not include the male offender.[24] Jean Mann was not one who sympathized with this attitude. What worried her were all the notice-board advertisements of 'masseuses', 'models', and 'companions' that went unchecked. She organized a deputation to see Mr Butler on this problem but without much result.[25]

Bessie Braddock, as a magistrate, had made a particularly close study of the judicial and penal systems of the country. In May 1956, after she had received a letter smuggled out of Walton gaol in Liverpool by a prisoner who complained of ill-treatment by prison officers, she was instrumental in getting a committee of inquiry

set up under Sir Godfrey Russell Vick Q.C. Sir Godfrey found some
of the charges justified (although he exonerated higher authority),
and as a result certain prison officers left the gaol.[26] Bessie was all
the more frustrated when in March 1957 during a debate on the
prison service she failed to catch the Speaker's eye. She raised the
matter on a point of order : 'Is it believed in this House,' she asked,
'that women know nothing about prisons. . . ? I am the only woman
who wanted to speak in the debate and I object to being kept out of
it.'[27]

At the Ministry of Pensions, Edith Pitt was still busily engaged
defending the Government's pensions policy, answering questions on
National Assistance, the 'ten shilling widow', and other categories
of elderly people outside the National Insurance Acts. She visited
the United States in the summer of 1959 to study social security and
industrial working conditions there, and in September of the same
year she went to Turkey to sign on behalf of the Government of the
United Kingdom the Anglo-Turkish Convention on Social Security.
She was a most conscientious minister and, until restrained by her
chief who was by this time Mr John Boyd Carpenter, worked regularly till 3 a.m. on her boxes. But, whatever the pressure of her work
in Whitehall and Westminster, she returned every week-end to
Birmingham to relieve her sister in the care of their old father.

About this time women ministers just missed having their own
country retreat or 'Chequers'. Miss Frances Scarborough, the candidate who in the 1935 election had tried to defeat Aneurin Bevan
at Ebbw Vale by song (p. 112), died and in her will left the residue
of her estate and Quiet Court, her house in Sussex, in trust for 'the
senior woman member of the Ministry of the Government of the
United Kingdom in order that she may have a retreat in which to
refresh her spirit, to learn of the trees and listen greatly to herself'.
But the benefactor's kind intention was frustrated by the fact that
she left inadequate funds, and when her will was contested by her
relatives Mr Justice Danckwerts found himself in difficulties in interpreting its terms; he knew, he said, what a woman was, but not
what a 'senior woman member' was, would it be senior by age or
rank? Therefore the well-intentioned gift failed.[28]

The issue of divorce was of great concern to women members, and
perhaps the most effective battle of all for justice for the victims
of broken marriages was waged by Joan Vickers. Winning a place
in the ballot for private bills in 1956 she took up one of the problems Edith Summerskill had attempted to deal with in her Women's

Disabilities bills : the question of defaulting husbands who fall into arrears with maintenance payments to their wives and choose to go to prison rather than pay up, with the result that their families have to rely on the support of the National Assistance Board. In March 1957 she introduced the second reading of her Maintenance Orders (Attachment of Income) Bill to make it possible on a court order for arrears of maintenance to be deducted from earnings.[29] She had a good deal of support inside and outside the House. But, after the second reading had been carried without a division and the bill committed to a Standing Committee, there was considerable opposition from lawyer M.P.s who feared this attachment of earnings might be extended to allow other debts to be collected; several deliberately boycotted the committee with the result that time after time it had to be adjourned for lack of a quorum until Joan eventually had to withdraw the bill. Mr Butler, the Home Secretary, was sympathetic, not least because no fewer than 2,000 defaulters were going to prison every year for arrears of maintenance and the charge to the State for the upkeep of deserted wives and children was running at a rate of £8 million a year. In December the Government introduced their own legislation for the attachment of earnings, the Maintenance Orders Bill, and Joan was given the honour of piloting this successfully through the House.[30] The value of her persistence in getting the measure carried was underlined in June 1959 when David Renton, Joint Under-Secretary of State at the Home Office, revealed that the effect of the Act had been 'immediate and striking', for after three months in operation the number of defaulters going to prison had fallen by well over half.[31]

There were many other directions in which women were active in this Parliament. The Rent Act of 1957, which decontrolled many classes of tenancies, engaged the interest of those with overcrowded urban constituencies such as Bessie Braddock, Joyce Butler, Lena Jeger and Freda Corbet. Jean Mann still devoted much of her time to the cost of living and food supplies and was also pressing for stricter regulations to control the weight and measurements of pre-packaged goods and to prevent accidents in the home. This last interest was shared by Pat McLaughlin who at the same time lost no opportunity to represent the interests of Ulster; on one occasion she dramatically threw down a symbolic red glove before initiating a debate on the industrial development of Northern Ireland,[32] but the gesture fell a trifle flat. 'Peterborough' of *The Daily Telegraph*[33] said the anticlimax recalled the occasion when Burke flung down a dagger in the Chamber and someone called out 'Where's the fork?'

Dr Summerskill drew applause from both sides of the House in January 1959 for a speech full of humanity and wisdom on the shortage of psychiatrists.[34] In March of the same year, when she was speaking on the manufacture of 'happy pills' and the drug industry in a debate on the estimates for the Ministry of Health, she had a frosty exchange with Irene Ward who resented her remarks about an absent Tory member. It culminated in Irene exclaiming: 'Oh, Edith, you really are an ass.'[35] There were protests from the Opposition benches but Mr Speaker diplomatically said that he had not heard a word.

Although Irene Ward lived up to her promise made at the beginning of this Parliament to make herself unpleasant to ministers whenever she thought it justified, her long unremitting service to Parliament and her constituents was rewarded by the D.B.E. in 1955. It may well be asked why Irene never reached the front bench, for some of the unruliest backbenchers (*vide* Ellen Wilkinson) have made first class ministers. But while she has shown herself to possess prodigious industry and a shrewd grasp of affairs, Dame Irene had always been rather too independent and obstinate in representing her particular interests for Conservative Prime Ministers to take the risk of giving her ministerial responsibility. Now in this Parliament she was often to be found, like a formidable Brunhilde, according to the Press, intervening on a wide range of matters. She attempted unsuccessfully to amend the Gas Act of 1948 so that the minimum charges should not impose undue hardship on elderly people with small incomes,[36] and she demanded to know why the Librarian of the House of Commons was advertising for male assistants only.[37] He gave as his excuse the rigours of all-night sittings and the fear that male members might be embarrassed by seeing women humping ladders. When Irene threatened to raise the matter again by carrying a ladder into the Chamber herself, the Librarian gave way with the result that there are now three or four efficient female assistants in the House of Commons Library. Irene took her concern that war-time secret operations should be accurately recorded a stage further by suggesting that an official history of the Special Operations Executive (SOE) should be written.[38] This proposal eventually resulted in the publication by the Stationery Office in 1966 of *SOE in France* by M. R. D. Foot, whch aroused great interest and controversy. Dame Irene even carried her campaigns into another place by uttering a cry of protest from below the bar when in 1958[39] their Lordships were debating the future of the Carl Rosa Opera Company of which she was a trustee.

In November 1957 Lady Tweedsmuir became the second woman after Florence Horsbrugh to move the Address in Reply to the Gracious Speech outlining the legislative programme for the session. In the course of her speech she said, 'For the first time the Government have faced the awful decision of having women in the Upper House. It is, alas, true that there are some in another place who maintain that women are unsuited to politics. They use the purely intellectual argument that they do not wish to meet them in the library!'[40]

She was referring to the Government's proposed legislation to create both men and women life peers. When the second reading of the Life Peerages Bill came to be debated the following spring Jennie Lee called it 'this dishonest, furtive bill, this bill which insolently leaves out of account those of us who do not believe in the House of Lords at all'.[41] In committee she moved an amendment to exclude women life peers saying the whole argument deployed by the Government reminded her of the Crazy Gang because hereditary peeresses were still to be excluded.[42] She was supported by Megan Lloyd George, Alice Cullen, Eirene White and Joyce Butler, but Bessie Braddock disagreed—she could see no objection to women being life peers, although she added: 'Speaking for myself there will be no chance of grabbing me for the House of Lords.'[43] Jennie Lee's amendment was lost by 302 votes to 59.

In the same month that the Life Peerages Bill was being debated another crucial by-election was fought at Kelvingrove following the death of the Conservative member, Mr Walter Elliot. His widow, Katherine (Kay) Elliot (later Dame Katherine Elliot D.B.E), a former chairman of the National Union of the Conservative and Unionist Associations, was adopted to defend the very marginal seat against the challenge of Mrs Mary McAlister, the Labour candidate and a State-registered nurse, an I.L.P. and Home Rule candidate. The Government was going through a bad patch; in January there had been what Mr Macmillan called 'a little local difficulty' when the Chancellor of the Exchequer, Mr Peter Thorneycroft, and two other Treasury ministers had resigned in disagreement over financial policy, and at the Rochdale by-election the Conservatives had come bottom of the poll. Mary McAlister captured Kelvingrove by 1,360 votes and entered the House of Commons to a warm welcome from her party and from the nursing profession which now had its first fully qualified representative at Westminster. But she was defeated at the general election eighteen months later. By a typical throw of the dice in this political game of snakes and ladders, her by-election opponent followed her to Westminster within a few months and has outlasted Mrs McAlister there, for in the autumn of 1958 Baroness Elliot of Harwood was among the first four women peers to take her seat in the House of Lords (see Appendix B(i)).

1958 House of Lords: A Seat, Place and Voice

IT IS now time to turn from the cut and thrust of the House of Commons to the more leisured, calmer atmosphere of another place. There on 21 October 1958 an event of historic importance is in progress. Into the richly decorated Barry Chamber of the House of Lords the Gentlemen Usher of the Black Rod, followed by Garter King of Arms and the Earl Marshal, is leading the procession of a new peer with two sponsors come to present the writ of summons. It is a sight familiar to their Lordships but this time it is strangely different, for though the figure walking between the sponsoring peers wears the same scarlet robes trimmed with miniver, on her head is a velour tricorne decorated with a rosette of gold lace. She is Baroness Swanborough, better known as Lady Reading, the first woman to present her writ of summons as a life peer. The benches in the Chamber and the galleries above are filled. There are several members of the House of Commons present, and the first woman to take her seat in the Lower House, Nancy, Viscountess Astor, is among the strangers to witness the reception of her counterpart in the House of Lords.

The procession makes its decorous way towards the Woolsack pausing at intervals to bow to the Lord Chancellor seated upon it in his black gown and full-bottomed wig. The Baroness kneels to present the writ and then at the Table the letters patent are read out, followed by the writ enjoining Baroness Swanborough that 'waiving all excuses [you] be personally present at our aforesaid Parliament with us and with the prelates, nobles and peers of our said Kingdom to treat and give your counsel upon the affairs aforesaid. . . .'

The oath is sworn and the new baroness is led to her place 'at the lower end of the Barons' Bench' where, at the commands of the Garter King of Arms, she and her sponsors rise and bow three times to the Lord Chancellor, the sponsor peers putting on and doffing their hats as they do so, while the peeress remains covered. As the solemn procession at last makes its way out of the Chamber behind the Woolsack all the peers signify their approval of this unique intro-

duction by a peculiar deep-throated growl of 'Hear, hear!' Perhaps
if this time the growls are a little greater in volume and a little
more prolonged than usual, it is to cover up, now that the irrevoc-
able step to admit women has been taken, echoes of harsh and fearful words about their possible admission spoken in this Chamber
over the past forty years. For this October day is the outcome of a
long and tangled struggle. While the door to the House of Commons
opened almost of itself to women once they had received the vote
in 1918, that to the House of Lords remained firmly shut against
them and the movement to prise it ajar was bedevilled by prejudice,
party politics and constitutional difficulties.

Following the Committee of Privileges' decision in the case of
Lady Rhondda in 1922 and the attempts of Mr Briant and Mrs
Wintringham to bring in a bill in the Commons to allow peeresses in
their own right to sit in the Upper House, the struggle for their
admittance had passed to the House of Lords itself where between
1924 and 1929 Viscount Astor tried no fewer than five times to introduce a Parliament (Qualification of Peeresses) Bill. And among its
opponents in these early days was none other than Lady Astor's old
enemy, Lord Banbury of Southam, who, with painful experiences
in the Lower House still fresh in his memory, opposed the second
reading of Lord Astor's first bill,[1] telling their Lordships: 'Over and
over again hon. members have said to me "We made a great mistake
when we admitted women to the House of Commons".' This bill was
interrupted by the dissolution of Parliament, but the following year
Lord Astor was assured of plenty of support outside Parliament
from the feminist societies and the peeresses themselves—then said to
be about twenty-one in number—who had organized a campaigning body which for the second reading of Lord Astor's bill[2] had the
temerity to send out its own three line Whip, signed by Lady
Rhondda, the Duchess of Norfolk and Lady Ravensdale among
others. Lord Astor's supporters in the Upper House included the
Duke of Atholl (husband of the M.P.), Lord Cecil of Chelwood and
the Archbishop of York. Lord Birkenhead led the opposition, basing
his argument on the undeniably historic fact that the House of Lords
was originally a feudal assembly required to do military or knightly
service for the Sovereign. It was never envisaged, this argument ran,
that females such as the abbesses (Notes: Pt I, Ch. 2, 8) who received
writs of summons should attend in person any more than they were
intended to lead their soldiers into battle; they acted through proxies.
In some letters patent it was expressly stated that a peeress would

have no right to a seat, place and voice; some peeresses however, such as Viscountess Rhondda and Baroness Ravensdale, whose fathers had no sons, were especially named in their fathers' patents of peerage. Nevertheless Lord Birkenhead maintained that all peeresses in their own right held their titles in order that 'physiologically they may act as a conduit pipe through which the blood of distinguished men may pass from one generation to another'. This time the measure was narrowly defeated by 80 votes to 78. Outside Parliament Lord Birkenhead's reference to 'a conduit pipe', imperfectly understood perhaps, gave offence in many quarters.

It was confidently expected that Lord Astor's third bill in 1926[3] would be successful, but it fared worse, 80 being content to 126 not content. This time Lord Banbury adroitly switched his argument to the fact that, since a committee had been set up to consider the reform of the Upper House in general, it would be premature to deal with this particular reform at the instance of a private member.

In February 1927 at a dinner given by the Women's Election Committee to the peeresses in their own right, Lord Astor prophesied that the most serious obstacle to the admittance of peeresses was now the proposed general reform of the House of Lords, for while majority opinion at last now agreed that there must be women members in the reformed House, reform might take some time to come.[4] He was correct. He amended his 1927 bill[5] to 'enable peeresses in their own right to sit and vote in certain cases in the House of Lords', having added the words 'in certain cases' in order to meet the objections raised during the discussion of previous bills, that letters patent of certain peerages specifically excluded them from the House of Lords; the bill had to be withdrawn pending the Government's proposals for the reform of the House of Lords. The Women's Freedom League and the Equal Rights Campaign Committee then forwarded a resolution to the Lord Chancellor and the Prime Minister, other prominent women signed a letter to *The Times*,[6] and in the House of Commons Lieutenant-Commander Kenworthy asked the Prime Minister whether he would consider enabling legislation, to which Mr Baldwin gave a flat 'No, sir.'[7]

Before Lord Astor moved his last unsuccessful bill in 1929[8] the Women Peers Committee had been set up to campaign for the admittance of peeresses to the Lords in advance of any other reforms. It had Mrs Helen Archdale as chairman and Mrs Pethick-Lawrence (Women's Freedom League), Miss Emily Phipps (National Union of Women Teachers), and Mrs Corbett Ashby (National

Union of Societies for Equal Citizenship) on its committee. When, in
July 1930, Lord Astor moved a resolution 'that in view of the attain-
ment of women to full enfranchisement, the membership of the House
of Commons, and to Cabinet and Ministerial rank in His Majesty's
Government this House would welcome a measure admitting them
to the House on the same terms as men',[9] the *Women's Leader*[10]
wrote hopefully : 'Possibly Amy Johnson's feat in the air may work
the miracle.' But their Lordships' defence of the most exclusive club
in London was proof even against Miss Johnson : the motion was
defeated by 55 votes to 49.

In November 1932 the National Government announced 'drastic
plans' for the reform of the House of Lords, including a reduction
in the number of hereditary peers who received writs and the creation of life peers with no bar to the admittance of women in either
category. A special committee was set up (under Lord Salisbury)
which made progress but the Government did not find it possible to
bring in a bill.

The argument was revived after the war when in March 1946
Lord Cecil of Chelwood moved in the Upper House 'that women
should be eligible to be made Peers on the same terms as men.'[11]
Lord Mansfield also put down a motion 'that Peeresses in their own
right should be eligible to sit and vote in this House. . . .'[12] Lord
Jowitt, then Lord Chancellor, said that if either resolution were
passed the Government would introduce the necessary legislation
to put it into effect, but opposition was still strong in all quarters
of the House. It was recalled, for instance, that Gladstone had said
that women in the Upper House would be 'disastrous : the majority
of peers would die of shock and the peeresses would die of boredom.'
Lord Cecil withdrew his motion and Lord Mansfield did not move
his. It was then that Mr Edward Iwi, a London solicitor, began to
organize a nation-wide petition to the House of Lords. Under a
clause of the Tumultuous Petitioning Act of 1661, then in force,
leave had to be obtained from three Justices in Quarter Sessions to
organize such a petition and the court had to satisfy itself that its
terms would not incite riots. In November 1947 leave was granted
by three Justices sitting at Middlesex Sessions to move the petition,
praying that women be given 'a seat, place and voice in the Peers'
House of Parliament.'

The movement behind the petition was non-party and included
several peeresses and Anglican bishops, Cardinal Griffen, the
Duchess of Atholl, Lord Horder, Miss Violet Markham, Mr Harold

Nicolson, Miss Sybil Thorndike and Miss Rebecca West, who all
signed a letter to *The Times*[13] in its support. Their letter was followed
by several others including one signed by the principals of the leading women's university colleges. Only Mr Quintin Hogg M.P.
sounded a dissident note, inquiring : 'Has the plot to relegate them
[the peeresses] to the political ghetto so far reserved for the eldest sons
of peers emanated solely from the passion of the moment for equality
of sacrifice ?'[14]

Signatures for the petition were collected throughout the country
and Miss Irene Edwards, already known as a county tennis player,
set off on a lecture tour to explain its aims. Thousands of people
signed the petition but it was never presented because on 27 July
1949 Lord Reading at last carried a motion (by 45 votes to 27) that
'In the opinion of this House . . . steps should be taken to obtain
leave to introduce legislation as soon as may be practicable to confer
upon women Peers, who under the existing conditions are not
qualified to take their seats in this House, the same rights, duties and
privileges as are enjoyed by male Peers having a seat, place and
voice in this House.'[15] The organizers therefore withdrew their
petition.

But, although their Lordship's opinions had changed, it became
clear during the debate on the motion that nothing was likely to be
done before a general reform of the House of Lords on which the
political parties still had difficulty in agreeing. As the Lord Chancellor remarked, 'whenever we debate this subject we get into the
most frightful muddle.' Prejudice was no longer the hindrance to
the admittance of women; it was now solely the question of general
reform. There followed another indignant letter in *The Times*[16]
from the heads of women's colleges.

The next phase in the struggle was initiated by Viscount Simon
who in 1953 introduced a bill to create a limited number of life
peers and which provided that women should be eligible to be created
Lords of Parliament on the same terms as men; it made no provision
for existing peeresses in their own right.[17] During the second reading
Lord Llewellin, a former M.P. for Uxbridge, announced his
opposition because he did not want 'bossy political women' disturbing the peace, for 'a lot of these ladies have a tremendous number
of bees under their bonnets'. This provoked a trenchant letter to *The
Times*[18] from Nancy Astor. While these deliberations were going on
the Conservative Government announced the convening of another
all-party conference on the reform of the Second Chamber, and the

second reading of Viscount Simon's bill was therefore adjourned *sine die*. But, though the Liberal Party accepted the invitation to attend the conference, the Labour Party rejected it. Impasse again.

By this time the peeresses' lobby had a powerful additional argument in that there was now a queen regnant; it was absurd that a woman could sit on the throne but not in the House of Lords. Early in 1957[19] an impressive joint letter signed by representatives of twenty-three interested societies was sent to all M.P.s and the Press, pointing out among other things that the eligibility of women for the Upper House had followed enfranchisement without any additional legislation in the United States, Australia, New Zealand, the Irish Free State, Austria, Belgium, Iceland, Czechoslovakia, Denmark, Germany, the Netherlands, Poland and Sweden.

The Conservative Government eventually decided that a measure of partial reform, by the creation of the life peerages already envisaged by Lord Simon and others, should be put in hand and proposals for this were announced in the Speech from the Throne in 1957 to which Lady Tweedsmuir referred in moving the Address in Reply (p. 203). The debate on these proposals held in the Upper House in October 1957[20] was interesting for the strong expression of antipathy from a small rearguard body of peers whose views were not very different from those of Lord Banbury and Lord Birkenhead in the twenties. Lord Glasgow summed up their objections quite honestly. 'The main point is', he said, 'that many of us do not want women in this House. We do not want to sit beside them on these benches nor do we want to meet them in the Library . . . we do not want it to become a House of Lords and Ladies.'

The Earl of Home (now Sir Alec Douglas-Home M.P.) for the Government said that the admission of women would be a recognition of the place that they commanded for themselves as a right in modern society. But the grumblers were not appeased and when the second reading of the bill took place in December,[21] Lord Airlie, Lord Chamberlain to the Queen Mother, announcing that 'I do not feel it [the House] will work if women are admitted,' moved an amendment to delete the provisions for creating women life peers. Lord Glasgow uttered a last desperate *cri-de-coeur* : 'This is about the only place left in the Kingdom where men can meet without women. For heaven's sake let us keep it like that !' In vain, for the overwhelming number of peers lived in the present century and the amendment was defeated by 134 votes to 30.

Although the Labour Party opposed the bill in the House of Com-

mons on the grounds that it left the Upper House overwhelmingly
hereditary with unimpaired powers to frustrate the will of the elected
representatives in Parliament, it passed through all its stages to become law in April 1958. After nearly forty years women had a seat,
place and voice in the Second Chamber, but not, ironically, those
who were peeresses in their own right, on whose behalf all the earlier
battles had been waged.

Naturally there was at once a good deal of speculation as to who
would be the first women to be created life peers. The names of
various eminent ladies were suggested including that of Lady Astor,
who told a meeting of the Suffragette Fellowship that summer : 'As
the first woman to take my seat in the House of Commons, I hope to
be the first to do so in the House of Lords'.[22] But her name was not
among those of the first four women peers announced shortly afterwards. They were Stella, Marchioness of Reading c.b.e., the head
and founder of the Women's Voluntary Services; Dame Katherine
Elliot, the widow of Walter Elliot M.P., and a Conservative; Mrs
Barbara Wootton, a Socialist and former Professor of Social Studies
at London University and Nuffield Research Fellow of Bedford College; and Baroness Ravensdale who, although a peeress in her own
right, accepted a life peerage in order to obtain her seat, place and
voice at the earliest opportunity. She had all along campaigned hard
for admittance and had once described their Lordships as 'a drowsy
lot of flies in a very hot room'. She was the third of her immediate
family to take her seat in Parliament being the eldest daughter of
Lord Curzon of Kedleston, the former Foreign Secretary and determined opponent of women's suffrage, and the sister of Lady Cynthia
Mosley, M.P. for Stoke from 1929 to 1931.

Immediately all the trappings and incidentals connected with the
admittance of women became of absorbing interest to the Press. It
was reported that a 'lounge powder-room' was being prepared for
the peeresses between the Earl Marshal's office and the West Front
Corridor, decorated with chintzes bearing the portcullis design. Then
there was the question of robes; a Court hairdresser expressed grave
doubts about the effect on the peeresses' hair-do's if they had to raise
their hats three times to the Lord Chancellor; Mr Norman Hartnell,
the Court dressmaker, was rumoured to be working in collaboration
with Garter King-of-Arms and Ede & Ravenscroft, the Court tailors,
on the designs for robes and a hat. In the end the peeresses wore the
same robes as the peers according to their rank and, as for the hat,
it was the tricorne already described which was designed 'to be worn

dead straight'.[23] It was found to the baronesses' relief that the robes could be borrowed from a pool. It was also decreed that they need not raise their hats.

And so, robed and hatted and impressive, on 21 October 1958 Baroness Swanborough and also Baroness Wootton of Abinger presented their writs of summons, to be followed the next day by Baroness Elliot of Harwood and Baroness Ravensdale of Kedleston. Their Lordships received them benignly as if those echoes of 'bossy political females', 'ladies with bees in their bonnets' had never been.

When Lady Elliot made her maiden speech early in November on the importance of the under-developed parts of Asia and Africa,[24] her reception was most friendly. As many people recalled, she was not, in fact, the first woman to speak in the Upper Chamber, for, apart from the interruptions of Miss Vivien Leigh[25] and Dame Irene Ward, other women had addressed their Lordships on divers matters. In 1937 Mr Gerard Clay had written to *The Times*[26] saying that he had a portrait of an ancestress, Elizabeth Robson, wife of an officer of the garrison of Gibraltar, who lived between 1695 and 1779, which bore the inscription : 'She was the only Lady who ever Spoke in the House of Lords, and came over from Gibraltar, to give testimony about the Slaves.' In 1869 a Miss Annabella Redden had addressed them for twenty-three days on a legitimacy claim, and in 1908 Miss Chrystal Macmillan (who contested Edinburgh as an Independent candidate in 1935), assisted by Miss Frances Simpson, spoke to their Lordships for four hours on behalf of the women graduates of the Universities of St Andrews and Edinburgh, who were appealing for the vote in the election of the universities' parliamentary representative. This was the first time the terrible words 'Votes for Women' were uttered in the House of Lords. The application was dismissed.[27]

As in the Commons, so in the Lords, women were accepted on terms of equality with good grace once the battle was done. The ladies themselves made an excellent impression, adding their knowledge and abilities to the conduct of affairs and the high level of debates so that in 1960 Lord Pethick-Lawrence was able to report under the headline : 'The Peeresses Make Good' that 'they have not disturbed the decorum of the House nor ruffled its susceptibilities.'[28]

There were a few minor adjustments to be made of course. Lady Wootton, as the only one of the original four women peers with a husband living, had to seek the advice of the Gentleman Usher of the Black Rod as to the rights of a 'male peeress', i.e. her husband, but with Black Rod's help suitable arrangements were made for him.

By November, at a reception given to the women peers by the Fawcett Society, Lady Swanborough was able to sum up the atmosphere of the House of Lords as follows: 'People move so slowly. . . . Nobody runs down passages or uses used envelopes: nobody does anything for himself if he can ask a gentleman with a gold chain to do it for him.'[29] The women had indeed entered into another place.

But the battle was not quite over. In January 1959 Lord Reading carried by 59 votes to 51 a motion to admit peeresses in their own right,[30] thus scoring a victory over the Conservative Government and the Labour Party. It was disclosed during the debate that there were still about twenty peeresses in their own right and that their average age was over seventy. Although the motion was carried the Government ignored it. It was not until four years later, when a further stage of reform to allow peers to renounce their peerages was passed, that these ladies were permitted to claim their rights to a seat, place and voice in the Upper House.

1959-1964 After Forty Years

IN 1959 soon after the election of a new Parliament, which for a third time returned a Conservative Government with a greatly increased majority, the fortieth anniversary of Lady Astor's introduction into the House of Commons was reached. It was a milestone from which to look back and measure the progress and changes since 1919. Much indeed had been achieved : women were firmly established in the House of Commons and had at last taken their place in the House of Lords. Whatever ill-informed commentators might say women had shown in both Houses that they were able to make a contribution on a wide range of subjects. Although the domestic side of affairs attracted a good deal of their attention, there were women such as Barbara Castle, Evelyn Emmet, Jennie Lee, Priscilla Tweedsmuir, Eirene White and Lady Elliot of Harwood capable of making worthy contributions on overseas matters; women such as Barbara Castle and Lady Wootton capable of dealing with economic affairs; and women such as Mervyn Pike, Eveline Hill and Irene Ward (who has considerable knowledge of the coal industry) with business experience. Even defence was no longer a closed book : Joan Vickers, as befitted a Plymouth representative, was knowledgeable on naval affairs and during this Parliament she became honorary secretary of the Conservative backbench naval sub-committee.

However two aspects of the situation were still regarded in certain quarters as unsatisfactory : there were far too few women M.P.s, and the range of ministerial posts to which they had been appointed seemed to many unduly limited to the domestic sphere—health, education, pensions, home affairs. In neither respect did the situation improve as a result of the 1959 General Election; indeed it could be said to have deteriorated.

As far as the numbers of women candidates and M.P.s were concerned the standards set by the 1955 election had not been maintained. Out of a total of 1,536 candidates there were only 81 women, as against 91 in 1955. Of these 39 had fought before.

	CONSERVATIVE	LABOUR	LIBERAL	OTHERS	TOTAL
1959	28	36	16	1	81
1955	*32*	*43*	*14*	*2*	*91*

More significantly it was the two main parties that had adopted fewer women; the only 'other' candidate was a Communist. Three former M.P.s had retired: Dame Florence Horsbrugh who, with one break from 1945 until 1950, had sat in the House since 1931 now accepted a life peerage and entered the House of Lords as Baroness Horsbrugh. Lady Davidson brought to an end a parliamentary career lasting from 1937; in January 1964 she entered the Upper House as Baroness Northchurch of Chiswick. Jean Mann, 'the housewife's M.P.', now approaching seventy, retired to write her entertaining memoirs—*Woman in Parliament*—after a comparatively short run of fourteen unbroken years. She had always upheld the official leadership of the Parliamentary Labour Party and for five years was a member of the National Executive Committee, until she resigned in 1957 following a clash with Harold Wilson over the appointment of a woman organizer for the Labour Party. She died in March 1964.

Of the candidates standing in this quiet election, fought in the halcyon weather of an Indian Summer on the maintenance of an affluent 'never-had-it-so-good' society, only two had been adopted for seats previously held by their parties. Mrs Margaret Thatcher, who as Miss Margaret Roberts had contested Dartford in 1950 and 1951 for the Conservatives, was adopted for Finchley, a plum that the retiring member had held with a majority of nearly 13,000; and Miss Betty Harvie Anderson, a veteran of the 1950, 1951, and 1955 elections, was selected as Conservative candidate for Renfrew East held by the former Conservative M.P. with a 16,000 majority.

At a meeting of Conservative parliamentary candidates held shortly before the election in an august Piccadilly club, where the women candidates had to report to the back entrance and be smuggled into the conference room by means of a service lift, a discussion about whether a candidate's religion need be entered on the application form sent to constituencies was brought to an abrupt halt when a little woman at the back of the room asked whether by the same token the candidate's sex could be omitted.

After forty years women candidates to the general public were still rarities and were treated to a good deal of publicity. Supporters and opponents alike admired their 'courage' and seemed rather surprised if they knew the right answers. There were still men at outdoor meetings who shouted 'Why doesn't your husband keep you at home?' and national newspapers still wanted to know what clothes they were wearing to attract support.

When the Conservative Government was returned with a majority of a hundred the swing to the right reduced the number of women members of Parliament to twenty-five (twelve Conservatives, thirteen Labour) for, in addition to the three who had retired, three Labour members had lost their seats and were replaced by two Conservatives and one Labour woman. Miss Elaine Burton lost Coventry South by 1,830 votes to the Conservatives, but she was not away from Westminster long, for she accepted a life peerage in 1962; Mrs Lena Jeger lost Holborn and St Pancras by 956 votes to Geoffrey Johnson Smith, the television commentator; and Mrs Mary McAlister lost Kelvingrove which reverted to the Conservatives by a 1,101 majority. Some former members who were returned had done extremely well in adverse circumstances. Mrs Barbara Castle, who was chairman of the Labour Party for this election year, had increased her former majority of 489 at Blackburn to 2,866, in spite of a stern fight in which the Conservatives made full play with her Cypriot exploits. Christopher Chataway, who was returned for Lewisham North, reminded the public in a party television broadcast that she had alleged that British soldiers 'tortured' Cypriot prisoners, and an action which Barbara brought against him after the election failed. Eirene White just held Flint East by 75 votes. One of the most spectacular results was that of Joan Vickers in Devonport where in a straight fight with Michael Foot she increased her majority from 100 to 6,454. Other women candidates lost by narrow margins in Norfolk South-West, Faversham, Watford and Leicester North-East.

In addition to the return of the two new Conservative members, Mrs Thatcher and Miss Anderson, the third new member, Mrs Judith Hart, converted a Conservative majority of 958 into one of 540 for Labour in Lanark, which except for two short breaks had always been Conservative. As well as good looks she and Margaret Thatcher had much in common. Both had been at universities: Margaret, the daughter of a Grantham grocer, won a bursary to Somerville College, Oxford where she became President of the University Conservative Club; Judith, a member of a Lancashire family, studied at the London School of Economics and London University, becoming chairman of the Cambridge University Labour Club when the L.S.E. was evacuated to Cambridge during the war; both had fought two previous elections; and both were now in their mid-thirties and married with young families. Margaret had been an industrial chemist before marriage, but was called to the bar in 1954 and since then had practised as a barrister specializing in taxation. Judith until her election had practised as a sociologist. Politically she was well to the left as a member of the Victory for Socialism group and had contributed articles on Scottish affairs to *Tribune*.

Miss Betty Harvie Anderson o.b.e., now in her mid-forties, had a different background as a Scottish landowner whose family had held their land since the fifteenth century. She had been an ATS officer during the war and was interested in army affairs. She had been a member of the Stirling County Council since 1945 and had contested three previous elections in West Stirlingshire and Sowerby. She is a good speaker but likes to keep out of the public eye. Soon after her election she married Dr J. F. P. Skrimshire but she continues to be known by her maiden name.

The new members were therefore of high quality and just the sort of youngish women for whom there was need in the House of Commons.

The ministerial appointments were disappointing. True, that three out of twelve Conservative women in the House should be given posts was gratifying, and Mervyn Pike's appointment as Assistant Postmaster-General (the first woman to hold this post) was considered interesting; but the two other junior ministers were just shuffled round: Edith Pitt went to the Ministry of Health as Parliamentary Secretary and Pat Hornsby-Smith took her place as Joint Parliamentary Secretary to the Ministry of Pensions and National Insurance. For Pat this might be regarded as demotion after the Home Office, although she was now created a Privy Councillor. Dame Irene Ward wrote to *The Daily Telegraph*[1] that the Treasury could benefit from a woman's guidance and added: 'I am devastated that the Prime Minister does not know how disturbed responsible women who deplore the deterioration of modern standards of behaviour will feel at the unimaginative decision to appoint women in his Government merely to do the chores of administration.'

Mervyn Pike settled down happily and successfully into the job of Assistant Postmaster-General and in November after a speech, in which she ranged briskly for half an hour over matters from alphabetical codes to slot machines,[2] six Labour M.P.s joined in congratulating her. Edith Pitt worked as hard as ever at the Ministry of Health but some critics reported that she had 'the manner of a pupil-teacher' at the dispatch box which did not please the House.[3] At the Ministry of Pensions Pat Hornsby-Smith was concerned with the implementation of the Government's scheme for graduated pensions which came into operation early in 1961. But in September after eleven years in Parliament she decided to seek a career in industry and voluntarily resigned her post though not her seat to take up a directorship in a large company. It was rumoured that she had for some time been concerned at the lack of future political prospects.[4] She was the first and, so far, the only woman minister to resign of her own accord and this created something of a stir in the Press. The Prime Minister wrote a letter of courteous regret but said he thought she had made 'a proper decision'. As 'Peterborough' of *The Daily Telegraph*[5] reflected: 'Mr Macmillan may not be exactly antipathetic to women in the Government, but he shows no great sign of being captivated by their talents.' 'Peterborough' felt that Pat had by now rated a department of her own. It was a disappointing end to a career for which so much had been expected. However Pat's services were rewarded by the D.B.E. and she has prospered in the industrial world to become chairman of a subsidiary company of Courtaulds, including among her directorships that of a unit trust —an unusual appointment for a woman.

In her place as Under-Secretary to the Ministry of Pensions and National Insurance Mr Macmillan appointed Margaret Thatcher at the age of thirty-six and after only two years as an M.P. She had done extraordinarily well in the House. In 1959 as a new member she had won a place in the ballot for private bills and had made her maiden speech in February 1960, introducing the second reading of her Public Bodies (Admission to Meetings) Bill which secured admission of the Press and other members of the public to the meetings of local authorities and other public bodies.[6] This was a vexed question which had been the subject of earlier but unsuccessful private members' bills, the most recent having been introduced four years before by Sir Jocelyn Simon, now Solicitor-General. As Margaret pointed out in her speech of introduction, the public had no right by common law or statute law to attend meetings of a wide range of public bodies and local authorities and, if the Press were also excluded (when, for instance, the council were sitting as a committee), could not keep account of what their elected representatives were doing; there had been one or two cases where this had caused much dissatisfaction. It was a brilliant speech delivered in all its complex details without recourse to notes and made a remarkable impression on both sides of the House. The Press found it of front bench quality and said that as a maiden speech 'it has not been and is unlikely to be excelled by any of her contemporaries new to the 1959 Parliament' for she 'had an instinct for the mood of the House which some members take years to acquire—and some may never acquire at all.'[7] In the Lords the bill was piloted through the various stages by another woman, Baroness Elliot of Harwood. This was the first time women in both Houses had co-operated in putting through a bill.

Edith Pitt's ministerial career came to an end in July 1962 when she was one of the ministers whom Mr Macmillan dispensed with in his purge. Without warning, she was summoned to the telephone during a meeting to be told that her resignation was required. Although she was created a D.B.E. on relinquishing her post, she never recovered from the abrupt manner of her dismissal. Many back-bench members found it impossible to forgive Mr Macmillan for sacrificing Edith.

In December 1962 Lady Tweedsmuir at last achieved office after sixteen years in the House of Commons by being appointed Under-Secretary of State at the Scottish Office on the resignation of Mr T. G. D. Galbraith, whose name had been mentioned in connection with the Vassall spy case (he was later completely exonerated). Her appointment was generally welcomed on both sides of the House. Early in this Parliament she had been accepted into the inner councils of the parliamentary party by being elected to the executive of the influential Conservative backbench 1922 Committee; as for the Labour members, many of them had always held she was 'a bonnie lassie in the wrong company'; the only surprise was that she had not been promoted much earlier.[8] In March 1963 Mervyn Pike was moved from the Post Office to the Home Office as Under-Secretary of State in place of Mr Charles Fletcher-Cooke who had resigned. She too was said to be 'one of the quieter women of Westminster' but 'good at her home work' and an efficient administrator.[9] She was active in the debates on the Children and Young Persons Bill[10] and helped to put through the Adoption[11] and British Nationality Bills[12] as well as speaking for the Government in a debate on *au pair* girls.[13]

On the Opposition front bench there were five women in 1959 :

Eirene White was spokesman on education, Edith Summerskill was back again as the expert on health, Alice Bacon shadowed Home affairs, Margaret Herbison, Scottish affairs, and Barbara Castle, slightly outside the normal run of domestic matters, studied the Ministry of Works and Public Buildings. But she did not perform this duty for long because of another and even fiercer conflict within the Labour Party after its defeat in the 1959 election. At the Party Conference at Blackpool shortly after the election, Barbara in the chair had echoed Aneurin Bevan's plea for unity, but by the time of the 1960 Party Conference at Scarborough all had changed: Aneurin Bevan was dead and the small left-wing section of the party, of which Barbara and Ian Mikardo were leading members, were dissatisfied with Hugh Gaitskell's leadership. The conference voted against the official Labour policy of supporting multilateral disarmament. During these discussions Barbara said pointedly: 'Nobody in this party will forgive any leader who sets out unnecessarily to split it on defence.' The Press reported that during the tremendous ovation which Gaitskell received after his 'fight, fight and fight again' reply, Barbara Castle was one of those on the platform who did not applaud him.

In the election for the Leader of the Parliamentary Party at the beginning of the new session she supported Harold Wilson in his challenge to Gaitskell and was reported as saying 'the re-election of Hugh Gaitskell would mean that the Labour Party had ceased to be socialist.'[14] In a defence debate in December 1960 Barbara Castle, Joyce Butler, Judith Hart and Jennie Lee were among those who abstained from voting with the Opposition.[15] Early in 1961 Jennie Lee wrote an article in *Tribune* complaining that the party had no leadership—'This is our Achilles heel. This is what is still lacking.'[16]

Dr Edith Summerskill also left the Opposition front bench in January 1961, but through no disagreement over policy for she had always supported the official leadership of the party. She decided at the age of fifty-nine to accept a life peerage, but she did not mean to retire. 'I am a working Parliamentarian', she told the Press, 'and I am just going in through another door.' Lady Wootton was one of her sponsors at her introduction and the following month, as Baroness Summerskill, she made her maiden speech on the health service, roundly condemning the rise in the health charges. In congratulating her Lord Amory said: 'Our characters are likely to benefit and be strengthened by her advice.'[17]

often finds after her earnings have been added to his that he has to pay supertax. This, they maintained, was the most powerful factor preventing professional women from returning to work.

The Employment of Women Bill (to regulate the employment of women after childbirth and thereby to safeguard their and their babies' health by protecting them from undue pressure to return to work too soon) had been introduced by Lord Balniel, a Conservative member, as a private bill. It had passed its second reading before women M.P.s and women's organizations became uneasy; then Joan Vickers and Judith Hart opposed it successfully in committee because they saw in it an infringement of personal liberty, if women, whatever their circumstances, were prevented by law from resuming their work for a specific length of time after a baby's birth, and because it might cause hardship to unmarried mothers.[36] Against such determined opposition Lord Balniel withdrew his clearly well-intentioned bill.

In 1964 Joan Vickers, who became Dame Joan Vickers with the award of the D.B.E. later that year, got a private measure to improve the conditions of employment of young people—the Young Persons (Employment) Bill on to the Statute Book.[37]

Even inside the Palace of Westminster, it seems, there were in the sixties some cases of discrimination. Although in the crowded conditions at Westminster the accommodation for lady members now compared favourably with that provided for men, there was still *apartheid* in the seating of spectators in that the Distinguished Strangers' Gallery was reserved for men, whereas Mr Speaker's Gallery was reserved for privileged women strangers, the wives of ministers, and so on.[38]

In overseas affairs the great question that arose during this Parliament was that of the possible entry of the United Kingdom into the Common Market on which opinion was sharply divided on both sides of the House. Evelyn Emmet spoke strongly in favour of Britain's entry, saying in a debate in 1961, 'The idea that we shall lose sovereignty if we go into the Common Market is a bogey that is being dressed up';[39] but Jennie Lee, for one, disagreed, saying in a debate on the European Economic Community later that year, 'No issue which has come before this House in my lifetime has been of greater importance.' She feared 'the polarization of world forces' and, speaking as one who did not find it too easy to live at peace with the relatively mild Whips of the Labour Party, she did not view incorporation into a wider community with favour.[40] Barbara Castle

I

agreed with her and in December 1962 she attacked the concessions which the Government was making in the negotiations conducted by Mr Edward Heath with the Common Market countries. 'This Government', she maintained, was willing, 'nay, anxious, pleading to be allowed to sell the passes of British interest and British freedom.'[41]

Before Lady Tweedsmuir's elevation to the Scottish office she was British delegate to the General Assembly of the United Nations in 1960 and 1961, serving on the Third Committee dealing with social, humanitarian and cultural affairs. She also went to Geneva in 1961 as leader of the British delegates on the United Nations Executive Committee which dealt with the programme of the High Commissioner for Refugees, and in May 1962 she was elected chairman of the committee's seventh session. Evelyn Emmet's work and knowledge of foreign affairs were also recognized when she was elected a vice-chairman of the Conservative back bench foreign affairs committee in 1963, the first woman to hold such a position.

On the other side of the House Judith Hart, in the interests of unity, ceased to take an active part in the Victory for Socialism group soon after she entered the House, but she caused some eyebrow-raising by attending within a few months the conference of the Women's International League for Peace and Freedom, a left-wing organization, where she urged that Britain should withdraw from NATO.[42] Although she sued the *Glasgow Herald* in 1963 for saying that she supported the anti-nuclear organization, the Committee of 100, (the action was settled out of court), she tried unsuccessfully to move the adjournment to discuss the raiding of the Committee's offices by the police in 1961,[43] and in the following year again unsuccessfully tried to initiate a debate on the nuclear tests on Christmas Island.[44] She was also very active in Commonwealth affairs as vice-chairman of the Movement for Colonial Freedom, another left-wing organization headed by Mr Fenner Brockway M.P. (now Lord Brockway) and of which Jennie Lee was treasurer.

Apartheid in South Africa provoked Barbara Castle and Lady Summerskill to stand in silent protest wearing black sashes outside Lancaster House in March 1961 during the Commonwealth Prime Ministers' Conference which resulted in South Africa leaving the Commonwealth. By now Barbara had established a formidable reputation on both sides of the the the House. 'In Tory eyes', according to the Press, 'as far as Mrs Barbara Castle is concerned the age of chivalry is dead. She has smashed the sex barrier; with her not even

the most condescending opponent dares risk any of the familiar
flannel about "the gracious lady in her usual charming way".[45]

Meanwhile progress was being made in the House of Lords. By
the end of this Parliament there were nine women peers. Besides
Florence Horsbrugh and Edith Summerskill, in April 1962 Elaine
Burton was introduced as Baroness Burton of Coventry by two
women peers, Baroness Wootton and Baroness Summerskill, and in
January 1964 Lady Davidson as Baroness Northchurch of Chiswick
was the first woman to join her husband in the Upper House. At
the same time Hugh Gaitskell's widow, Dora, was introduced, with
many friends from both Houses present, as Baroness Gaitskill of
Egremont in the County of Cumberland, the first woman to be
honoured in this way as a tribute to her husband. She has taken
an active part in the deliberations of the House.

Lady Horsbrugh became the first woman member of a Royal
Commission in 1961 when she sat with the Lord Chancellor and one
other peer giving the Royal Assent to bills.[46] (Members of a Royal
Commission must be both peers and Privy Councillors.) In the same
year Lady Wootton became a member of the Council of Tribunals
which acts as an advisory body to administrative tribunals and
statutory inquiries. At the beginning of the session in 1962 Lady
Elliot of Harwood was the first woman to move the Address in
Reply to the Queen's Speech in the House of Lords.[47] She earned a
rich compliment from Lord Dynevor who seconded the Address; he
reminded the House that now the 'garrison warmly welcomes the
besiegers and that they now play a valuable and integral part in your
Lordships' affairs', while Lord Alexander of Hillsborough was even
more gallant: 'She has set a standard for women as a whole', he
said, 'and not merely as one of the peeresses of this House. I hope it
will mean that there will be still further expansion in the use, in
public life, of the womanhood of our country.'

Most of those who had sat in the Commons carried on their main
interests as before. Lady Summerskill, for instance, contributed frequently to health debates and again waged war on professional boxing, finding greater support in the Upper House, for when in 1962
she introduced a private bill to ban boxing promotions it failed by
only six votes.[48] The following year she piloted the Married Women's
Property Act on to the Statute Book.[49] This embodies one of the provisions of her earlier unsuccessful Women's Disabilities bills, making
it law that savings from housekeeping money should belong in equal
shares to husband and wife. Florence Horsbrugh spoke on educa-

tion[50] and housing[51] and in 1962 conducted a private inquiry into rent levels in Scotland. Lady Burton contributed to the debates on the Weights and Measures Bill and, with Lady Elliot, to those on the Hire Purchase Bill.[52]

The more one studies British parliamentary history the more one is struck by the ironic twists and turns that have evolved the present Parliament. The admittance of peeresses in their own right has been one of the most ironic for, after all the striving, petitioning and arguments in the past to get them 'a place, a seat, and a voice' in the Upper House they were at last admitted under a further measure of reform, which also gave hereditary peers of the male sex the right to renounce their peerages. When the Peerage Bill was debated in the House of Commons in June 1963, Jennie Lee opposed it, as she had opposed the Life Peerage Act, because she was against the hereditary principle and thought the abolition of the House of Lords would be an excellent method of obtaining more accommodation for the House of Commons.[53] Evelyn Emmet, who had been a member of the Joint Committee, welcomed the bill. It would, she pointed out, at last make it possible for the United Kingdom to sign the United Nations Covenant on the Political Rights of Women which had been passed ten years before when she was a delegate to the United Nations.[54] Because this country was one of the few that barred women from its Upper Chamber it had not been able to sign. When the bill was passed only three peeresses took their seats in November 1963.[55] All of them were by now elderly; the first was Baroness Strange of Knokin, aged seventy-nine, followed by Baroness Audley and Lady Beaumont (who took the oath at the same time as her husband, Lord Howard of Glossop). She was propelled into the Chamber in a wheelchair, recalling the introduction of Lady Apsley into the House of Commons in 1943.

None of the hereditary peeresses have taken much part in the debates of the House so far. The first to speak, two years later in July 1965, was Lady Strange of Knokin who made a short, constructive speech on the health and welfare services and the care of the elderly in rural areas. She was warmly congratulated by her son, Viscount St Davids, and Edith Summerskill who revealed that Lady Strange was now over eighty. 'The noble lady must be extremely happy,' she said.[56]

But we have gone ahead of the dissolution of this Parliament in October 1964, which brought to an end a long period of Conservative Government. Although women no longer had a harder task than their male colleagues simply because they were women, and therefore targets for extra correspondence and requests, they shared with the men the greatly increased pressures of modern political life that made their job as demanding as any that women tackle. They continued to speak at meetings throughout the country and to be active in their constituencies, answering a heavy correspondence: Pat Hornsby-Smith revealed at the end of this Parliament that in fifteen years as an M.P. she had interviewed no fewer than 17,000 constituents and taken up 12,000 cases with ministries.[57] Sometimes the pressures became too great. In 1961 Alice Bacon was seriously ill in hospital with thrombosis and was away from Westminster for several months; in 1960 Margaret Herbison, who had been a member of the National Executive Committee of the Labour Party since 1948 and chairman for the year 1956–7, did not stand for re-election to it because she wanted to spend some time with her mother who was seriously ill. She was re-elected to the NEC in 1961.

To the political correspondent of *The Times*,[58] recalling in 1962 that there had been only seventy-six women M.P.s in forty-three years, it was 'still a man's world for women politicians. . . . On any view', he wrote, 'the women politicians have all the big cards stacked against them when they take the high road to Westminster and so it will continue.' During this period a very strange comment came from no less a person than Lady Hylton-Foster, the wife of Mr Speaker and daughter of an earlier Speaker, who was reported in the *Sunday Express* in 1960 as saying: 'I cannot think why they do it. I just do not understand them. Women do not have enough education to become politicians. I know that many Labour Members of Parliament who have had no education have done extremely well, but they have bothered to find out things for themselves and read up what they don't know. Women don't.' This statement was raised as a breach of privilege by Mr Emrys Hughes, a Labour member, and the Speaker found himself in the embarrassing position of having to be judge in his wife's case; after due reflection he found there was not a breach.[59] Today Baroness Hylton-Foster of the City of Westminster sits in Parliament herself.

1964-1966 Prospects Widen

THE TWO General Elections of 1964 and 1966 in which the electorate at first hesitantly and then decisively established a Labour Government in office with a large turnover of seats, unlike those of 1923, 1929, and 1945, made very little difference to the representation of women in the House of Commons, for the gains on the Labour side were balanced by retirements and Conservative losses. In 1964 the initial swing to the left did raise the number of women M.P.s from twenty-six to twenty-nine, but eighteen months later the election of 1966 brought the figure down to twenty-six again. More significantly too the number of candidates adopted by the two major parties continued their downward trend.

	CONSERVATIVE	LABOUR	LIBERAL	OTHERS	TOTAL
1966	21	30	20	10	81
1964	24	32	25	9	90
1959	*28*	*36*	*16*	*1*	*81*

Before the General Election of 1964 there had been much concern in both major parties at their failure to adopt more women candidates. Mr Selwyn Lloyd, by now an elder statesman of the Conservative Party, went on a tour of the constituency parties in 1963 and in his report repeated the recommendation that every Conservative Association choosing a candidate should include at least one woman and one trade unionist on every short list.[1] It is doubtful whether this recommendation was everywhere carried out. Lucille Iremonger, the writer and wife of Mr Tom Iremonger, Conservative M.P., described in an article in *The Sunday Times* in April 1964[2] her own experience and that of other women in both parties when they appeared before selection committees. It was not, she wrote, until she reached the short list as one of four (the other three were men) out of ninety-six candidates applying for a safe Conservative seat 'that I realized that it is not possible to ignore the fact of being a woman'. Married women, she found, were asked whether they contemplated neglecting their husbands, their children and grandchildren, and their homes. 'But single women are faced with a blunt "Why aren't you married? Isn't it rather odd?" (Bachelors, however, are rapturously received).' She did not in the end contest either the 1964 or 1966 elections.

Olive R. Cruchley writing in *Labour Woman* before the 1964 election recalled sadly that in 1950 forty Labour women had fought. 'If we had progressed steadily, we might by now have been able to muster about sixty candidates', more of whom might have been successful. Women, she said, must help women, for it would be 'unthinkable if the Conservatives were to overtake us . . . the movement must be careful to translate theories into better practice.'

The number of Liberal women fluctuated according to the total figure which the party decided to put forward at each election, but in spite of the fact that they included women of first-class ability, such as Miss Nancy Seear, a lecturer at the London School of Economics and in 1966 President of the Liberal Party, who that year contested her sixth election, and the lively Miss Manuela Sykes who had fought five, no Liberal woman was adopted for a seat which she had any real prospect of winning. The Independent candidates were mostly Communists (four in 1964 and a record number of six in 1966).

As a result of these two elections several familiar faces vanished and some new ones appeared at Westminster. In 1964 Mrs Patricia McLaughlin (U.U., Belfast West) did not stand for re-election because of poor health. Mrs Eveline Hill, after fourteen years in Parliament during which her knowledge of local government affairs had been invaluable to the Conservative Party, lost her marginal seat at Wythenshawe, Manchester. After the 1964 General Election Mrs Evelyn Emmet (Conservative, East Grinstead) was given a life peerage in the Dissolution Honours and went to the House of Lords as Baroness Emmet of Amberley. In 1966 Lady Gammans (Conservative, Hornsey) and Mrs Harriet Slater (Labour, Stoke-on-Trent) retired, two prominent women members died and two others lost their seats. Dame Edith Pitt, Conservative M.P. for Edgbaston, died suddenly at the age of fifty-nine in January 1966, and in May Lady Megan Lloyd George died at the age of sixty-four, greatly mourned by her Carmarthen constituents. She had been made a Companion of Honour in the 1966 Dissolution Honours. Both these ladies had been appointed in November 1965 to the Chairman's Panel of Committees, the first women to be appointed since Mrs Florence Paton in the post-war Parliament. Dame Patricia Hornsby-Smith and Lady

Tweedsmuir were both casualties of the swing to the left in the 1966 election.

The new members who took their seats as a result of the two elections belonged with one exception to the Labour Party. In 1964 Mrs Lena Jeger returned to Parliament having won back Holborn and St Pancras which she had represented from 1953 to 1959. Five women gained seats : Mrs Anne Kerr (Rochester and Chatham), a former actress aged thirty-nine and a strong advocate of nuclear disarmament; Mrs Margaret McKay (Clapham), a former Women's Organizer of the Trades Union Congress, aged fifty-three; Mrs Renée Short (Wolverhampton East), a journalist of forty-six who had fought an all-woman battle against Mrs Miranda Greenaway, Conservative (which prompted 'a man in a bus queue to complain 'of course, there's nothing to choose between them, they're both ruddy women').[3] In addition there were the two Shirleys—astonishingly alike in background : both daughters of famous mothers, both in their early thirties, both married, and both educated at St Paul's School for Girls and Somerville College, Oxford. The Hon. Dr Shirley Summerskill, daughter of Lady Summerskill, formerly practised medicine and Shirley Williams, daughter of Vera Brittain and Professor George Catlin, was formerly general secretary of the Fabian Society.

In the 1964–6 Parliament there were eighteen Labour and eleven Conservative women members. The Conservatives were reduced to ten when Mrs Emmet left the Commons.

In 1966 the new members were Miss Joan Lestor (Labour, Eton and Slough) a nursery-school teacher aged thirty-five, Mrs Gwyneth Dunwoody (Labour, Exeter), aged thirty-six, mother of three children, who described herself as a 'housewife' and joined both her newly elected husband and her mother, Lady Phillips, at Westminster. There have now been married couples sitting together in both Houses of Parliament but the combination still to be achieved is that of a true 'pair'—a man and wife sitting on opposite sides of either House. That final peak of marital independence may yet be scaled.

The third new member in 1966 was Mrs Jill Knight (Conservative, Edgbaston) another 'housewife' aged forty-three with a young family, whose adoption for her safe seat was both a tribute to her long record of work for her party and the esteem in which her supporters had held her predecessor, Edith Pitt.

After the 1966 General Election there were nineteen Labour

women members (eighteen after the death of Lady Megan) and seven Conservative women members in the House of Commons.

All the newly elected women who reached Westminster in this short period were of high calibre, had considerable political experience, and had contested seats before. Although several of them were women in their thirties or early forties, the average age of women M.P.s had risen rather than fallen since 1959 when it was forty-seven and a half; in 1964 it was fifty-one and in 1966, fifty-two. This is naturally because the senior M.P.s were getting older at each election. Following the 1966 election Mrs Alice Cullen was the oldest woman M.P. at seventy-four, and the youngest was Shirley Summerskill aged thirty-four.

In the Upper House the number of women peers rose considerably so that by the 1966 General Election they numbered seventeen. In December 1964, in addition to Baroness Emmet, the former Mrs Henry Brooke, vice-chairman for many years of the National Union of Conservatives and Unionist Associations, became Baroness Brooke of Ystradfellte; also in 1964 Lady Violet Bonham-Carter, the veteran Liberal politician and daughter of Mr Asquith, the former Prime Minister, who had twice stood for Parliament unsuccessfully, at last reached Westminster as Baroness Asquith of Yarnbury; and the same year Mrs Norah Phillips, widow of Morgan Phillips a former General Secretary of the Labour Party, took her seat as Baroness Phillips of Fulham. In 1965 three widows of distinguished men took their seats; Baroness Plummer of Topplefield, widow of Sir Leslie Plummer, the Labour M.P., Baroness Spencer-Churchill, and Baroness Hylton-Foster, widow of the former Speaker. In January 1966 another woman of great distinction, who had twice stood for election, Mrs Mary Stocks, the former head of Westfield College and well known as a broadcaster and as the biographer of Eleanor Rathbone, presented her writ of summons as Baroness Stocks of the Royal Borough of Kensington and Chelsea. (For other life peers created up to January 1967 see Appendix B.)

In December 1965 Lady Wootton was appointed to the panel of Deputy Chairmen of Committees, and in February 1966 became the first woman to sit on the Woolsack. She described it as 'very comfortable' but denied that there was anything very remarkable about sitting on it : 'Nobody was very astonished. People take it for granted now that women should do all these things.'[4] In the New Year Honours Lady Summerskill was made a Companion of Honour.

It must be recorded that as in the House of Commons in the

1920s so in the Lords in the 1960s the vexed question of millinery cropped up—and who was to raise it but that most hat-conscious lady, Baroness Burton : by Standing Order 24 dating back to 1621 members of the House of Lords must speak 'standing and uncovered'. This rule goes back to the time when peers generally wore their hats because the Chamber was draughty, but it irked Lady Burton who put the matter before the Committee of Procedure of which Lady Wootton (generally hatless) was a member. It was soon able to report that peeresses who wished to should be allowed to wear their hats when speaking.[5]

The great break-through in this period was in the range and number of ministerial appointments. In 1964 and 1966 women on the Labour benches were well rewarded for their services in Opposition : in 1964 no fewer than seven (out of eighteen) were given appointments and for the first time women were entrusted with responsibility for overseas affairs. The major appointment in 1964 was that of Mrs Barbara Castle (Blackburn), the former Bevanite rebel who had always worked closely with the Prime Minister, Harold Wilson. As Minister of the newly created Ministry of Overseas Development and a Privy Councillor she became the fourth woman to reach Cabinet rank. In January 1966 she was transferred to an even more formidable and testing appointment as Minister of Transport following the resignation of Mr Tom Fraser. Nevertheless Press and public took her appointment fairly calmly. Barbara's ability on the back benches had long been recognized; the secret of her successful career, according to the *New Statesman* of 7 January 1966, was the fact that she had 'always accepted the business of politics on men's terms' attacking hard and expecting no quarter. 'In attack', reported the paper, 'she provides one of the most awesome sights the House of Commons has to offer.'

Both Margaret Herbison (Lanarkshire North) and Alice Bacon (Leeds South East) continued to follow parallel careers by being appointed to ministries which they had shadowed in Opposition : Margaret became Minister of Pensions and National Insurance (later Social Security) and Alice, Minister of State at the Home Office. Both became Privy Councillors, Margaret in 1964 and Alice in 1966.

Mrs Eirene White (Flint East) was another woman to break new ground. In 1964 she became Parliamentary Secretary to the Colonial Office and in 1966 she was moved to the Foreign Office as one of the four Ministers of State. Even in an egalitarian age, accustomed to women on the High Court Bench, a Russian female astronaut in

space, and stateswomen rising to high positions abroad, the appointment of the first woman to assail the masculine heights of the British
Foreign Office created a mild sensation.[6]

Another interesting appointment was that of Miss Jennie Lee
(Cannock) as Parliamentary Secretary to the Ministry of Works and
Public Buildings with special responsibility for the Arts, a post that
was in 1966 brought under the Ministry of Education and Science.[7]
She was perhaps the Minister who was happiest of all for somehow,
while funds were low in other departments, she managed to persuade
the Prime Minister, of whom like Barbara Castle she had always
been a firm supporter, to allow increased grants for the Arts in both
1965 and 1966; she was able to announce that the Royal Phil-
harmonic Orchestra would be saved; a large sum set aside for litera-
ture; the National Theatre, the Royal Opera House and the London
Library helped; and that plans were to be made for some kind of
'university of the Air'. Reporters found presiding over all this benefi-
cence a handsome, stately Jennie, in sharp contrast with the fiery
girl of the pre-war years or the embittered Bevanite of the post-war
period.

The ability of Mrs Judith Hart (Lanark) was recognized by her
appointment as Under-Secretary of State for Scotland in 1964
and her promotion in 1966 to the post of Minister of State at the
Commonwealth Relations Office. Mrs Shirley Williams (Hitchin)
also won early promotion. After being P.P.S. to the Minister of
Health in the 1964 Parliament she became in 1966 Parliamentary
Secretary to the Ministry of Labour at the age of thirty-five.[8] For
the first time women were appointed as Whips: in her last Parliament Mrs Harriet Slater became a Lord Commissioner of the
Treasury, and in 1965 Lady Phillips was appointed Baroness in
Waiting and was the first woman to occupy a ministerial position
in the Upper House.[9]

It was reported that Mrs Bessie Braddock (Liverpool Exchange)
was also offered a post in 1964 but declined it, preferring to remain
on the back benches as the first woman chairman of the House of
Commons Kitchen Committee.[10]

In Opposition women also broke new ground. In 1964 Sir Alec
Douglas-Home, then Leader of the Opposition, appointed Mrs
Margaret Thatcher (Finchley) and Miss Mervyn Pike (Melton) to
shadow portfolios which they had held in office, pensions and General
Post Office affairs respectively. In 1965 Mr Edward Heath appointed
Mrs Thatcher to cover housing and land affairs which had then

been incorporated into a short-lived ministry. He also gave Lady Tweedsmuir (Aberdeen South) some responsibility for foreign affairs —a role which she was well able to play—thus anticipating the Government's appointment of a woman in this hitherto masculine sphere. After the new ministerial appointments had been announced following the General Election in 1966, and the Press was commenting that the only other great Whitehall Everest after the Foreign Office that women had yet to conquer was the Treasury, Mr Heath announced that among his spokesmen for Treasury and economic affairs would be Mrs Thatcher. Her first speech in the Budget debate was considered an outstanding success.[11] Miss Mervyn Pike was appointed in 1966 to be the Opposition spokesman on the social services.

And so the barriers to ministerial promotion come tumbling down in the sixties. By the time of the next general election it is likely that women will have been members of Parliament for over fifty years. There are still very few of them—a mere 25 out of 630—and the signs are that, far from increasing, the number of women parliamentary candidates is falling, but the prospects for those who do manage to climb the rough, uneven path to Westminster are now much broader. Parents of politically precocious daughters might do well to have them photographed posing outside the door of Number 10.

In Conclusion

IT IS now possible to look back over a period of nearly fifty years since Lady Astor first took her seat in the House of Commons and to try to answer the questions which were posed at the beginning of this book. What kind of women have become members of Parliament? What has been their contribution? And why, after nearly half a century, are there still so few of them?

What kind of women have become M.P.s?

The majority have belonged to the left; of the 83 women who have taken their seats in the House of Commons since 1919, 47 have been Labour, 31 Conservative, 4 Liberal (including Lady Megan Lloyd George who subsequently joined the Labour Party) and one Independent.

The average age of the 67 women who have revealed it is forty-five. Only two women under thirty have entered Parliament: Jennie Lee at twenty-four and Megan Lloyd George at twenty-seven. At the other end of the scale Dr Ethel Bentham, sixty-eight, and Mrs Caroline Ganley, sixty-six, were the two oldest women to be elected. 44 have been married, 13 widowed, and 26 single at the time they entered Parliament (a few changed their status while they were M.P.s). It follows from their average age that few of the married women have been the mothers of young families; in fact from information available only 17 have had children of school age or under when they were elected, and 20 married women and widows have been childless.

Educationally their standard has always been high and only 6 claim to have had only elementary education, leaving school at fourteen or fifteen; all the others have had secondary education of some kind and 29, a high proportion, have been to a university. The graduates have included women from working-class backgrounds such as Jennie Lee, Ellen Wilkinson, Margaret Herbison and Freda Corbet who have won their way to a university. It does not seem however that there has been any kind of 'old girls' network' in operation, unless it is of Old Paulines. Most leading girls' public schools such as Roedean and Cheltenham Ladies' College have yet to send a woman to Westminster; Wycombe Abbey has sent one (Mary Pickford), and though St Paul's Girls' School in Hammersmith has the proud record of having had five former pupils in the House of Commons—Mavis Tate, Eirene White, Anne Kerr, Shirley Summerskill, Shirley Williams—all but one of these women come from the left so it is unlikely that their school background has exerted undue influence in their favour. As regards the universities, London and Oxford lead, claiming 8 each to Cambridge's 5. At Oxford, Somerville has returned 5, Lady Margaret Hall 2, St Hugh's 1; at Cambridge, Newnham has returned 3 and Girton 2.

The professions of women entering the House of Commons (some have changed them later) have been :

Schoolteacher	10
Trade union or political organizer	8
Journalist or writer	6
Farmer, landowner	4
Civil Servant	3
Welfare Officer	3
Doctor	3
Actress	2
Barrister	2
Company Director	2
Secretary	2
Economist	1
Industrial Relations Consultant	1
S.R.N.	1
Organizing Secretary	1
Sociologist	1
University Lecturer	1

The remaining women have had no declared professions and have sometimes described themselves as 'housewives', meaning apparently that they were married women leading domestic lives, but in a great majority of cases this has been an over-simplification because of the amount of public or political work which they have undertaken outside their homes. No fewer than 40 women M.P.s have served on local government bodies, which seem to have been a useful training ground for national politics.

What most women M.P.s have had in common then (apart from

the fact that a surprising number of the most prominent have had red hair and been small in stature) is a good education and a professional or middle-class background. They have also had politics in their blood, having been reared in families with strong political connections or a record of public service. Apart from these they have really been remarkable for their individuality. Only in the 1931–5 era, and in the 'housewife era' of 1945–50 could it be said that many of them conformed to a type. The others have shown a great diversity of character, ranging from the formidable intellectuals of the Eleanor Rathbone, Susan Lawrence school to the 'woman-next-door' type of Jean Mann; from the dedicated, aloof aristocrat like the Duchess of Atholl to the warm-hearted, impetuous Irene Ward; from Jennie Lee, daughter of a miner and a Labour rebel of the far left, to Cynthia Mosley, daughter of a marquess, a Labour rebel springing from Tory circles. Indeed, although there have been so few of them, women have in one sense provided a microcosm of what Parliament should be, drawn from all manner of human beings.

What have women contributed to Parliament?

Eleanor Rathbone prophesied in 1936 'that those who expect women's contribution [to Parliament] to be something completely *sui generis*, utterly different from the contribution of men, will be disappointed.'[1] Tracing the history of women members over the years it is impossible to find that their work has differed radically from that of men; what is striking is the breadth of interests which this small group has managed to embrace and the fact that since the late 1920s women have had a contribution to make on nearly every major issue before Parliament. The battles they have fought for their own sex have been but a small proportion of their total effort. While inevitably expressing 'the women's point of view' they have, like their male colleagues, made full use of whatever talents and experience they brought with them into Parliament. It is indeed those qualities of intellect and knowledge not necessarily peculiar to women that have made the more successful of them so valuable or outstanding: Mrs Wintringham for her knowledge of agriculture, Eleanor Rathbone for her work for family allowances and refugees, Barbara Castle for her grasp of economics and overseas affairs—and so one could continue quoting examples. By the same token it might be said that the brilliant and charming Megan Lloyd George never realized the high hopes that were held out for her because she chose to confine her interests too narrowly to local and regional matters.

Those who hold that women's primary function in Parliament is to deal with 'women's issues',[2] are imposing upon them a restriction quite out of keeping with their duties as members, which will deny to Parliament a source of ability that it can ill afford to do without.

If women have been remarkable for any particular qualities it is perhaps for their dedication to their parliamentary duties—only three or four at the most have shown themselves unsuited to be M.P.s —and their high degree of independence and courage in expressing it. Although the House of Commons accepted them with the traditional impartiality and courtesy which it extends to all new members, giving them complete equality from the beginning, and providing them with facilities which, if not ideal, compare favourably with those the male members enjoy, it was, and still is, very much a man's club. It took, particularly in the early days, a great deal of courage for a woman to stand up in this nearly all-male assembly and express unorthodox or unpopular views. Even Lady Astor was far more terrified than she allowed her colleagues to know. 'It was not easy,' was the Duchess of Atholl's understatement about her speech on female circumcision. 'It was not easy,' recalled Mavis Tate of Lady Astor's and her own decision to vote against the Chamberlain Government in the Norway debate of 1940. It cannot have been easy for Thelma Cazalet-Keir to divide the House on the equal pay issue in 1944; for Jennie Lee and Barbara Castle to oppose official Labour policies in the post-war years; for Irene Ward to sit blandly on the Treasury Bench demonstrating on behalf of the fixed income groups.

Another tribute that should be paid to women members is that, though they have had to live from the first under the arc lamps of almost world-wide news coverage, they have, with very few exceptions, never sought publicity. This reticence has given some commentators the impression that they were not being a success or pulling their weight, whereas in reality they have been working effectively. Among the most important requirements for an M.P. of either sex have always been good stamina and a strong constitution both physical and mental. There have been some like Ellen Wilkinson and Mavis Tate who have sacrificed their health.

As ministers women have so far proved themselves competent but not outstanding. The four who were full ministers before 1964 all had to face difficulties of one kind or another, so that it is not easy to judge their true potentialities. Of the junior ministers, Susan

Lawrence stands out for her ability, but she did not have long in office before the economic disaster of 1931. But in the share-out of appointments women have done well; 22 out of the 83 returned to Parliament have occupied ministerial positions, several of them occupying more than one post. They have enjoyed a rather unfair advantage in this over their male colleagues as a result of games-manship between governments seeking to present a progressive 'image' by their appointment of women, although until 1964 they confined them to domestic affairs. Harold Wilson's appointment in that year of Mrs Castle and Mrs White to deal with overseas affairs was an important development for women M.P.s, indicating that in future their abilities may earn recognition in whatever sphere they lie.

Within their own party Labour women seem to have been able to exert rather more influence than their Conservative colleagues. Five seats are reserved for women on the National Executive Com-mittee of the Labour Party which has some policy-making powers. Most prominent Labour women M.P.s have served on the NEC and Susan Lawrence, Ellen Wilkinson, Barbara Castle, Alice Bacon, Margaret Herbison and Edith Summerskill have all occupied the chair of the party. In the Conservative Party policy is decided by the leader of the party and his front bench colleagues in Parliament; only one woman (Florence Horsbrugh) has reached Cabinet status and comparatively few have been at any one time junior ministers (see Appendix A) or Opposition spokesmen. Lady Davidson, Dame Edith Pitt, Lady Tweedsmuir, Miss Harvie Anderson are the only women who have so far been elected to the executive committee of the 1922 Committee, the influential backbenchers' group. Within their party organization very few Tory women M.P.s have occupied leading positions : of the twelve women who since 1926 have been chairmen of the National Union of Conservative and Unionist Associations, presiding over the annual party conference, only two, the Countess of Iveagh and Mrs Emmet, have been members of Parliament; since 1930 there has always been a woman Vice-Chair-man of the Conservative Party Organization appointed by the party leader, but Lady Iveagh has been the only M.P. to occupy this office. Therefore whereas in the Labour Party women M.P.s have taken an active part in policy decisions and some of them have been prominent in support of various candidates for the party leader-ship, Conservative women M.P.s have never emerged as leaders of any ginger group or members of any inner or 'magic' circle; in the leadership changes of 1963 and 1965 no woman M.P. was mentioned as playing an influential part in support of a particular candidate.

This distinction is again reflected in the political groups attached to the parties. While Labour Party women M.P.s such as Shirley Williams have been an integral part of the Fabian Society and others have been closely connected with various pressure groups such as Victory for Socialism or the Movement for Colonial Freedom, no Conservative woman who is now an M.P. has taken a leading role in the Bow Group, the Monday Club or PEST (Pressure for Economic and Social Toryism) in which in any case young men seem to play far the greater part. Perhaps this is because the all-male club tradition is stronger among Conservatives than Socialists. Women politicians are not eligible for the Tory political clubs such as the Carlton, the Constitutional or the Junior Carlton,[3] or for the political dining clubs, the United and Cecil and the Coningsby; and the only Tory women's club, the Ladies' Carlton, closed its doors some years ago owing to financial difficulties. This exclusion is a depriva-tion because all the men's clubs are centres where M.P.s and pros-pective parliamentary candidates meet to dine with party leaders and discuss policies and tactics informally. They can be the forcing grounds for influential pressure groups.

The House of Lords, to which women have been admitted com-paratively recently, has allowed an even more widely drawn group to contribute their experience to Parliament, including some who have sought in vain to enter the House of Commons. After a long struggle and many harsh and peevish words women's acceptance has been as courteous, kind and unruffled as it was in the Lower House, and they have contributed to the high level of the debates.

Therefore while women cannot and would not wish to claim that they have brought about any dramatic changes in Parliament, their presence even in such small numbers must have had a profound effect, making the two assemblies more genuinely representative of the country as a whole; in both Houses women have been able to bring a wider point of view to bear upon the deliberations. As mem-bers of the House of Commons and the House of Lords they have not fallen short of the standards set by their colleagues; in some respects they may have enhanced them.

Why are there still so few women M.P.s?

There is no simple explanation for this, nor is it a phenomenon confined to Britain : in several other Western countries the numbers of women in the legislatures are not only small but declining.[4] Naturally in the early days in Britain prejudice played its part; selection committees looked without favour on untried female candidates and feared their effect on an electorate that until 1929 was predominantly male. There were other difficulties too : most women lacked political or local government experience; they were handicapped by financial considerations; not only was it an expensive business nursing a constituency for those earning their own living (and they were not as well paid as today) but candidates were generally expected to contribute to election expenses, and once elected an M.P.'s salary was only £400 a year. Some Labour candidates were sponsored by trade unions but in the Conservative Party the situation was even more difficult because constituencies had every inducement to adopt wealthy candidates (see p. 125-6 for Mrs Tate's difficulties).

Although a woman is still generally reckoned to have to be a little better than a man to achieve adoption, from the 1930s it has not been really difficult for a woman of good qualifications and sufficient determination to find a seat to contest, provided she is willing to take on a constituency that has little chance of returning her. The real hurdle is to get adopted for a winnable seat, even for those women with experience of fighting several elections. This is illustrated by the fact that the majority of women members of all three parties first reached Parliament either by winning over constituencies held by their opponents or by standing for newly created divisions in which the results were unpredictable, as the table below shows :

WOMEN MEMBERS OF PARLIAMENT
1919–66

	CONSERVATIVE	LABOUR	LIBERAL	TOTAL
First elected to a constituency formerly represented by a relative[5]	9	4	2	15
First elected to a constituency held by candidate's party (but not by a relative) at previous election	8	6	1	15
First elected after winning over newly created division or one previously held by opponents	14	37	1	52

The choice of candidates is in all parties determined by local committees and not by party headquarters, whose role, in theory at any rate, is simply to ensure that all candidates available for selection come up to the required standard. There are complaints from time to time that constituency selection committees do not include sufficient women but there is no evidence of this. In any case it is a moot point whether women on the committee assist the chances of a woman candidate; they have been known to prefer men.

The attitude to the adoption of women candidates varies slightly in the different parties. The Labour Party, which from its inception has always favoured electoral equality, has over the years generally sponsored more women candidates than either of the other parties. But a high proportion of them have had to fight difficult seats and, as the above figures show, they have adopted fewer women for seats already held by their party than the Conservatives have.[6] The great majority of their women M.P.s, including those of the calibre of Mrs Shirley Williams, have made more than one attempt to enter Parliament before winning a seat on an electoral swing. In the past the trade unions have been said to have been conservative (with a small 'c') about nominating women. Today however Labour Party officials deny that there is any appreciable prejudice over the selection of women and Mr R. H. Underhill, Assistant National Agent, explains the smaller numbers recently adopted to fight elections by saying: 'One of the factors may be that the women who might be interested in a candidature find that when in the appropriate age group they have family responsibilities.'[7] He has no record of those willing to stand in 1966 who failed to be adopted.

The Conservative Central Office has since the war let it be known that it regards the small number of women candidates as unsatisfactory and has frequently urged constituencies to include women among their short-listed candidates. Thirty-three Conservative women who were willing to stand failed to be adopted to fight the 1966 General Election.[8] Some Conservative spokesmen have put the blame for the discrimination fairly and squarely on the shoulders of the local committees, particularly those composed of elderly or middle-aged men and women. But the chairman of the party, Mr Edward du Cann M.P., believes that 'It is a misconception to suggest that this is exclusively due to prejudice on the part of constituency selection committees. Society being at the stage of development it is, there are many members of the general public, as distinct from party workers, who hold a prejudice against women politicians for purely traditional reasons.' He agrees that this prejudice is far less manifest among younger people.[9]

In the Liberal Party, with its small number of seats in the House of Commons, the position is rather different and the number of women candidates has fluctuated according to the overall number which the party decides to sponsor at each election. Mr P. C. Chitnis, the General Secretary, while admitting the small number of women among the Liberal candidates in 1966, reports that women on the approved list were adopted in roughly the same proportion as men and that only six were unsuccessful in finding seats whereas twenty were adopted. He deduces from this that there is little prejudice against women in Liberal selection committees.[10] This may well be so, but competition for seats in the Liberal Party is obviously less intense than in the other two parties.

The general picture then is that while the Labour and Liberal party organizations claim that discrimination against women is lessening, the Conservative Party makes no secret that it is still difficult for a woman candidate to be selected for a winnable seat; the Conservative Party moreover continues to lag behind the other parties, as it has done since 1918, in adopting women candidates.

It is beyond the scope or intention of this book to make any detailed statistical comparison between the election results of male and female candidates. Mr J. F. S. Ross in his book *Elections and Electors*, published in 1955, devoted a chapter to 'Women in Parliament' in which by analysis of results in various seats he proved pretty conclusively that to the majority of electors the sex of the candidates is immaterial, concluding that 'on the day of the election it is the party that counts with the overwhelming majority of voters'.[11] This has been borne out more recently by findings of the Gallup Poll. In 1958 and again in 1965 the following question was put to a national cross-section of the adult population aged twenty-one and over: 'If the party of your choice nominated a generally well-qualified person who happened to be a woman, would you vote for her?'

In November 1958, 76 per cent and in September 1965, 78 per cent answered yes.

These findings, while not supporting Mr du Cann's views mentioned above, do correspond with the experience of the candidates themselves: once she is adopted by a constituency party a woman rarely finds any bias against her.[12] Indeed she enjoys a rather unfair advantage over a man in that her supporters are apt to rally to her, admiring her 'courage' and adopting her as 'our Mary' or whatever her name may be; even male opponents often show that inborn courtesy or what Lady Astor, quoting Henry James, called the 'dauntless decency' for which the British are remarkable. A woman candidate attracts a good deal of publicity and is therefore at an advantage in becoming known to her constituents; there are very few places these days which she is barred from entering, and because she is a woman she is much in demand to open bazaars and fêtes of local organizations, which brings her into contact with a wide circle of people. Her only handicap is sometimes said to be that she does not have a wife to share her social duties, but husbands also make useful political consorts as the late Mr Jack Braddock and Mr Denis Thatcher have proved. In conducting a regular 'surgery' or advice service a woman is generally very capable, receiving perhaps more confidences than a man and often more than she really desires. ('Please find a wife for my Willie', wrote a constituent to Jean Mann. 'He's forty and I want to see him settled.'[13]) Women often speak effectively, in language which the electorate understands; they seldom make the pompous kind of political speeches which Peter Sellers has satirized so well. Moreover women are often good listeners and, contrary to popular opinion, listening is quite half a politician's job.

From all the evidence so far collected it therefore seems doubtful whether women fare any differently from men at the polls. The *Gallup Analysis of the Election '66* produced some figures[14] which appear to provide *prima facie* evidence that *Conservative* women did worse, and *Labour* women better, than men but, apart from this being very unlikely, it is inconclusive since it does not take into account many important factors, such as local conditions, which are essential for arriving at any definite verdict. It may be assumed that if prejudice does exist against women as candidates it is not based on any valid reasons and is more in the mind of the party selector, who would perhaps prefer a man to a woman candidate for quite personal and emotional reasons, rather than in that of the elector who is more interested in the party than the sex of the candidate.

The recent fall in the number of new women candidates fighting their first elections in the two main parties indicates however that there are causes other than prejudice for their remaining such a minority. The figures for 1959, 1964 and 1966 reveal the extent of the decline :

WOMEN PARLIAMENTARY CANDIDATES

	CONSERVATIVE		LABOUR	
	TOTAL	NEW	TOTAL	NEW
1959	28	12	36	16
1964	24	4	32	10
1966	21	5	30	7

This fall in the number of new parliamentary candidates, who generally find comparatively little difficulty in being adopted to fight a first unwinnable contest, is taking place at a time when an increasing number of women are participating in local government. Since the war all three parties have made themselves responsible for the candidates' election (but not personal) expenses and the comparatively high levels of remuneration both in Parliament (a member's salary is £3,250) and outside have removed the financial obstacles for many. But there are obstacles of a different kind: young women marry earlier and even if they have co-operative husbands and families, and are prepared to sacrifice their home life, there is still the difficulty of finding and keeping reliable domestic help. Then there is the age factor, as Mr Underhill, the Labour Assistant National Agent, pointed out. Recently constituencies have shown themselves anxious to adopt candidates under forty, the very age when married women have domestic ties. Moreover even when her children are grown up a woman with a husband and a home is less likely to be mobile than a man, and her geographical range in seeking a seat is more limited. These problems are all deterrents but they are not insuperable and do not apply to the single woman. Here an observation by Mr Chitnis, the Liberal General Secretary, is relevant: that 'whereas it is quite natural for a certain type of man to consider standing for Parliament this is not yet true of women.'[15] This does seem to be the heart of the matter: women themselves are not at the present time eager to come forward in increasing numbers, and possibly to many who might make suitable parliamentary candidates the idea never occurs.

In general in Britain there is very little in the upbringing or the schooling of the average girl without a political background to give her the idea of a parliamentary career, for the old suffragette stimulus urging women on to prove themselves in securing political equality has gone. The point has been made. Women can, and do make good members of parliament and ministers of the Crown. They can sit on the High Court Bench, be ejected into space, or, in various parts of the world, become Prime Ministers; it is no longer a matter for surprise. Now that nearly all doors are open to them, as Dame Kathleen Courtney said in a remarkable speech at the Centenary Dinner of the Fawcett Society in May 1966, 'women can be themselves'; they can choose the way of life that suits them best. To many the path to Westminister may be too long and hard and uncertain to be attractive. Until they decide otherwise and come forward in greater numbers it is unlikely that there will be many more women members in the House of Commons.

Notes

Unless otherwise stated all *Hansard* references are to the House of Commons.

PART ONE

CHAPTER I

1. The pamphlet was written by Arthur Charles Gronno and published by the Manchester Branch of the Women's National Antisuffrage League
2. *Hansard* Vol. xciii, 22 May 1917, Col. 2133; 23 May 1917, Col. 2323
3. *The Times*, 13 May 1918
4. *Hansard* Vol. cx, 23 October 1918, Col. 813–22
5. ibid. Col. 833–56
6. *The Times*, 24 October 1918
7. *Hansard* Vol. cx, 4 November 1918, Col. 1867–84
8. ibid. 6 November 1918, Col. 2186–2202
9. ibid. (H. of L.) Vol. xxxii, 15 November 1918, Col. 140–54
10. 23 October 1918
11. To avoid confusion Unionist candidates will be classified as Conservative throughout the book
12. *The Times*, 4 December 1918
13. ibid.
14. Christabel Pankhurst, *Unshackled*, p. 294
15. 14 December 1918
16. *The Star*, 16 October 1918
17. Later Dame Millicent Fawcett
18. Quoted in *The Times*, 12 December 1918
19. *The Prison Letters of Constance Markievicz*, p. 205–6
20. *The Times*, 12 December 1918
21. 4 December 1918
22. 12 December 1918
23. *The Prison Letters of Constance Markievicz*, p. 188
24. 10 December 1918
25. *The Prison Letters of Constance Markievicz*, p. 193
26. 30 December 1918
27. Colin Cross, *The Fascists in Britain*, pp. 180, 193

CHAPTER 2

1. *The Times*, 4 November 1919
2. Maurice Collis, *Nancy Astor*, p. 62
3. ibid. pp. 62–3
4. *The Times*, 4 November 1919
5. ibid.
6. ibid. 15 November 1919
7. ibid. 29 November 1919
8. ibid. The writer seems to have been mistaken. Certain abbesses received writs of summons to Parliament in the thirteenth or fourteenth centuries but it is doubtful that they attended in person
9. Maurice Collis, *Nancy Astor*, pp. 70–1
10. *Hansard* Vol xcvii, 15 August 1917, Col. 1168. It was over these railings that a banner proclaiming 'VOTES FOR WOMEN' had been flung in 1914. After dismantling, one of the grilles was given to the London Museum
11. ibid. Vol. cx, 23 October 1918, Col 857
12. Maurice Collis, *Nancy Astor*, p. 75
13. *The Times*, 2 December 1919
14. Maurice Collis, *Nancy Astor*, p. 72
15. *The Times*, 2 December 1919
16. ibid.
17. B.B.C. TV interview 7 October 1962
18. Vera Brittain, *Lady Into Woman*, p. 50
19. *Hansard* Vol. cxxii, 4 December 1919, Col. 656
20. ibid. Vol. cxxiii, 23 December 1919, Col. 1250
21. ibid. Vol. cxxv, 24 February 1920, Col. 1621
22. ibid. Col. 1623–31
23. Maurice Collis, *Nancy Astor*, p. 82
24. *The Times*, 25 February 1920
25. Thomas Jones, *A Diary with Letters 1931–1950*, p. xxxvii
26. *Hansard*, Vol. cxxvi, 18 March 1920, Col. 2500
27. ibid. Vol. cxxv, 27 February 1920, Col. 2071
28. ibid. Col. 2111–3
29. ibid. Vol. cxxvii, 14 April 1920, Col. 1792–5
30. ibid. Vol. cdix, 28 March 1945, Col. 1390
31. ibid. Vol. cxxix, 19 May 1920, Col. 1566–8
32. ibid. Vol. cxxx, 18 June 1920, Col. 1696–7

CHAPTER 3

1. *Hansard* Vol. cxli, 6 May 1921, Col. 1402–7
2. ibid. Vol. cxxxix, 9 March 1921, Col. 489

3. ibid. Vol. CXL, 22 April 1921, Col 2270 *et seq.*
4. Maurice Collis, *Nancy Astor*, p. 95
5. *The Times*, 24 September 1921
6. 3 November 1921
7. *Hansard* Vol CXLVII, 2 November 1921, Col. 1732
8. Mary D. Stocks, *Eleanor Rathbone*, p. 142
9. *The Daily Telegraph*, 18 May 1922
10. Quoted by the *Manchester Guardian*, 2 December 1944
11. *Hansard* Vol. CXLVIII, 9 November 1921, Col. 466
12. ibid. Vol. CLII, 28 March 1922, Col. 1272
13. ibid. Vol CLV, 14 June 1922, Col. 352
14. ibid. (H. of L.) Vol. XLIX, 2 March 1922, Col. 286 *et seq.*; 30 March 1922, Col. 1012 *et seq.*; Vol. LI, 4 July 1922, Col. 248 *et seq.*

CHAPTER 4
1. Maurice Collis, *Nancy Astor*, p. 99–100
2. ibid. p. 107
3. ibid. p. 108
4. ibid. p. 109–10
5. *Hansard* Vol. CLXI, 9 March 1923, Col. 915
6. ibid. Vol. CLXV, 29 June 1923, Col. 2802
7. *The Daily Telegraph*, 2 July 1923
8. *Hansard* Vol. CLXVI, 13 July 1923, Col. 1759 *et seq.*
9. Maurice Collis, *Nancy Astor*, p. 117
10. *Hansard* Vol. CLXIII, 23 April 1923, Col. 116
11. 8 June 1923
12. 8 June 1923
13. *Hansard* Vol. CLXVIII, 15 November 1923, Col. 544
14. Mr Stanley Baldwin decided to go to the country at the end of 1923 on his protectionist policy
15. 2 July 1923

CHAPTER 5
1. 8 December 1923
2. In fact 84 women had done so
3. Maurice Collis, *Nancy Astor*, p. 119
4. *Political Quarterly*, April/June 1932, (article on Women in Politics)
5. Duchess of Atholl, *Working Partnership*, p. 126–7
6. ibid. p. 134
7. ibid. p. 135–6
8. *Daily Chronicle*, 18 December 1923

9. 8 December 1923
10. Article by Margaret Bondfield in *The Labour Woman*, 15 November 1947
11. Margaret Bondfield, *A Life's Work*, p. 245
12. ibid. p. 250
13. *Hansard* Vol. CLXIX, 16 January 1924, Col. 214
14. ibid. Col. 438
15. ibid. Col. 601
16. Margaret Bondfield, *A Life's Work*, p. 254
17. ibid. p. 255
18. *Hansard* Vol. CLXIX, 18 February 1924, Col. 1289
19. Maurice Collis, *Nancy Astor*, p. 120
20. *Hansard* Vol. CLXX, 29 February 1924, Col. 863 *et seq.*
21. ibid. Vol. CLXXI, 25 March 1924, Col. 1143
22. ibid. 4 April 1924, Col. 2659
23. ibid. Vol. CLXIX, 15 February 1924, Col. 1218
24. ibid. Vol. CLXXV, 2 July 1924, Col. 1376
25. ibid. Vol. CLXIX, 13 February 1924, Col. 898
26. Maurice Collis, *Nancy Astor*, p. 121
27. *Hansard* Vol. CLXX, 4 March 1924, Col. 1258
28. ibid. Vol. CLXXVII, 9 October 1924, Col. 741
29. ibid. Vol. CLXXVI, 30 July 1924, Col. 2050
30. ibid. Vol. CLXX, 27 February 1924, Col. 635
31. *Daily Chronicle*, 31 January 1924
32. ibid. 10 April 1924
33. Duchess of Atholl, *Working Partnership*, p. 139

CHAPTER 6

1. Both Margaret Bondfield and Ellen Wilkinson had visited the Soviet Union, but before they entered Parliament
2. *The Daily Telegraph*, 12 March 1925, reported Mrs Wintringham as saying : 'I personally preferred committee work to Parliamentary work, but I found it very difficult to do conscientious work on a number of committees . . .'
3. 1 November 1924
4. *The Observer*, 9 February 1947
5. Maurice Collis, *Nancy Astor*, p. 132
6. *Hansard* Vol. CLXXIX, 10 December 1924, Col. 242
7. 11 February 1925
8. 15 February 1925
9. *Hansard* Vol. CLXXX, 11 February 1925, Col. 174
10. Widows, Orphans and Old Age Contributory Pensions Bill, second reading, *Hansard*, Vol. CLXXXIV, 18 May 1925, Col. 173 *et seq.*

11. ibid. Vol. CLXXXII, 3 April 1925, Col. 1735
12. ibid. 6 April, Col. 1837
13. ibid. Vol. CXCVI, 10 June 1926, Col. 1798
14. ibid. Col. 1822
15. ibid. Vol. 197, 22 June 1926, Col. 252
16. ibid. Col. 318
17. ibid. Vol. CCIV, 1 April 1927, Col. 1623
18. ibid. Vol. CLXXXIII, 5 May 1925, Col. 815
19. ibid. Vol. CLXXXIX, 8 December 1925, Col. 263
20. ibid. Vol. CLXXXV, 29 June 1925, Col. 2020
21. ibid. Vol. CXCIII, 16 March 1926, Col. 335 (Economy [Miscellaneous Provisions] Bill)
22. ibid. 26 March 1926, Col. 1535
23. ibid. Vol. CXCVII, 28 June 1926, Col. 1022
24. See *Hansard*, Index for 1926, (Vol. CCI) under her name
25. *Hansard* Vol. CCXXIII, 27 November 1928, Col. 287
26. 29 November 1928
27. *Hansard* Vol. CCXXVI, 12 March 1929, Col. 989
28. ibid. Vol. CCXXII, 15 November 1928, Col. 1230
29. ibid. Vol. CCXXV, 27 February 1929, Col. 2039–40
30. ibid. Vol. CCXXVI, 6 March 1929, Col. 386
31. 21 November 1927
32. *Hansard* Vol. CCXI, 15 December 1927, Col. 2567
33. 8 May 1930
34. *Hansard* Vol. CCXVIII, 13 June 1928, Col. 1104 *et seq.*
35. ibid. Vol. CLXXXIX, 17 December 1925, Col. 1802
36. Duchess of Atholl, *Working Partnership*, p. 158
37. *Hansard* Vol. CLXXX, 20 February 1925, Col. 1503 *et seq.*
38. Arthur H. Booth, *British Hustings 1924–1950*, p. 76–7
39. *Hansard* Vol. CCXI, 1 December 1927, Col. 677–8
40. ibid. Vol. CCXV, 29 March 1928, Col. 1359–1482
41. ibid. Vol. CCXXIII, 4 December 1928, Col. 1029
42. ibid. 11 December 1928, Col. 1919
43. 13 December 1928
44. *Hansard* Vol. CCXXII, 13 November 1928, Col. 692–4
45. ibid. Vol. CCXXIV, 4 February 1929, Col. 1409; *Manchester Guardian*, 5 February 1929
46. *Hansard* Vol. CCXVII, 15 May 1928, Col. 913
47. ibid. Vol. CCXXVI, 13 March 1929, Col. 1166
48. 14 March 1929
49. Hugh Dalton, *Call Back Yesterday*, p. 210
50. 23 March 1929
51. *The Daily Telegraph*, 25 February 1929
52. *Manchester Guardian*, 23 March 1929

53.　*Hansard* Vol. ccxxvii, 25 April 1929, Col. 1114
54.　*Daily Telegraph*, 20 November 1928
55.　*Evening Standard*, 20 November 1928

PART TWO

CHAPTER I

1.　23 October 1928
2.　*The Observer*, 25 November 1928
3.　*Manchester Guardian*, 14 July 1927
4.　*The Daily Telegraph*, 15 February 1929
5.　*Manchester Guardian*, 20 March 1928
6.　6 November 1927
7.　30 April 1929
8.　*Hansard* Vol. ccxviii, 21 June 1928, Col. 1735
9.　6 September 1930
10.　*Manchester Guardian*, 4 June 1929
11.　Hugh Dalton, *Call Back Yesterday*, p. 215
12.　Margaret Bondfield, *A Life's Work*, p. 278
13.　ibid. p. 277
14.　ibid. p. 278
15.　ibid. p. 279
16.　ibid. p. 279
17.　A copy of this document is in the possession of the Fawcett Library
18.　12 June 1929
19.　Mary Agnes Hamilton, *Remembering My Good Friends*, p. 180
20.　Arthur H. Booth, *British Hustings 1924–1950*, p. 90
21.　*Hansard* Vol. ccxxxi, 6 November 1929, Col. 1103
22.　Mary Agnes Hamilton, *Up-Hill All the Way*, p. 46
23.　*Hansard* Vol. ccxxxii, 27 November 1929, Col. 1424
24.　ibid. 4 December 1929, Col. 2467
25.　*Manchester Guardian*, 3 March 1930
26.　Hugh Dalton, *Call Back Yesterday*, p. 240
27.　Edith Picton-Turbervill, *Life is Good*, p. 188
28.　ibid. pp. 197, 181, 244, 269
29.　ibid. p. 186
30.　ibid. p. 186–8
31.　*The Daily Telegraph*, 27 November 1929
32.　6 December 1929
33.　*Hansard* Vol. ccxxix, 9 July 1929, Col. 767
34.　ibid. Vol. ccxxxii, 29 November 1929, Col. 1816

35. Mary D. Stocks, *Eleanor Rathbone*, p. 129
36. ibid. p. 48
37. *The Spectator*, 11 January 1946
38. *Hansard* Vol. ccxxx, 22 July 1929, Col. 972
39. Mary D. Stocks, *Eleanor Rathbone*, p. 146

CHAPTER 2

1. *Hansard* Vol. ccxxxii, 21 November 1929, Col. 737
2. ibid. 3 December 1929, Col. 2249
3. ibid. Vol. ccxxxvii, 28 March 1930, Col. 783
4. ibid. Vol. ccxl, 18 June 1930, Col. 487
5. ibid. Vol. 234, 5 February 1930, Col. 1923
6. Margaret Bondfield, *A Life's Work*, p. 300
7. *Hansard* Vol. ccxli, 18 July 1930, Col. 1627; Vol. ccxlv, 1 December 1930, Col. 1827; Vol. ccxlviii, 16 February 1931, Col. 901
8. Article by Ian Mackay, *News Chronicle*, 25 October 1947
9. Edith Picton-Turbervill, *Life is Good*, p. 216
10. *Hansard* Vol. ccxxxi, 31 October 1929, Col. 462–70
11. ibid. Vol. ccxxxiv, 31 January 1930, Col. 1451
12. ibid. Vol. ccxxxi, 12 November 1929, Col. 1733
13. ibid. Vol. ccxxxiii, 11 December 1929, Col. 599
14. Duchess of Atholl, *Working Partnership*, p. 177–8
15. *Hansard* Vol. ccxlvii, 3 February 1931, Col. 1715
16. ibid. Vol. ccxlviii, 20 February 1931, Col. 1641
17. ibid. Vol. ccxlv, 2 December 1930, Col. 1989
18. ibid. 19 November 1930, Col. 551
19. 19 November 1930
20. *Hansard* Vol. ccxlvii, 4 February 1931, Col. 1815
21. Edith Picton-Turbervill, *Life is Good*, p. 209
22. *Hansard* Vol. ccxlv, 28 November 1930, Col. 1675
23. *Manchester Guardian*, 21 February 1931
24. 16 August 1931
25. Maurice Collis, *Nancy Astor*, p. 173
26. Letter dated 3 March 1931 quoted by *The Times*, 5 March 1931
27. Mary Agnes Hamilton, *Up-Hill All the Way*, p. 54
28. *Hansard* Vol. ccxliv, 31 October 1930, Col. 415
29. Unemployment Insurance (No. 4) Bill, ibid., Vol. ccliv, 26 June 1931, Col. 773
30. Unemployment Insurance (No. 3) Bill, ibid., 8 July 1931, Col. 2101
31. Margaret Bondfield, *A Life's Work*, p. 302

32. *Review of Reviews,* November 1931
33. *Hansard* Vol. CCLV, 21 July 1931, Col. 1275
34. Edith Picton-Turbervill, *Life is Good,* p. 257–8
35. *Hansard* Vol. CCLVI, 23 September 1931, Col. 1757
36. Mary Agnes Hamilton, *Remembering My Good Friends,* p. 247
37. *Daily Herald,* 7 February 1931
38. *Lord Morrison of Lambeth: An Autobiography,* p. 125–6
39. Harold Nicolson in *Diaries and Letters 1930–39,* p. 98, records on 11 December 1931 : '. . . Cimmie [Cynthia] wants to put a notice in *The Times* to the effect that she dissociates herself from Tom's fascist tendencies . . .'
40. *Hansard* Vol. CCXXXVII, 7 April 1930, Col. 1843
41. 22 March 1930
42. 2 May 1931
43. *Daily Herald,* 11 May 1931

CHAPTER 3

1. *Political Quarterly,* April/June 1932
2. ibid.
3. *The Daily Telegraph,* 3 November 1931; 16 June 1934
4. *Hansard* Vol. CCLIX, 10 November 1931, Col. 70
5. ibid. Col. 81
6. ibid. 16 November 1931, Col. 615
7. ibid. Col. 592
8. ibid. Vol. CCLXV, 4 May 1932, Col. 1204
9. ibid. 5 May 1932, Col. 1387
10. ibid. Vol. CCLIX, 18 November 1931, Col. 950
11. ibid. Vol. CCLX, 23 November 1931, Col. 72
12. ibid. Vol. CCLXVI, 30 May 1932, Col. 923
13. ibid. Vol CCLXV, 3 May 1932, Col. 1019
14. ibid. Vol. CCLXVIII, 11 July 1932, Col. 994
15. ibid. Vol. CCLXIV, 13 April 1932, Col. 883
16. ibid. Vol. CCLXVIII, 12 July 1932, Col. 1190
17. ibid. Vol. CCLXI, 12 February 1932, Col. 1167 *et seq.*
18. ibid. Vol. CCLXV, 11 May 1932, Col. 1972
19. ibid. Vol. CCXC, 7 June 1934, Col. 1202 *et seq.*
20. ibid. Vol. CCLXXVI, 28 March 1933, Col. 940
21. Duchess of Atholl, *Working Partnership,* p. 194
22. *Hansard* Vol. CCXCVIII, 11 February 1935, Col. 1688
23. ibid. Vol. CCCII, 4 June 1935, Col. 1810
24. ibid. Vol. CCLXXIV, 22 February 1933, Col. 1718
25. ibid. Vol CCLXXVI, 13 April 1933, Col. 2762
26. ibid. Vol. CCLXXX, 5 July 1933, Col. 394

27. ibid. Vol. cccLII, 12 October 1939, Col. 633
28. ibid. Vol. cccI, 2 May 1935, Col. 638
29. ibid. Vol. cccv, 24 October 1935, Col. 387
30. ibid. Vol. ccLXXXVI, 8 March 1934, Col. 2129
31. ibid. Vol. ccLXXXVIII, 10 April 1934, Col. 245
32. ibid. Vol. ccLXXII, 2 December 1932, Col. 1191
33. ibid. Vol. ccLXXXVII, 23 March 1934, Col. 1562
34. 25 June 1932
35. 29 July 1933
36. 29 October 1932
37. Quoted by *The Daily Telegraph*, 16 June 1934. This parliamentary record ceased publication during the Second World War
38. *The Daily Telegraph*, 9 November 1932
39. ibid. 16 June 1934
40. *Hansard* Vol. cccIV, 23 July 1935, Col. 1633

CHAPTER 4

1. 22 January 1935
2. *The Times*, 29 November 1935
3. *Manchester Guardian*, 17 June 1936
4. 16 November 1935
5. *The Daily Telegraph*, 1 November 1935
6. Note by William Rees-Mogg concerning the 1935 election in the correspondence columns of *The Sunday Times*, 10 April 1966; letter by him to the author of 13 April 1966 recalling his memories of Mrs Tate's stand on rearmament
7. Thomas Jones, *A Diary with Letters 1931–50*, p. 293–4
8. ibid. p. 295–6
9. 30 October 1936
10. *Hansard* Vol. cccxVII, 3 November 1936, Col. 14
11. Thomas Jones, *A Diary with Letters 1931–50*, p. 330
12. Duchess of Atholl, *Working Partnership*, p. 203
13. *Hansard* Vol. cccxVII, 5 November 1936, Col. 337
14. Duchess of Atholl, *Working Partnership*, p. 207
15. C. R. Attlee, *As It Happened*, p. 94
16. Hugh Dalton, *The Fateful Years*, p. 108
17. ibid. p. 210–3
18. Mary D. Stocks, *Eleanor Rathbone*, p. 244
19. Thomas Jones, *A Diary with Letters 1931–50*, p. 350
20. *Hansard* Vol. cccvII, 4 December 1935, Col. 194
21. *Hansard* Vol. cccxxxVII, 27 June 1938, Col. 1540. Lady Astor was upsetting some of her party colleagues too. For a revealing

K

incident see Harold Nicolson, *Diaries and Letters 1930–39*, p. 326–7

22. Thomas Jones, *A Diary with Letters 1931–50*, p. 359
23. Gollancz, 1938
24. *Hansard* Vol. cccxxvi, 19 July 1937, Col. 1901
25. ibid. Vol. cccxxviii, 1 November 1937, Col. 654
26. *The Times*, 29 April 1938
27. *Hansard* Vol. cccxxxix, 5 October 1938, Col. 360
28. ibid. 6 October 1938, Col. 520
29. Mary D. Stocks, *Eleanor Rathbone*, p. 235
30. ibid. p. 251
31. Duchess of Atholl, *Working Partnership*, p. 229
32. *Hansard* Vol. cccx, 30 March 1936, Col. 1713
33. ibid. Vol. cccxxxvi, 1 June 1938, Col. 2115
34. ibid. Vol. cccxlv, 5 April 1939, Col. 2816
35. ibid. Vol. cccx, 1 April 1936, Col. 2017
36. ibid. 6 April 1936, Col. 2477
37. ibid. Vol. cccxxii, 8 April 1937, Col. 385 *et seq.*
38. ibid. Vol. cccxvii, 11 November 1936, Col. 998
39. ibid. 4 November 1936, Col. 75
40. ibid. Vol. cccxxxv, 6 May 1938, Col. 1208 *et seq.*
41. Hugh Dalton, *The Fateful Years*, p. 222–5
42. Inheritance (Family Provision) Bill; *Hansard* Vol. cccxxxviii, 13 July 1938, Col. 1388
43. ibid. Vol. cccxxix, 1 December 1937, Col. 2082
44. Marriage Bill; ibid. Vol. cccxvii, 20 November 1936, Col. 2107 *et seq.*
45. *Daily Herald*, 30 October 1941
46. *Hansard* Vol. cccxxvi, 13 July 1937, Col. 1119
47. ibid. Vol. cccxlii, 16 December 1938, Col. 2355
48. ibid. Vol. cccxxix, 29 November 1937, Col. 1746
49. ibid. Vol. cccxxxviii, 12 November 1937, Col. 2052
50. ibid. Vol. cccxxxv, 28 April 1938, Col. 360
51. ibid. Vol. cccxxxvii, 16 June 1938, Col. 393
52. ibid. Vol. ccclii, 29 September 1939, Col. 1642
53. ibid. Vol. cccl, 4 August 1939, Col. 2892
54. ibid. Vol. ccclii, 24 August 1939, Col. 35

CHAPTER 5

1. *Hansard* Vol. ccclii, 12 October 1939, Col. 629
2. ibid. Col. 632
3. Thomas Jones in *A Diary with Letters 1931–50*, p. 457 gives an

account of a luncheon party at Lady Astor's London house at which Lloyd George was 'produced for inspection and to be tested for his fitness to return to the helm of the ship of state.' He seems to have passed the test to everyone's satisfaction

4. 9 February 1947. Other accounts have it that it was Mr Attlee who first proposed to the Parliamentary Labour Party that the Opposition should force a division
5. *Hansard* Vol. CCCLXXXV, 25 November 1942, Col. 756
6. Hugh Dalton, *The Fateful Years*, p. 320
7. 27 May 1940
8. *The Daily Telegraph*, 11 October 1940
9. *Hansard* Vol. CCCLXXII, 10 June 1941, Col. 79
10. ibid. Vol. CCCLXXXVII, 23 March 1943, Col. 1513
11. ibid. Vol. CCCLXX, 20 March 1941, Col. 375
12. ibid. Col. 315/400
13. ibid. Vol. CCCLXXVI, 2–4 December 1941, Col. 1034–95, 1153–1216, 1285–1354
14. ibid. 2 December 1941, Col. 1095–6
15. ibid. Vol. CCCLXXVIII, 5 March 1942, Col. 817–900
16. ibid. Vol. CCCLXXVII, 3 February 1942, Col. 1042
17. ibid. Vol. CCCLXXVIII, 24 February 1942, Col. 18
18. ibid. Vol. CCCLII, 24 October 1939, Col. 1253
19. ibid. Vol. CCCLXXIX, 30 April 1942, Col. 1057
20. ibid. Vol. CCCLXXXV, 25 November 1942, Col. 750 *et seq.*
21. ibid. Vol. CCCLXXXVIII, 7 April 1943, Col. 624
22. ibid. Vol. CCCXCVI, 18 January 1944, Col. 31
23. ibid. Vol. CCCLXXI, 7 May 1941, Col. 838
24. ibid. Vol. CCCLXXXVII, 3 March 1943, Col. 556; Vol. CCCLXXXVIII, 20 April 1943, Col. 1532–3
25. ibid. Vol. CCCXCVIII, 28 March 1944, Col. 1356
26. ibid. 30 March 1944, Col. 1588–9
27. 5 April 1944; 19 June 1944
28. *Hansard* Vol. CDVIII, 8 March 1945, Col. 2275 *et seq.*
29. For a moving account of the effect of her visit on the inmates of the camp see a letter by H. Redlich in *The Times*, 14 October 1946
30. *Hansard* Vol. CCCLXXXIX, 19 May 1943, Col. 1156
31. ibid. Vol. CCCLXXXVII, 23 March 1943, Col. 1598
32. *Manchester Guardian*, 4 January 1946
33. Hugh Dalton, *The Fateful Years*, p. 459–60
34. *The Times*, 2 December 1944
35. ibid. 15 December 1944
36. *News Chronicle*, 15 June 1945
37. *The Observer*, 3 May 1964

PART THREE

CHAPTER I

1. Letter quoted by the *Manchester Guardian*, 5 July 1945
2. 22 April 1945
3. *The Braddocks*, p. 88–9
4. 27 July 1945
5. C. R. Attlee, *As It Happened*, p. 153
6. *Hansard* Vol. CDXV, 16 November 1945, Col. 2616
7. ibid. Vol. CDXIV, 10 October 1945, Col. 292
8. *Manchester Guardian*, 15 February 1946
9. 5 July 1960
10. Jean Mann, *Woman in Parliament*, p. 36
11. *New York Times*, 10 July 1946
12. *Hansard* Vol. CDXIV, 17 October 1945, Col. 1255
13. ibid. Vol. CDXV, 2 November 1945, Col. 876
14. 4 January 1946
15. Obituary notice by Miss Helen Darbishire, *The Times*, 31 January 1946
16. Mary D. Stocks, *Eleanor Rathbone*, p. 185
17. Jean Mann, *Woman in Parliament*, p. 13
18. *The Daily Telegraph*, 1 March 1946
19. ibid.
20. *Manchester Guardian*, 6 July 1949
21. *Hansard* Vol. CDXLV, 12 December 1947, Col. 1418 *et seq.*
22. ibid. 16 December 1947, Col. 1638
23. ibid. Vol. CDXXXIII, 25 February 1947, Col. 2018 *et seq.*
24. Speech in London, 6 October 1949
25. *The Times*, 22 January 1949
26. *Hansard* Vol. CDLVII, 10 November 1948, Col. 1552
27. ibid. Vol. CDLXI, 21 February 1949, Col. 1604
28. ibid. Vol. CDXLVII, 26 February 1948, Col. 2101
29. *The Braddocks*, p. 145–6
30. *Hansard* Vol. CDXXXIX, 26 June 1947, Col. 768
31. ibid. Col. 773
32. ibid. Vol. CDXLI, 6 August 1947, Col. 1582
33. ibid. Vol. CDXXXIII, 26 February 1947, Col. 2146
34. *Manchester Guardian*, 7 February 1947
35. *New York Times*, 7 February 1947
36. Education Bill, second reading, *Hansard* Vol. CDXVIII, 1 February 1946, Col. 1256
37. *The Times*, 29 October 1945; *Hansard* Vol. CDXV, 31 October 1945, Col. 553–8

38. Quoted by the *Manchester Guardian*, 8 October 1945
39. Quoted by the *Daily Herald*, 21 January 1931
40. *The Times*, 4 December 1946
41. *The Daily Telegraph*, 21 May 1947
42. *Hansard* Vol. CDXXXIV, 11 March 1947, Col. 1193
43. ibid. Vol. CDLI, 31 May 1948, Col. 698
44. ibid. Vol. CDXXXIII, 21 October 1947, Col. 12
45. ibid. Vol. CDLIX, 17 December 1948, Col. 1555
46. *The Braddocks*, p. 210–2
47. *Hansard* Vol. CDLIV, 19 July 1948, Col. 189
48. ibid. Vol. CDLXX, 12 December 1949, Col. 2441
49. ibid. Vol. CDXXX, 18 November 1946, Col. 526
50. ibid. Vol. CDXLVIII, 22 March 1948, Col. 2662
51. ibid. Vol. CDXXX, 18 November 1946, Col. 595
52. She gained the title on her father's ennoblement in 1945
53. National Service Bill, *Hansard* Vol. CDLVIII, 1 December 1948, Col. 2126
54. *Manchester Guardian*, 12 November 1948
55. *Hansard* Vol. CDLXVI, 28 June 1949, Col. 988
56. ibid. Vol. CDXXXIII, 19 February 1947, Col. 1248

CHAPTER 2

1. *Hansard* Vol. CDLXX, 15 December 1949, Col. 2983
2. *The Socialist Case* (1946 edition), p. 258
3. 30 June 1947
4. *Daily Herald*, 29 November 1947; *The Daily Telegraph*, 5 February 1948
5. Quoted by the *Manchester Guardian*, 17 February 1950
6. *Hansard* Vol. CDLXXIV, 1 May 1950, Col. 1437
7. ibid. Vol. CDLXXII, 6 March 1950, Col. 45
8. *Lanarkshire Clarion*
9. *Hansard* Vol. CDLXXXV, 9 March 1951, Col. 926
10. ibid. Vol. CDLXXXIII, 26 January 1951, Col. 487
11. ibid. Vol. CDLXXXII, 13 December 1950, Col. 1175
12. ibid. Vol. CDLXXX, 2 November 1950, Col. 379
13. ibid. Vol. CDLXXVI, 19 June 1950, Col. 850
14. 27 November 1950
15. 14 December 1949
16. As reported in *The Times*, 7 February 1950

CHAPTER 3

1. Hugh Dalton, *High Tide and After*, p. 374
2. 7 March 1952

3. *The Times*, 15 March 1952
4. *Hansard* Vol. CDXCIV, 29 November 1951, Col. 1842, 1847 *et seq.*
5. *Manchester Guardian*, 1 December 1951
6. *Hansard* Vol. CDXCIX, 24 April 1952, Col. 880
7. *Manchester Guardian*, 28 June 1952; see also *Hansard* Vol. DXXXI, 26 July 1954, Col. 144 *et seq.*
8. *The Times*, 18 October 1954; *Manchester Guardian*, 19 October 1954 and 22 October 1954, which quotes an open letter to Miss Horsbrugh's successor in *The Schoolmaster and Woman Teacher's Chronicle* as saying that in spite of difficulties there had been no personal antagonism between Florence Horsbrugh and the N.U.T. (National Union of Teachers), 'indeed we have good cause to recognise her courage, her pertinacity and fighting qualities . . .'
9. *Hansard* Vol. DIII, 2 July 1952, Col. 509 *passim*; 11 July 1952, Col. 1776
10. Housing Repairs and Rents Bill, second reading, *Hansard* Vol. DXXI, 30 November 1953, Col. 789
11. *The Braddocks*, p. 109
12. *Hansard* Vol. DII, 27 June 1952, Col. 2788
13. ibid. Vol. DXXVIII, 1 June 1954, Col. 1078
14. ibid. Vol. D, 16 May 1952, Col. 1765–857
15. ibid. Vol. DXI, 19 February 1953, Col. 1438, Vol. DXVIII, 21 July 1953, Col. 194 (*inter alia*)
16. ibid. Vol. DXXVIII, 25 May 1954, Col. 204
17. Second readings : ibid. Vol. CDXCIX, 25 April 1952, Col. 899; Vol. DXV, 8 May 1953, Col. 807
18. ibid. Vol. CDXCVI, 20 February 1952, Col. 237
19. ibid. Vol. DXXIII, 12 February 1954, Col. 1513
20. ibid. Vol. DXXI, 4 December 1953, Col. 1484
21. ibid. 2 December 1953, Col. 1164
22. ibid. Vol. DVII, 19 November 1952, Col. 1873
23. ibid. Vol. DIX, 8 December 1952, Col. 202; Vol. DXIII, 23 March 1953, Col. 602; Vol. DXVI, 26 June 1953, Col. 2273 *et seq.*
24. ibid. Vol. CDXCVIII, 26 March 1952, Col. 726 *et seq.*
25. *Hansard* Vol. DXXVII, 18 May 1954, Col. 1957
26. ibid. 20 May 1954, Col. 2311 *et seq.*
27. ibid. Vol. DXXV, 31 March 1954, Col. 206
28. ibid. Vol. DXIV, 27 April 1953, Col. 1760
29. *The Daily Telegraph*, 12 June 1953
30. *Hansard* Vol. DXX, 3 November 1953, Col. 10
31. ibid. Vol. DXXIV, 25 February 1954, Col. 605
32. ibid. Vol. CDXCVII, 5 March 1952, Col. 559
33. *The Times*, 17 December 1954

34. ibid. 22 November 1954
35. As reported in *The Daily Telegraph*, 7 September 1953
36. *The Times*, 16 December 1954
37. *Hansard* Vol. DXXXVIII, 22 March 1955, Col. 1881

CHAPTER 4

1. *Notes on Procedure*, p. 8
2. Quoted by *The Times House of Commons, 1955*, p. 19
3. *Hansard* Vol. DXLVI, 23 November 1955, Col. 1467
4. ibid. Col. 1480
5. ibid. Col. 1527
6. ibid. Vol. DLI, 18 April 1956, Col. 1101
7. ibid. Vol. DLVIII, 31 October 1956, Col. 1480
8. *The Times*, 18 January 1957
9. *The Star*, 28 January 1957
10. *Hansard* Vol. DLXIII, 28 January 1957, Col. 656
11. *The Daily Telegraph*, 4 December 1956
12. *Hansard* Vol. DLXXII, 25 June 1957, Col. 75
13. *The Times*, 23 September 1958
14. *Hansard* Vol. DXLVII, 14 December 1955, Col. 1175
15. ibid. 21 December 1955, Col. 2035
16. ibid. Vol. DCX, 27 July 1959, Col. 219
17. 16 November 1958
18. *The Times*, 1 October 1956
19. *The Daily Telegraph*, 16 February 1959
20. 'Peterborough' in *The Daily Telegraph*, 19 January 1957
21. Death Penalty (Abolition) Bill, second reading, *Hansard* Vol. DL, 12 March 1956, Col. 822
22. ibid. Vol. DXC, 27 June 1958, Col. 36 *et seq.*
23. First reading, ibid. Vol. DLXXVIII, 20 November 1957, Col. 399
24. Second reading, ibid. Vol. DXCIX, 29 January 1959, Col. 1267
25. Jean Mann, *Woman in Parliament*, p. 77–9
26. *The Braddocks*, p. 98–101; *Hansard* Vol. DLIII, 31 May 1956, Col. 427; Vol. DLIV, 14 June 1956, Col. 746
27. ibid. Vol. DLXVI, 13 March 1957, Col. 1202
28. *The Times*, 12 February 1957; 22 March 1958
29. *Hansard* Vol. DLXV, 1 March 1957, Col. 1543
30. Second reading, ibid. Vol. DLXXIX, 12 December 1957, Col. 1563
31. ibid. Vol. DCVII, 18 June 1959, Col. 632–3
32. ibid. Vol. DXCVII, 18 December 1958, Col. 1320
33. 19 December 1958
34. Mental Health Bill, second reading, *Hansard* Vol. DXCVIII, 26 January 1959, Col. 726

35. ibid. Vol. DCI, 12 March 1959, Col. 1469–82 *et seq.* primly gives this as 'Do not be an ass, Edith !' but the exclamation as reported in *The Times* sounds more natural
36. ibid. Vol. DLVIII, 24 October 1956, Col. 647
37. ibid. Vol. DXLIII, 30 June 1955, Col. 503
38. ibid. Vol. DXCVII, 11 December 1958, Col. 121
39. *The Times*, 27 November 1958
40. *Hansard* Vol. DLXXVII, 5 November 1957, Col. 8
41. ibid. Vol. DLXXXII, 13 February 1958, Col. 610
42. ibid. Vol. DLXXXV, 25 March 1958, Col. 350
43. ibid. Col. 373–6

CHAPTER 5

1. *Hansard* (H. of L.) Vol. LVIII, 17 July 1924, Col. 696 *et seq.*
2. ibid. (H. of L.) Vol. LXI, 21 May 1925, Col. 428
3. ibid. (H. of L.) Vol. LXIV, 24 June 1926, Col. 568
4. *The Times*, 25 February 1927
5. *Hansard* (H. of L.) Vol. LXVI, 12 April 1927, Col. 916
6. 14 July 1927
7. *Hansard* Vol. CCXI, 5 December 1927, Col. 981
8. ibid. (H. of L.) Vol. LXXII, 5 February 1929, Col. 848
9. ibid. (H. of L.) Vol. LXXVIII, 16 July 1930, Col. 498
10. 4 July 1930
11. *Hansard* (H. of L.) Vol. CXXXIX, 4 March 1946, Col. 1019
12. ibid. (H. of L.) Col. 1036
13. 7 November 1947
14. *The Times*, 10 November 1947. Mr Quintin Hogg was an interested party since he had to leave the Commons on succeeding his father as the second Lord Hailsham. In 1963 he renounced his peerage and re-entered the House of Commons as the member for St Marylebone
15. *Hansard* (H. of L.) Vol. CLXIV, 27 July 1949, Col. 581
16. 7 December 1949
17. Second reading ibid. (H. of L.) Vol. CLXXX, 3 February 1953, Col. 133
18. 5 February 1953
19. 22 March 1957
20. *Hansard* (H. of L.) Vol. CCV, 30 October 1957, Col. 581 *et seq.*; 31 October 1957, Col. 683 *et seq.*
21. ibid. (H. of L.) Vol. CCVI, 3 December 1957, Col. 609
22. Quoted by Jean Mann, *Woman in Parliament*, p. 52
23. *The Daily Telegraph*, 14 October 1958
24. *Hansard* (H. of L.) Vol. CCXII, 4 November 1958, Col. 160

25. In 1957 Miss Vivien Leigh, the actress, made a protest about the demolition of the St James's Theatre and was escorted from the Chamber by Black Rod. There were some earlier interruptions too. Lady Mary Wortley Montagu describes in a letter of 1738 how 'a tribe of dames' led by the Duchess of Queensberry and the Duchess of Ancaster invaded the Lords during a closed session and made a great disturbance which was 'the reason why poor Lord Hervey spoke so miserably'

26. 27 September 1937

27. Correspondence in *The Times* by Mr W. M. Lodge, 2 October 1937, and Miss Chrystal Macmillan, 10 November 1958

28. *Calling All Women*, July 1960

29. *The Daily Telegraph*, 20 November 1958.

30. *Hansard* (H. of L.) Vol. ccxiii, 21 January 1959, Col. 612

CHAPTER 6

1. 29 October 1959

2. *Hansard* Vol. dcxiii, 13 November 1959, Col. 751

3. Article by Norman Shrapnel, *Guardian*, 16 November 1959

4. In an article in *Punch*, 9 May 1962, she wrote, 'Why are other doors barred to us? Why are finance committees so often the preserve of the male? . . . Why when women are the largest consumer spenders can't we have a woman Under-Secretary at the Board of Trade? . . .'

5. 1 September 1961

6. *Hansard* Vol. dcxvi, 5 February 1960, Col. 1350

7. 'Peterborough' in *The Daily Telegraph*, 6 February 1960

8. *The Times*, 4 December 1962; *Guardian*, 4 December 1962

9. *Guardian*, 4 March 1963

10. *Hansard* Vol. dclxxx, 5 July 1963, Col. 773 *et seq.*

11. Second reading, ibid. Vol. dcxc, 28 February 1964, Col. 821

12. Second reading, ibid. Vol. dclxxxviii, 5 February 1964, Col. 1291

13. ibid. Vol. dcxcv, 15 May 1964, Col. 815

14. Jean Mann, *Woman in Parliament*, p. 182

15. *Hansard* Vol. dcxxxii, 16 December 1960, Col. 839–40

16. 10 February 1961

17. *Hansard* (H. of L.) Vol. ccxxviii, 13 February 1961, Col. 628

18. 5 May 1964

19. *Hansard* Vol. dcxvi, 2 February 1960, Col. 816–7

20. ibid. Vol. dcxxx, 23 November 1960, Col. 1121

21. *Guardian*, 24 November 1960

K*

22. *Hansard* Vol. DCXXXVIII, 20 April 1961, Col. 1522
23. ibid. Vol. DCXLIX, 21 November 1961, Col. 1284
24. ibid. Vol. DCLIX, 7 May 1962, Col. 144–5
25. ibid. Col. 31
26. ibid. Vol. DCLXII, 4 July 1962, Col. 590 *et seq.*
27. ibid. Vol. DCXXXI, 1 December 1960, Col. 595
28. ibid. Vol. DCLX, 1 June 1962, Col. 1826
29. ibid. Vol. DCXLII, 13 June 1961, Col. 324
30. ibid. Vol. DCLXXXIV, 12 November 1963, Col. 13
31. ibid. Vol. DCXXV, 29 June 1960, Col. 1509–14
32. ibid. Vol. DCXXXVIII, 11 April 1961, Col. 145–6
33. ibid. Vol. DCLXXIX, 20 June 1963, Col. 661
34. ibid. Vol. DCXLIV, 19 July 1961, Col. 1256
35. ibid. Vol. DCLXXV, 2 April 1963, Col. 251
36. ibid. 5 April 1963, Col. 826–874
37. ibid. Vol. DCXCV, 13 May 1964, Col. 426
38. Women members now had the room on the terrace and two other small rooms. In the rebuilt House of Commons, occupied in 1960, there is no Ladies' Gallery as such
39. *Hansard* Vol. DCXL, 18 May 1961, Col. 1642
40. ibid. Vol. DCXLV, 2 August 1961, Col. 1545
41. ibid. Vol. DCLXIX, 13 December 1962, Col. 684
42. Jean Mann, *Woman in Parliament*, p. 34–5
43. *Hansard* Vol. DCL, 6 December 1961, Col. 1391
44. ibid. Vol. DCLIX, 8 May 1962, Col. 216–8
45. *The Daily Telegraph*, 8 October 1964
46. 9 May 1961
47. *Hansard* (H. of L.) Vol. CCXLIV, 30 October 1962, Col. 6
48. ibid. (H. of L.) Vol. CCXL, 10 May 1962, Col. 347–408
49. Second reading, ibid. (H. of L.) Vol. CCLIII, 26 November 1963, Col. 633 *et seq.*
50. ibid. (H. of L.) Vol. CCXXXVII, 8 March 1962, Col. 1219
51. ibid. (H. of L.) Vol. CCLIX, 29 June 1964, Col. 445
52. ibid. (H. of L.) Vol. CCXLVIII, 8 April 1963, Col. 827; Vol. CCLIII, 10 December 1963, Col. 1163–76
53. ibid. Vol. DCLXXIX, 27 June 1963, Col. 1678
54. ibid. Vol. DCLXXIV, 28 March 1963, Col. 158
55. Lady Rhondda had died in 1958. For hereditary peeresses who have subsequently taken their seats see Appendix B(ii)
56. *Hansard* (H. of L.) Vol. CCLXVII, 7 July 1965, Col. 1355–7
57. *The Daily Telegraph*, 8 October 1964
58. 28 May 1962
59. *Hansard* Vol. DCXXI, 11 April 1960, Col. 890; 12 April 1960 Col. 1087

CHAPTER 7

1. Selwyn Lloyd Report on the Party Organization, 1963, para. 10 which, dealing with the work of the Conservative Standing Advisory Committee on candidates, reads, 'I also hope that they will ensure that to a greater extent than up to now among those attending for final interview one of the women applicants and one of the Trade Unionist applicants are included.' This recommendation is also embodied in the summary of recommended points on p. 34

2. 26 April 1964

3. *The Daily Telegraph*, 9 October 1964

4. *Evening Standard*, 17 February 1966

5. *Hansard* (H. of L.) Vol. CCLXXI, 20 December 1965, Col. 878

6. She was not to hold it for long since in January 1967 she was appointed Minister of State for Welsh Affairs

7. In February 1967 she was promoted to Minister of State, Department of Education and Science, though she declined to draw her increase in salary. In June 1966 she was made a Privy Councillor

8. She was further promoted in January 1967 when she became a Minister of State, Department of Education and Science

9. In the House of Lords Government Whips have junior ministerial responsibilities and speak from the front bench for various departments

10. *The Sun*, 22 October 1964

11. *Hansard* Vol. DCCXXVII, 5 May 1966, Col. 1890

CHAPTER 8

1. *Our Freedom and Its Results*, p. 34

2. This view still seems to be held by some politicians. In an interview with Kenneth Harris, reported in *The Observer* Colour Supplement of 16 January 1966, Mr Edward Heath, Leader of the Opposition, when asked whether he would 'like to see more women in politics?' replied, 'Yes, I would, in the House of Commons and outside it at all levels, *so long as they are providing what women can, and not just duplicating what men can do*, which probably would lead to them not making a woman's contribution anyway.' (The italics are the author's.)

3. The Constitutional Club and, more recently, the Junior Carlton Club have decided to accept a limited number of women as associate members, but they must be either wives or daughters of members

4. In the United States, for example, the House of Representatives (435 members) had 17 women members in 1956 and 10 in 1964; the West German Bundestag (497 members) 45 in 1963 and 38 in 1965; the French National Assembly (627 members) 22 in 1951 and 8 in 1963

5. These figures include the three 'warming pan' members (Mrs Hilton Philipson, Mrs Hugh Dalton, Mrs Walter Runciman) who were returned for seats for which their husbands had been selected.

6. The Conservative Party has in fact adopted nine women in this category; Mrs Elaine Kellett was adopted to contest the marginal Conservative held division of Buckingham in the 1964 General Election, but failed to hold it

7. Letter to author 9 May 1966

8. Letter to author from Mr Edward du Cann M.P., Chairman of the Conservative Party, 1 July 1966

9. ibid.

10. Letter to author 28 April 1966

11. p. 266

12. The case of Dr Pearl Hulbert at Colchester in 1948 (see p. 171) seems to have been exceptional

13. Article 'My Post Bag' by Jean Mann, *Labour Woman*, February 1958

14. Table 5, p. 27

15. Letter to author 28 April 1966

Bibliography

Astor, Michael. *Tribal Feeling*. John Murray, 1963

Atholl, Katherine, Duchess of. *Women and Politics*. Philip Allan, 1931 : *Searchlight on Spain*. Penguin Books, 1938 : *Working Partnership*. Arthur Barker, 1958

Attlee, C. R. *As It Happened*. William Heinemann, 1954

Bailey, S. D. (editor). *The Future of the House of Lords: A Symposium* (Chapter on Women and the House of Lords by Edward Iwi) Hansard Society. 1954

Beveridge, W. H. *Power and Influence*. Hodder & Stoughton, 1953

Bondfield, Margaret. *A Life's Work*. Hutchinson, 1950

Booth, Arthur H. *British Hustings 1924–1950*. Muller, 1956

Braddock, Jack and Bessie. *The Braddocks*. Macdonald, 1963

Brittain, Vera. *Lady into Woman*. Dakers, 1953

Collis, Maurice. *Nancy Astor*. Faber & Faber, 1960

Coxhead, Elizabeth. *Daughters of Erin*. Secker & Warburg, 1965

Cross, Colin. *The Fascists in Britain*. Barrie & Rockliffe, 1961

Dalton, Hugh. *Call Back Yesterday: Memoirs 1887–1931*. Muller, 1953 : *The Fateful Years: Memoirs 1931–1945*. Muller, 1957 : *High Tide and After: Memoirs 1945–60*. Muller, 1962

Douie, Vera. *Daughter of Britain*. George Roüald, Oxford, 1950

Fulford, Roger. *Votes for Women*. Faber & Faber, 1957

Gallup Analysis of the Election '66. The Daily Telegraph, 1966

Hamilton, Mary Agnes. *Margaret Bondfield*. Leonard Parsons, 1924 : *Mary Macarthur*. Leonard Parsons, 1925 : *Remembering my Good Friends*. Jonathan Cape, 1944 : *Up-Hill All the Way*. Jonathan Cape, 1953

Jones, Thomas. *A Diary with Letters, 1931–1950*. Oxford University Press, 1954

Kamm, Josephine. *Rapiers and Battleaxes: The Women's Movement and its Aftermath*. Allen & Unwin, 1966

Lee, Jennie. *This Great Journey*. McGibbon & Kee, 1963

Leonard, R. L. *The Pan Guide to the General Election*, Pan Books, 1964

Mann, Jean. *Woman in Parliament*. Odhams, 1962

Markham, Violet. *Return Passage*. Oxford University Press, 1953

Middlemas, Robert Keith. *The Clydesiders*. Hutchinson, 1965

Morrison of Lambeth, Herbert. *An Autobiography*. Odhams, 1960

Nicolson, Harold. *Diaries and Letters 1930–1939*. Collins, 1966

O'Faolain, Sean. *Life of Constance Markievicz*. Jonathan Cape, 1934

Pankhurst, Christabel. *Unshackled: The Story of How Women Won the Vote*. Hutchinson, 1959

269

Picton-Turbervill, Edith. *Life is Good*. Muller, 1939

Ponsonby, Colonel Sir Charles. *Ponsonby Remembers*. Alden Press, 1965

Rathbone, Eleanor. *Family Allowances: A New Edition of the Disinherited Family*. Allen & Unwin, 1949

Ranney, Austin. *Pathways to Parliament*. Macmillan, 1965

Richards, Peter G. *Honourable Members*. Faber & Faber, 1959

Roper, Esther (editor). *The Prison Letters of Constance Markievicz*. Longmans, Green, 1934

Ross, J. F. S. *British Journal of Sociology*. Vol. IV. No. I, March, 1953 (Chapter on Women and Parliamentary Elections) : *Elections and Electors*. Eyre & Spottiswoode, 1955

Stocks, Mary D. *Eleanor Rathbone: A Biography*. Gollancz, 1954

Strachey, Ray (editor). *Our Freedom and its Results*. Hogarth Press, 1936

Summerskill, Edith. *Letters to My Daughter*. Heinemann, 1957 : *A Woman's World*. Heinemann, 1967

Warwick, Frances, Countess of. *Ebb and Flow*. Hutchinson, 1929

Wilkinson, Ellen. *The Town that was Murdered*. Gollancz, 1939

Wood, Ethel. *Mainly for Men*. Gollancz, 1943

In addition to *Hansard* I have drawn from the Press, the records of the Fawcett Library, relevant pamphlets issued by the party organizations and books of general reference such as *The Times House of Commons* issued by The Times Publishing Company for every election since and including 1929, *Dod's Parliamentary Companion, Vacher's Parliamentary Companion, Dictionary of National Biography*, etc.

Appendices

Appendix A. Women Members of the House of Commons (1918–January 1967)

* = Cabinet Minister   P.P.S. = Parliamentary Private Secretary

Name	Dates	Party	Constituency	Appointments
ADAMSON, Mrs J. L.	1938–46	Lab.	Dartford	1940–5 P.P.S. to Minister of Pensions, 1945–6 Parliamentary Secretary, Ministry of Pensions
ANDERSON, Miss M. B. Harvie o.b.e. (Mrs J. F. P. Skrimshire)	1959—	Cons.	Renfrewshire, East	
APSLEY, Lady Viola	1943–45	Cons.	Bristol Central	
ASTOR, Viscountess C. H.	1919–45	Cons.	Plymouth, Sutton	
ATHOLL, Duchess of d.b.e.	1923–38	Cons.	Perth and Kinross	1924–9 Parliamentary Secretary, Board of Education
BACON, The Rt Hon. Alice c.b.e.	1945—	Lab.	Leeds S.E. (formerly Leeds N.E.)	1964— Minister of State, Home Office
BENTHAM, Dr Ethel	1929–31	Lab.	Islington E.	
BONDFIELD, The Rt Hon. Margaret G. H.	1923–24	Lab.	Northampton	1924 Parliamentary Secretary, Ministry of Labour
	1926–31	Lab.	Wallsend	1929–31 Minister of Labour*
BRADDOCK, Mrs E. M.	1945—	Lab.	Liverpool Exchange	
BURTON, Miss E. (Baroness Burton)	1950–59	Lab.	Coventry South	

Name	Dates	Party	Constituency	Appointments
BUTLER, Mrs J.	1955–7	Lab.	Wood Green	1965–6 P.P.S. to Minister of Land and Natural Resources
CASTLE, The Rt Hon. Barbara	1945—	Lab.	Blackburn	1945–51 P.P.S. to President of Board of Trade 1964–6 Minister of Overseas Development* 1966— Minister of Transport*
CAZALET-KEIR, Mrs T. (Miss T. Cazalet)	1931–45	Cons.	Islington E.	1938–40 P.P.S. to Parliamentary Secretary of Board of Education 1945 Parliamentary Secretary, Ministry of Education
COLMAN, Miss G. M.	1945–50	Lab.	Tyneside	
COPELAND, Mrs I.	1931–35	Cons.	Stoke-on-Trent	
CORBET, Mrs F.	1945—	Lab.	Camberwell, Peckham (formerly N.E.)	
CULLEN, Mrs A.	1948—	Lab.	Glasgow, Gorbals	
DALTON, Mrs R.	1929	Lab.	Bishop Auckland	
DAVIDSON, Viscountess D.B.E. (Baroness Northchurch)	1937–59	Cons.	Hemel Hempstead	
DUNWOODY, Mrs G.	1966—	Lab.	Exeter	
EMMET, The Hon. Mrs E. (Baroness Emmet)	1955–64	Cons.	East Grinstead	

Name	Constituency	Party	Dates	Offices
FORD, Mrs P.	Down North	U.U. (Cons.)	1953–55	
GAMMANS, Lady	Hornsey	Cons.	1957–66	
GANLEY, Mrs C. S.	Battersea South	Lab.	1945–51	
GOULD, Mrs B. Ayrton	Hendon North	Lab.	1945–50	
GRAVES, Miss M.	Hackney South	Cons.	1931–35	
HAMILTON, Mrs M. A.	Blackburn	Lab.	1929–31	1930–1 P.P.S. to Chancellor of Duchy of Lancaster (subsequently Postmaster General)
HARDIE, Mrs A.	Glasgow, Springburn	Lab.	1937–45	
HART, Mrs J.	Lanark	Lab.	1959—	1964–6 Under-Secretary of State, Scottish Office 1966— Minister of State, Commonwealth Relations Office
HERBISON, The Rt Hon. Margaret	Lanark North	Lab.	1945—	1950–1 Joint Under-Secretary of State, Scottish Office 1964— Minister of Social Security (formerly Pensions and National Insurance)
HILL, Mrs E.	Manchester, Wythenshawe	Cons.	1950–64	
HORNSBY-SMITH, The Rt Hon. Dame Patricia D.B.E.	Chislehurst	Cons.	1950–66	1951–7 Parliamentary Secretary, Ministry of Health 1957–9 Joint Parliamentary Under-Secretary, Home Office 1959–61 Joint Parliamentary Secretary, Ministry of Pensions and National Insurance

Name	Party	Dates	Constituency	Appointments
HORSBRUGH, The Rt Hon. Florence G.B.E. (Baroness Horsbrugh)	Cons.	1931–45	Dundee	1939–45 Parliamentary Secretary, Ministry of Health 1945 Parliamentary Secretary, Ministry of Food
		1950–59	Manchester, Moss Side	1951–4 Minister of Education*
IVEAGH, Countess of	Cons.	1927–35	Southend	
JEGER, Mrs L.	Lab.	1935–59	Holborn and St Pancras S.	
	Lab.	1964—	Holborn and St Pancras S.	
JEWSON, Miss D.	Lab.	1923–24	Norwich	
KERR, Mrs A. P.	Lab.	1964—	Rochester and Chatham	
KNIGHT, Mrs J.	Cons.	1966—	Birmingham, Edgbaston	
LAWRENCE, Miss A. S.	Lab. Lab.	1923–24 1926–31	Poplar Poplar	1924 P.P.S. to President of Board of Education 1929–31 Parliamentary Secretary, Ministry of Health
LEE, The Rt Hon. Jennie (Mrs Aneurin Bevan)	Lab. Lab.	1929–31 1945—	Lanark North Cannock	1964–5 Parliamentary Secretary, Ministry of Public Buildings and Works 1965–7 Joint Parliamentary Under-Secretary of State, Department of Education and Science 1967— Minister of State, Department of Education and Science

Name	Years	Party	Constituency	Notes
LESTOR, Miss J.	1966–	Lab.	Eton and Slough	
LLOYD GEORGE, Lady Megan C. H.	1929–51 1957–66	Lib. Lab.	Anglesey Carmarthen	
McALISTER, Mrs M.	1958–9	Lab.	Glasgow, Kelvingrove	
McKAY, Mrs M.	1964–	Lab.	Clapham	
McLAUGHLIN, Mrs P.	1955–64	U.U. (Cons.)	Belfast West	
MANN, Mrs J.	1945–59	Lab.	Coatbridge and Airdrie	
MANNING, Mrs E. L.	1931 1945–50	Lab. Lab.	Islington E. Epping	
MARKIEVICZ, Countess	1918–22	Sinn Fein	Dublin, St Patrick's	*(Did not take seat)*
MIDDLETON, Mrs L.	1945–51	Lab.	Plymouth, Sutton	
MOSLEY, Lady Cynthia	1929–31	Lab.	Stoke-on-Trent	
NICHOL, Mrs M. W.	1945–50	Lab.	Bradford North	
NOEL-BUXTON, Lady	1930–31 1945–50	Lab. Lab.	Norfolk North Norwich	
PATON, Mrs F.	1945–50	Lab.	Rushcliffe	
PHILIPSON, Mrs M. Hilton (Miss Mabel Russell)	1923–29	Cons.	Berwick-on-Tweed	

Name	Dates	Party	Constituency	Appointments
PHILLIPS, Dr M.	1929–31	Lab.	Sunderland	
PICKFORD, The Hon. M. C.B.E.	1931–34	Cons.	Hammersmith N.	
PICTON-TURBERVILL, Miss E.	1929–31	Lab.	The Wrekin	
PIKE, Miss M.	1956—	Cons.	Melton	1958–59 P.P.S. to Joint Parliamentary Under-Secretary of State, Home Office 1959–63 Assistant Postmaster General 1963–64 Joint Under-Secretary of State, Home Office
PITT, Dame Edith D.B.E.	1953–66	Cons.	Birmingham, Edgbaston	1955–59 Joint Parliamentary Secretary, Ministry of Pensions and National Service 1959–62 Parliamentary Secretary, Ministry of Health
QUENNELL, Miss J.	1960—	Cons.	Petersfield	1962–64 P.P.S. to Minister of Transport
RATHBONE, Miss E.	1929–46	Ind.	Combined English Universities	
REES, Mrs D.	1950–51	Lab.	Barry	1950–51 P.P.S. to Minister of National Insurance
RIDEALGH, Mrs M.	1945–50	Lab.	Ilford North	
RUNCIMAN, Mrs H.	1928–9	Lib.	St Ives	
RUNGE, Mrs N.	1931–5	Cons.	Rotherhithe	

Name	Party	Constituency	Years	Office
SHAW, Mrs C. M.	Lab.	Ayr	1945–46	
SHAW, Mrs H. B.	Cons.	Bothwell	1931–35	
SHORT, Mrs R.	Lab.	Wolverhampton East	1964—	
SLATER, Mrs H. c.b.e.	Lab.	Stoke-on-Trent N.	1953–66	1964–66 Lord Commissioner of the Treasury (Whip)
SUMMERSKILL, The Rt Hon. Edith (Dr Edith, now Baroness Summerskill)	Lab.	Fulham West	1938–55	1945–50 Parliamentary Secretary, Ministry of Food; 1950–51 Minister of National Insurance
SUMMERSKILL, The Hon. Dr S.	Lab.	Warrington	1955–60	
	Lab.	Halifax	1964—	
TATE, Mrs M.	Cons. Cons.	Willesden West Frome	1931–35 1935–45	
TERRINGTON, Lady	Lib	Wycombe	1923–4	
THATCHER, Mrs M.	Cons.	Finchley	1959—	1961–64 Joint Parliamentary Secretary Ministry of Pensions and National Insurance
TWEEDSMUIR, Lady (Lady Grant)	Cons.	Aberdeen S.	1946–66	1962–64 Joint Parliamentary Under-Secretary of State, Scottish Office
VICKERS, Dame Joan D.B.E.	Cons.	Plymouth, Devonport	1955—	

Name	Dates	Party	Constituency	Appointments
WARD, Dame Irene D.B.E.	1931-45	Cons.	Wallsend	
	1950—	Cons.	Tynemouth (formerly Tyneside)	
WARD, Mrs S. A.	1931-35	Cons.	Cannock	
WHITE, Mrs E.	1950—	Lab.	Flint East	1964-66 Parliamentary Secretary, Colonial Office 1966-67 Minister of State for Foreign Affairs 1967— Minister of State, Welsh Office
WILKINSON, The Rt Hon. Ellen	1924-31	Lab.	Middlesbrough	1929-31 P.P.S. to Parliamentary Secretary, Ministry of Health
	1935-47	Lab.	Jarrow	1940 Parliamentary Secretary, Ministry of Pensions 1940-45 Parliamentary Secretary, Ministry of Home Security 1945-47 Minister of Education*
WILLIAMS, Mrs S. V. T. B.	1964—	Lab.	Hitchin	1964-66 P.P.S. to Minister of Health 1966-67 Parliamentary Secretary, Ministry of Labour 1967— Minister of State, Department of Education and Science
WILLS, Mrs E. A.	1945-50	Lab.	Birmingham, Duddeston	
WINTRINGHAM, Mrs M.	1921-24	Lib.	Louth	
WRIGHT, Mrs B. (Mrs Rathbone)	1941-45	Cons.	Bodmin	

Appendix B. Women Members of the House of Lords (*January 1967*)

(i) Life Peers

Baroness Asquith of Yarnbury D.B.E.	(Lady Violet Bonham-Carter)	1964
Baroness Brooke of Ystradfellte D.B.E.	(Dame Barbara Brooke)	1964
Baroness Burton of Coventry	(Miss Elaine Burton)	1962
Baroness Elliot of Harwood D.B.E.	(Dame Katherine Elliot)	1958
Baroness Emmet of Amberley	(The Hon. Mrs Evelyn Emmet)	1964
Baroness Gaitskell of Egremont	(Mrs Dora Gaitskell)	1964
Baroness Horsbrugh of Horsbrugh P.C., G.B.E.	(Dame Florence Horsbrugh)	1959
Baroness Hylton-Foster of the City of London	(Lady Hylton-Foster)	1965
Baroness Northchurch of Chiswick D.B.E.	(Viscountess Davidson)	1964
Baroness Phillips of Fulham	(Mrs Norah Phillips) *Baroness in Waiting*	1964
Baroness Plummer of Topplefield	(Lady Plummer)	1965
Baroness Ravensdale of Kedleston	(deceased 1966)	1958
Baroness Serota of Hampstead	(Mrs Beatrice Serota)	1967
Baroness Sharp of Hornsey D.B.E.	(Dame Evelyn Sharp)	1966
Baroness Spencer-Churchill of Chartwell G.B.E.	(Lady Churchill)	1965
Baroness Stocks of the Royal Borough of Kensington and Chelsea	(Mrs Mary Stocks)	1966
Baroness Summerskill of Kenwood P.C., C.H.	(Dr Edith Summerskill)	1961
Baroness Swanborough G.B.E.	(Stella, Marchioness of Reading)	1958
Baroness Wootton of Abinger	(Mrs Barbara Wootton)	1958

(ii) *Hereditary Peeresses who have received the Writ of Summons*

Countess of Erroll*
Countess Seafield*
Countess of Sutherland*
Baroness Audley

Baroness Beaumont
Lady Kinloss
Lady Nairne
Baroness Strange of Knokin

* Peeresses who have obtained leave of absence

C. *Private Members' Bills introduced by Women Members of Parliament which became Law*

Year	Member	Bill
1923	Lady Astor	Intoxicating Liquor (Sales to Persons under Eighteen) Bill
1927	Mrs Hilton Philipson	Nursing Homes (Registration) Bill
1929	Miss Susan Lawrence	Bastardy (Witness Process) Bill
1929	Duchess of Atholl	Illegitimate Children (Scotland) Bill
1931	Miss E. Picton-Turbervill	Sentence of Death (Expectant Mothers) Bill
1937	Miss F. Horsbrugh	Methylated Spirits (Sale by Retail) Scotland Bill
1937	Miss I. Ward	Poor Law (Amendment) Bill
1938	Miss E. Wilkinson	Hire Purchase Bill
1938	Miss F. Horsbrugh	Adoption of Children (Regulation) Bill
1950	Mrs B. Castle	Criminal Law (Amendment) Bill
1952	Miss E. Burton	Disposal of Uncollected Goods Bill
1953	Miss I. Ward	Rights of Entry (Gas and Electricity Boards) Bill
1953	Lady Tweedsmuir	Protection of Birds Bill
1954	Lady Davidson	Protection of Animals (Anaesthetics) Bill
1958	Miss M. Pike	Drainage Rates Bill
1960	Mrs M. Thatcher	Public Bodies (Admission to Meetings) Bill
1960	Dame Irene Ward	Nurses (Amendment) Bill
1962	Dame Irene Ward	Penalties for Drunkenness Bill
1963	Mrs P. McLaughlin	Public Lavatories (Turnstiles) Bill
1964	Miss H. Harvie Anderson	Animals (Restriction of Importation) Bill
1964	Miss J. Vickers	Young Persons (Employment) Bill
1965	Mrs L. Jeger	British Nationality Bill

Index

Date Due